MW00938911

LEAVING
SALT LAKE CITY

MATTHEW TIMION

LEAVING SALT LAKE CITY

—

Copyright © 2013 Matthew Timion
All rights reserved.

First Edition April 15, 2013
published by Matthew Timion via Createspace

Edited by Nicole Yabut

ISBN: **1480232068**
ISBN-13: **978-1480232068**

This book is protected under the copyright laws of the United States of America. Any reproduction or other unauthorized use of the material or artwork herein is prohibited without the express written permission of the author.

This book is a memoir, and it should be understood that the events detailed in this story are the author's recollection and perception. While names have been changed, the events in this book actually happened. The author has used every resource at his disposal to ensure the accuracy of the time line of the events.

For further information please see the Author's Note at the end of the book.

DEDICATION

For my son Manny.
Your ability to triumph over adversity inspires me daily.

| ONE |

June 28, 2007

It was six in the morning. I snapped awake, anxious and shaking, unsure if my nightmare was real or not.

It was real. The night before had really happened.

My wife had called me on the phone last night and told me she knew I was cheating on her. She was away on a business trip in Oregon and had called me, accusing me of things that would end our marriage. She *knew* I did those things.

I stood up and got out of bed. Our two dogs jumped out of bed and wanted to go outside. I would never see those dogs again.

My wife, Jessica, was done with me. She apparently knew the horrible things I had done. I took the dogs outside and relived the night before over and over in my mind trying to find a way to fix the situation. I needed to do something - anything - to keep my life the way it had been for years. I couldn't lose her. I couldn't lose my wife.

Oh my God. I was going to lose my wife. It was an impossible thought, and yet it seemed like a real possibility. Shit. I was going to lose my wife. I was going to lose my family.

I walked into the house and was greeted by my son Manny, who Jessica and I adopted just a week before. A short four-year-old boy now had my last name. I had to catch my breath. I couldn't breathe. I could lose him too.

How did it all come to this? Jessica and I were so in love. We worked and built our life together; knowing we would always be at each others' side. It felt like the life we had built was going to be taken away in an instant.

I remembered when I first met Jessica in early May of 2004. I was living in California while she was in Utah. We both belonged to an online community of former Mormons. We were hoping to find other people to connect with to validate the emotional turmoil we experienced after leaving our religion. One day I saw a new person to the group post a message online. Her picture was cute, and, filled with post-divorce lust and flirtatious admiration, I sent her a message.

Quickly we started talking more and more. Within a few weeks she was on an airplane to visit me.

I stood in the Ontario, California airport waiting for her to come down the escalator. We were sending each other text messages when I saw her at the top of the stairs. She was there looking around for me with her bleached blonde hair and busty bosom. Her tight pink t-shirt proclaimed "Jesus loves you and your tattoos," while she looked around herself. She called my cell phone. "Where are you?" I had stopped behind a pillar, awestruck, as I admired her from afar for a moment longer. I emerged from my reverie and walked up to her.

"Hi," she said, as she fell into my arms. She began kissing me right then and there. Her big soft lips felt amazing. I didn't even notice the hundreds of people walking around the airport watching us lock lips. The woman I had met online was next to me, and I knew I was the luckiest man in the world. I knew nothing could spoil the weekend we had planned. I had finally met someone that made the pain and heartache I experienced in leaving Mormonism and divorcing my first wife worth it. I was ready for Jessica.

The perfect woman I met at the airport eventually became my wife. I moved from Southern California to Utah to be with her. We eventually adopted a child together and became a family. The life I had always wanted was finally mine. We were happy.

But that morning, the morning after she called me, we were not happy. The joy and bliss of our relationship was gone. It was replaced with fear and confusion. I can only imagine what it felt like for her.

"I know what you did," she had told me the night before. Her voice still echoed in my thoughts. "I've talked with fourteen friends, and all of them have told me things you've done!"

I had to stay busy. I had to do something - anything - to get those thoughts off of my mind.

I put cereal in a bowl for our son Manny. He sat in front of the television watching Spongebob unaware of the devastation surrounding me.

The night before Jessica accused me of having sex with her nineteen year old cousin. "You child molester! I'm taking Manny and you'll never see him again!" I looked at Manny eating his breakfast. I knew I might experience a life without him; I might never raise him into the man he should be.

Everything I had worked for was crashing down on me because of a phone call.

How could this have happened? What went wrong? I sipped my coffee with shaking hands knowing having a stimulant in my system wasn't the best idea. What was I supposed to do though? How was I supposed to behave?

"Dad, I want some ice cream!" Manny yelled. Manny called cantaloupe "ice cream," so I stood up and prepared a few slices for him to eat while watching television. Thank God Manny was there to distract me, if even for a few minutes at a time. Uninterrupted obsession would have been the end of me.

I sat back down in my chair not knowing what would happen next. I couldn't fathom the "proof" Jessica had about my infidelity, but I knew nothing good could come from it.

I had a fleeting thought about running. I could take Manny and leave; escape the craziness that had become my life over the last twelve hours. I decided instead to stay and hope Jessica could see reason. I loved her. I loved our family. The last thing I ever wanted was a life without her and our newly adopted son.

I thought back to the first time she told me she loved me.

I walked into our bedroom and saw her things all around. There were her clothes. Her shoes. A picture of her mother on the wall. I refused to live without her. She was my entire world.

Waiting for her to return from her work trip, I worked on coming up with something, some story, to make the pain go away. I tried to figure out a way to stop the accusations and threats. I just wanted her to know I loved her. I wanted her to understand that Manny and I were her family.

Until then I could only watch Spongebob with a four year old, pretending not to hurt, pretending not to be terrified of what the next few days might turn into.

Then she barged into the house.

PART 1

| TWO |

Christmas Day, 2004

I was on the road; moving to my new home in Salt Lake City. My girlfriend Jessica was by my side. She had flown to California to make the trip with me. Catching a glimpse of her whenever I could, I knew there was something more to Jessica than her good looks.

Reflecting back, I was too embarrassed to say what that something more was. She was the third woman named Jessica I had dated. I was an atheist, and I knew the nature of the universe was random, but a part of me felt a sense of destiny in dating Jessica. This relationship was a cosmic sign that I had finally met the *right* Jessica, and that perhaps my affection for previous Jessicas was a higher power's way of directing me to the right path. In hindsight, I should have realized that Jessica was the most popular female baby name in America for children born in the 1970s. If I had dated Catholic women, I am sure that I would have been just as surprised at the recurrence of the name Mary in my dating life - and found it just as significant - as I did the name Jessica.

Driving the moving truck to Salt Lake City, we passed the time discussing our childhoods. Jessica was an absolutely fascinating woman. Her parents had met when her dad was a Mormon missionary in Chile. He returned to Chile after his two-year missionary service and married Jessica's mother. They spent a number of years in Chile and eventually moved back to the United States when Jessica's father's job was transferred. Jessica told me about the difficulty of moving to America at the age of ten years old and having to learn English quickly.

Jessica's ability to learn English so quickly without a

foreign accent amazed me. As a Mormon missionary, I spent two years living in the Philippines speaking nothing but Filipino, and my accent as a Filipino speaker is still very thick. I was awed by her native accent. She would tell stories often about how difficult it was for her to adjust to American life, diet, and culture. Her father's parents never liked her siblings or her, and they would usually treat them differently than the other grandchildren in the family. Jessica attributed her grandfather's disdain to the unchangeable reality that her mom was Chilean and had darker skin. Thus her mother, and by extension, Jessica and her siblings, were considered "lesser" by her white grandfather.

There is a common racist undertone in the Mormon culture, which has roots in an old Mormon doctrine that the less faithful were once cursed with dark skin. According to this controversial teaching, all people with black skin are in fact descendants of Cain, he who killed Abel in the Bible. While these teachings have no real basis in official Mormon doctrine, they had been part of Mormon culture for almost one hundred and fifty years. When I heard her white grandfather disliked her family for having a different skin color, it made complete sense to me.

My father and her mother both died at around the same time. We were almost the same age when we lost our parents. I had finally found a kindred spirit, one who knew what it was like to lose someone so young. She made my heartache feel justified. I didn't have to explain to her the pain of leaving Mormonism, my subsequent divorce, or the death of a parent. She simply understood.

Jessica's ability to empathize made her everyone's instant friend. Her personality made her the center of everything. She was the most popular person in our group of friends; the one who threw the best parties that everyone insisted on attending. I was beyond thrilled, being nothing more than a computer geek, that the popular girl wanted me as much as I wanted her. I

wanted to take a picture of us together and send it to every
ex-girlfriend I had ever had. A picture wouldn't had done justice
to how she made you feel around her, however. That was
something you had to experience for yourself.

As we drove, the temperature outside changed from warm,
to brisk, to cold. We arrived in Salt Lake City and pulled up to
the house I had purchased sight unseen. Jessica had found the
house for us; I had bought it with my money, knowing we would
live there together. It was on the west side of town, which was
often considered a bad neighborhood. This reputation was
probably because of the high percentage of immigrants in the
area, but we were okay with that. In fact, we prefered it. We
were better than the suburban white-bread families who were
afraid of Hispanics and Polynesians. The misunderstood were
our people. We fit in better with them than in a neighborhood
with white picket fences.

While preparing for my arrival, Jessica had been living
in our new house with her two dogs and a cat for a month. She
had spent the time painting, pulling out carpet, and redoing the
ceilings. At around one o'clock in the afternoon the trip to our
new home was over. We pulled into the driveway. The ground
was frozen solid, but there was no snow. It was quite the change
from Southern California, but it was a change I was happy about,
one I had signed up for.

Looking around my new city I was amazed at how many
giant SUVs I saw. Having just moved from Southern California,
I was used to people living beyond their means, but the
motivation for these lavish displays was different. While not a
doctrine preached from the pulpit, I had always noticed how
many faithful Mormons attributed financial success to spiritual
righteousness. God blessed the faithful with material *things* and
punished the unfaithful with poverty. Luckily one did not need to
be faithful to appear pious. One only needed a credit card. Even
if one lacked religious devotion, the giant SUV cemented his or

her reputation as the most righteous person on the block.

The next morning I awoke early, eager to begin unpacking the moving truck and then returning it to its owners. Jessica handed me a cup of coffee. As I began to consume the only thing that could make me think straight, a steady stream of people began knocking on our door. It was the morning after Christmas, and, before I could put on my pants, my new bungalow was filled with no less than twenty people. Was it Mormons coming to welcome me to the neighborhood? Were they going to offer to help on condition that I attended church the following week? No, the small assembly in my house were all *former* Mormons eager to help.

As Mormons we had oftentimes been guilted into doing this exact same duty by being reminded that service is next to Godliness. I had hated when new people moved into my congregation. I had hated volunteering to unload a moving truck, but I had done it anyway. These people, walking around my house seemingly unaware of my blue pajamas, were all there of their own free will to help an *un*spiritual brother unload furniture. Their presence reminded me again of our shared identity and that the community I had lost when leaving Mormonism had been replaced by a community of people just like me.

Jessica vanished into the basement and came back up holding a box. "Where should I put these?" she asked.

"What are those?" I was uncertain of the contents of the box. She was clutching the box like it might explode if she dropped it.

"This is my collection of shot glasses I stole from bars."

Jessica had a knack for stealing from restaurants and bars. It was normal for her to steal shot glasses, silverware, or even pictures off of the walls. They were mementos from places she had been on wonderful evenings. She hung the Absinthe picture she had lifted from a club in our dining room. Seeing the new artwork in our dining room, I thought of how happy I was she hadn't brought the giant "Road Closed" sign that had served as a headboard from her apartment. Thankfully the orange construction cones were nowhere to be found either.

Her innocent kleptomania was not abnormal. What was abnormal was that you would steal things too when you were with her. There was something about Jessica that made you do things you would never normally consider. Stealing, verbally abusing someone, excessive drinking, or making out with a member of the same gender in front of twenty other people. ("Spin the Bottle" was a common party game for this group of former Mormons.) You would do these things around Jessica, and you would keep doing them as long as you received her approval.

***

To understand the dynamics of my new kindred spirits, one must understand a little bit more about Mormonism. Mormonism is a religion of leadership. Everyone has a leader, all the way up to the President of the Church (revered by the membership as being a living prophet). Even the President of the Church has a leader: Jesus Christ himself. Within individual congregations there are multiple levels of leadership that report to a larger geographical leadership who also report to an even higher geographical leadership. Ascending the hierarchy, each leader has progressively more authority and is perceived to be more divinely inspired, adding more and more weight to his words.

Taking orders from your leaders is ingrained into Mormon theology, and, as a result, is a cornerstone of the cultural identity of Mormonism. It should be no surprise then that ex-Mormons, despite rejecting the religion and all it stands for, seek out similar forms of leadership, even if the overt hierarchy is not there. Having spent years as Mormons, listening to a church hierarchy, it was only natural to want structure.

***

The leadership in the ex-Mormon community was not appointed by God, like the Mormon leadership, nor was the leadership formally declared. One man, Lester, seemed to be the voice of the group due largely to his lifetime of unique experiences. Lester was openly gay, an artist, heavily tattooed, an eccentric, and had met celebrities. His life reflected what most of us wanted our lives to be. He handed out wisdom instead of insults. Lester always expressed an understanding of hatred, having experienced so much of it himself. While most sought him for guidance and counsel, others still preferred to make their own life decisions without Lester's approval.

Two camps began forming slowly in our community. Those who seemed to be stuck on Mormonism (culturally or theologically) gravitated towards Lester. The other camp, those who had moved on from Mormonism years prior, considered Lester and his followers to be rather silly. It was not until years later that I understood that both groups were one and the same.

Jessica, in her own right, was also a leader in the community. She was not a wise sage, as many viewed Lester, but the embodiment of fun and partying. People looked up to her with awe and excitement, partially because of the interesting life she led, but mostly because she made you feel younger, sexy, and fun when you were around her. She had a way of bringing out the party animal in all of us, something we were mostly too reserved to do for ourselves.

I always interpreted Jessica's command of a group as a result of her being a natural leader. This was likely a major factor in why so many people came to help us move in. Many people came that day, and they didn't leave right away either.

After a few hours of unpacking, unloading and getting settled, the house was mostly all set up. Some friends stayed, and some friends left. Those who stayed consumed beer, which always appeared to be the holy communion of former Mormons.

Mormons spend their entire lives on a strict diet. They cannot consume alcohol, coffee, tea, tobacco, or illegal drugs. This dietary law is based on a revelation the founding prophet received. Because of this, when Mormons leave the church, they often jump off the deep end with consumption. Many ex-Mormons start drinking, smoking pot, smoking cigarettes, and usually engage in risky sexual behavior.

We were making up for lost time. While I never experienced it first hand, I hear most people get all their "partying" out of their system during their teenage and college years. Because most of us former Mormons were away on two year missions during prime partying years, we felt the need to cram as much and as many of the lost experiences into as short a time as possible.

As adults, fully *recovered-from-Mormonism* adults, we could afford to buy good microbrews and expensive pot. We were adult teenagers experiencing a second adolescence. Since I had had no real experience with which to contrast the behavior of my new community, everything we did was normal.

This was how adults lived. Real adults.

I had moved into my new home. Salt Lake City was going to be my homebase for the rest of my life. I was going to live and die there. I was going to raise a family there. I was happy.

| THREE |
Letting Go of the Past
March 2005

I spent the next few months adjusting to living in Salt

Lake City with a live-in girlfriend, which took some getting used to because I'd never had a live-in girlfriend before. I telecommuted to my office in Southern California while Jessica worked for the Air Force a few miles from our house. It was a great situation. She would leave, I would work, and then she would come home. Life was exactly like it was supposed to be: routine and a little boring, but stable since we were both making decent money. I took advantage of our financial situation to pay off my debts and save a rainy day fund.

I finally felt like an adult: I owned a house where I lived with my girlfriend, two dogs, and a cat. I was free from Mormonism although my idea of what an adult *should be* still reflected being part of and surrounded by Mormon culture since I was eighteen. I was doing something real and meaningful by being part of our small family in our house. I was fortunate to have Jessica living this experience with me. She had spent a considerable amount of time "in the world," outside of Mormonism's grasp, so not only was she my partner, but she could be my guide. I was living the way I was supposed to live. I had come a long way and I was terribly proud of myself.

As perfect as my life seemed, my American Dream hadn't prepared me for how much of an adjustment it was to move in with someone. We had to figure out rules, expectations, and roles. Did we both do the dishes, or did just one person? Who was supposed to pick up after her dogs? They were her dogs after all and not mine. Who was supposed to clean the furniture? It was my furniture and not hers. We were young and in love. How often should we have sex? How messy around the house was I allowed to be with her? Figuring out new roles and rules is completely normal when two people move in, but sometimes it felt like we were trying to build a life during an earthquake.

These adjustments took a toll on both of us. I started wondering what I got myself into. She began to passive-aggressively criticize my lack of dusting or sweeping up the dog hair. Many of her criticisms would start with the phrase, "You're here all day, you can clean." She seemed to forget that I was working too. We were both questioning whether we were in over our heads.

Jessica came home one day and had a panic attack. "My friends ask me if we're dating, and I honestly don't have an answer for them." She was right. We had never defined the relationship with a title. I had assumed living together would be evidence enough of our relationship status. I didn't know if it even needed a title, but I didn't want her to feel like a roommate with benefits so some sort of definition needed to happen. I told her, "Of course you're my girlfriend, Jessica," secretly unsure if it was what I really wanted.

Her constant drinking and partying wore on me. I wasn't used to people drinking every night, and honestly it frightened me. My father had died when I was sixteen from alcoholism. I have always been afraid the same could happen to me, so I avoided alcohol as well as I could. I had a drink here or there, but I was twenty-six and proud that I had never been drunk before. I wore it like a badge of honor. While everyone else around me was getting drunk, I smugly looked at them knowing that I was the only sober one around. This left me picking up after them, coordinating rides, or stopping them from breaking something important to me.

I tried looking for a new point of view. I was barely twenty-six, and she was twenty-four. We had both left a controlling religion, and we had each recently divorced a Mormon spouse. We had enough combined baggage to make us question why we hopped into a relationship.

I started sharing my concerns about Jessica with my friend Bryce. I had met him online as well, and he more or less ran the online community where I had met her. He and I had a lot in common, and we would often times spend hours just chatting. I told him I didn't think Jessica and I were going to last, and I felt the relationship was going to end within a few weeks. I knew our annual ex-Mormon trip to Las Vegas was coming up, and I asked him to watch my cat while I went to Las Vegas with the other ex-Mormons. He agreed, and then told me he had something to tell me, something he wished he had told me before I moved to Utah.

"I'm only telling you this because you're thinking of leaving Jessica, but did you know that she and I used to date?"

"No." My heart was racing. What did he mean?

"Yeah, while you were still in California, we dated."

"What do you mean by dated?" I was hoping for a liberal definition of the word *date.*

"Dinner, movies, sex, you know, the normal."

To say that I was shocked would be an understatement. I had had no clue. I put the pieces together and realized that Jessica had explained away some rumors a few months before.

One night Jessica, Bryce, and a girl named Amy all went out for dinner. They drank a lot and ended up at Amy's apartment where Amy went to bed. Amy was a little upset because she and Bryce had dated, and they had broken up a week before. Amy had kept checking in on the other two, who were sleeping in the living room. According to Jessica they spent the next few drunken hours just giggling and being silly. After telling me this, Jessica warned me that any other version of the story I might hear was simply Amy being upset and jealous. Everyone was jealous of Jessica. I had no reason to disbelieve her so I started seeing Amy as a bit of a nut. This was exactly how Jessica wanted me, and everyone else, to see Amy.

The real story was that Jessica and Bryce had sex that night in Amy's living room, according to Bryce. The "rumors" Amy was telling everyone were in fact true, but after a while no one believed her and as a consequence a number of Amy's friendships were ruined.

"How often did you have sex?" I had to have more information.

"Very often, usually without protection. In fact, when Jessica got pregnant a few months ago, I was so relieved when she had the abortion because I was afraid the baby would come out looking like me."

This was the final straw for me. I could understand the difficulty of a long distance relationship and her inability to be completely faithful during that time period. I even understood why she was sleeping with two of us in the same time period (at least once she slept with both of us during the same day). I was far away, and he was close by. What I could not understand, however, was how she had handled her accidental pregnancy.

In July of 2004, Jessica and I had only been dating for a few months when she became pregnant. She had promised me that if she ever got pregnant she would have an abortion. We both had felt we were both too young and that the relationship was too new. When she became pregnant I was assured that I was, without a doubt, the father. I trusted her.

Upon finding out about her indiscretion with Bryce I realized I might not have been the biological father of her unborn baby. All along she had been sleeping with someone else on a regular basis without protection.

Bryce forwarded me a number of email exchanges he and Jessica had where they were planning dates, planning sex, or discussing the secretive nature of their relationship. They had both agreed that it was something I was to never know about.

It was late at night when I learned about Jessica's secret cheating past. I went to bed with my head swimming with everything I had learned. Waking her up and screaming at her seemed like a better idea than trying to sleep. I easily spent the next three or four hours in bed stewing. The next morning while Jessica was at work I sent off a number of cryptic emails to her letting her know I knew what was going on. She put the pieces together really quickly and rushed home.

"I am so sorry." She apologized before I said anything to her.

"How many times did you sleep with him?"

"Just once."

"You are telling me that you are being honest, and then you just lie to my face."

I couldn't think straight. I needed a cigarette, so I went outside, into the bitter Utah cold and smoked. She went outside with me. I confronted her with what I knew, and she minimized it. She said it didn't happen as often as Bryce claimed and that they had always used protection. The accidental pregnancy had to have been mine due to math and when we slept together. When I asked her why she had sent a certain email or had said something else in a chat message, she denied ever having said or sent those things.

"Bryce probably changed my chat log or my email. I would have never said those things."

I knew she was lying.

Jessica told me if I wanted to end the relationship and have her move out, she would understand. She just wanted to know what I wanted and what to expect. It was as though she had prepared for that moment, either out of anticipation of the truth coming out or from having been in a similar situation before. Her matter of factness bothered me. I couldn't think straight with this new knowledge. How could she be so calm about it? I told her I needed time to think about what I wanted next, which meant for the time being we were together, but on the verge of the relationship being over.

I spent an unhealthy amount of time scouring through emails. I keep all of my emails. It's the pack-rat inside of me that thinks I might need that email one day. I reconstructed time lines and tried to "prove" to her she was lying. I knew she was lying, and she knew she was lying. For whatever reason it was important for me to show her that her lying was unmistakably obvious.

Over a period of a few weeks I reconstructed her entire relationship with Bryce in extreme detail. Her memory of their relationship always became hazy whenever I confronted her with information that caught her in a lie. I persisted. Looking back, all I wanted from her was an admission of guilt, an admission that she had lied and caused me pain. Instead, she had selective amnesia. After I showed her how her story didn't add up, she agreed with me that her story did not match up with the facts. She then gave me the most baffling justification I have ever received, one I would become all too familiar with over the next few years.

"You're right Matt, that doesn't add up. I don't know. I just don't remember it like that."

I don't know. As if claiming ignorance about painful events somehow magically removed the transgressions from existence. At the time I didn't know if she was trying to trick me, play the victim card, or if perhaps her memory was so horrible she really didn't know. Maybe the person in front of me wasn't the person who did all of those horrible things. Perhaps she forgot them because they were caused by some factor beyond my understanding. A part of me bought it. She didn't know.

Trying to figure out her motivations made me look at mine. My Encyclopedia Brown adventure of proving her lies and trying to figure out "why" made me look at myself and ask the same questions. What I discovered about myself was that I had entered the relationship expecting it to end. I had been planning for a way out, an escape, since the relationship was new. This was an obvious issue with me and my ability to be in an adult relationship. After my first divorce I had gone into defensive mode. Knowing it *would* end one day made everything safer somehow. Her mistakes notwithstanding, I knew building an emotional escape pod from the relationship was part of the problem too.

We spent those weeks of not knowing our future, not talking about anything serious and definitely not touching each other in bed. We walked on eggshells as I kept thinking about a topic that pained me. It had been a few weeks since I had discovered her indiscretion, and I just needed the uncertainty and confusion to end. I needed to move on knowing she was committed to me now, not with Bryce, not with anyone else.

One Saturday morning I surprised her in the shower by joining her. It was the first time we had had sex since finding out about her lies and unfaithfulness. We both understood I had accepted her apology and that we were moving on, together. We talked about it more afterwards. I told her that while I was disgusted with what happened, I was willing to let it go for the sake of our relationship. This time, I was really going to try to make a relationship work instead of always planning my escape. I was jumping in headfirst. It felt liberating to put everything on the line and have blind faith in someone for the first time in years. This relationship was going to be perfect and nothing like the marriage I had ended with my first wife. I was making this choice myself, not simply following the teachings of the church, so I knew it would be perfect.

It was March of 2005, and I weighed 200 pounds. At 5'10" I knew I was too heavy. We decided to repair the relationship and make our health a priority. I needed to lose weight. So did she.

| FOUR |
Trying Again for the First Time
April 2005

Our relationship felt new. It felt exciting. It was as though we were at Disneyland for the first time; as if we had never been there one hundred times and never had gone on a ride. For the first time ever, I was making every effort for my relationship to succeed. After all, I had moved to Utah to be with Jessica. I had uprooted my life to be around her, to be with her, to start a life with her. I wondered if I had known all along that we would end up together. Luckily for me we were willing to *really* put the effort into our relationship and do whatever we could to make our future a reality.

Our renewed dedication to each other brought not only complete honesty, but also a focus on making ourselves more healthy. We wanted a long happy life together so both of us had to be alive for a long time. Luckily for me, Jessica had once trained as a professional Mixed Martial Arts fighter a few years before I had met her. She told me stories about fighting professionally and would often brag of her third degree black belt in Brazilian Ju-Jitsu.

Her stint as a professional fighter had been short lived, mainly due to the backlash from her family and the objectification she experienced for being a female fighter. She told me that one night Joe Rogan (the host of a popular reality television show and the commentator on Mixed Martial Arts tournaments) had asked to sleep with her after a fight. She slyly gave Joe Rogan the hotel room key that another man (who was trying to sleep with her) had just given her. The world of professional fighting was not for her.

Because of her extensive training, she knew how to work out properly, and we did. We ate right, we exercised, and we supported each other. We worked not only towards a healthier *us* emotionally, but physically as well. I was working at home still, telecommuting for my job in Southern California. She ditched the idea of driving to work and bought a bicycle. We had become urban; commuting on our bikes and working at home. We focused on our health because we both wanted a future together.

Our renewed relationship did not go unnoticed in the

ex-Mormon community. We were still popular. Some people wanted to be like us. Other people wanted to be around us. Jessica and I were strong together. Jessica's previous indiscretions were unknown to the rest of the community and so was all of the turmoil we had experienced. It was better that they didn't know. If I no longer cared about the past then why should her mistakes be public knowledge?

"OH MY GOD! You have to come see this!" Jessica yelled from the basement. I was upstairs making dinner. "Get your ass down here now!" I ran downstairs into the study where both of our computers sat. I spent over eight hours a day working in that room.

"What is it?" Jessica was laughing hysterically. She could not contain herself.

"Look what I just posted!" Her laughter continued. I saw what she had posted on the Internet and laughed with her. We had a long tradition of posting online as alter-egos. We were professionals at baiting people and then insulting them. This hobby was never something I had done before Jessica. Her apparent zeal and talent for it made joining her so much easier.

A few months before she and I had joined our friend Bryce (while they were sleeping together) in baiting and insulting people in our small online community. We were the worst. If someone posted a genuine thought on the Internet, all three of us would insult the person who shared had shared his or her most intimate moments with the Internet. We never posted such negative remarks using our real names or even our known pseudonyms. We shared one name, and it made people furious.

Eventually the truth of who we were came out, and we all stopped immediately. Well, Jessica never stopped. Her hobby was toying with people and seeing what kind of reaction she could get from them. She wanted to know just how far she could push them before they would break. I still welcomed the entertainment while I felt uncertain about the damage of what she was doing. Truthfully, without Jessica's influence I might never have even entertained the idea of participating in online harassment. She was teaching me how to be *normal*. I wanted to be funny and popular like she was. Stirring up drama usually made her happy, and a happy Jessica meant a happy Matt. I loved laughing together.

We were not alone in our online harassment. CaptainAwesome8, also known as Vince, participated too, and he came to visit Utah from out of state. Vince had custody of his daughters in North Carolina so he came to Utah to drop his daughters off for their summer visit with their mother. He was part of our community, although most people did not like him. His negativity was too much for people to handle.

I have heard it said that former Mormons can leave Mormonism, but they cannot leave Mormonism alone. If this was ever true of a person, it was true of Vince. He was the type of guy who could be either the greatest defender or the greatest critic of whatever movement you belonged to. He either promoted or destroyed others' beliefs on the Internet. He had had his sights on the Mormon Church for years. We welcomed him into our home.

He was tall, handsome, and he had a great head of hair. He spoke with confidence, and he was nothing like we expected him to be. In person Vince was a normal guy. Was there some demon inside of him that made him act out online? Online he was one of the meanest people we knew. His presence alone made people leave online message boards. His very friendship often made others question their affiliation with us.

But Jessica and I liked Vince. He was doing exactly what we had been doing. He was pointing out flaws in people who could not see them in themselves. Honestly, what he did went beyond pointing out flaws. It was all extremely entertaining as long as his anger was never directed towards us. We were safe as long as we were on his side.

He came over, thankful that we let him stay with us, and laughed. He brought a compact disc of his favorite band. It was a "thank you" gift for letting him stay for free at our home. Lots of people came and went from our home. We always let people stay with us, especially if they were a part of our tight-knit group of former Mormons. Our house was the place to be. Everyone idolized us. When all of the dirty laundry from our past was out in the open I felt that we were so strong that we could move past all of the nonsense. We were so *above* everyone else that poking fun at them online was something we easily did. We enjoyed it.

We had Vince with us to talk about our superiority with more. He was just like us, although I'm certain he was slightly darker. Either way his objective was the same as our objective online.

A part of me never liked what we did, but I knew it brought Jessica so much joy. I had initially joined the community of former Mormons to heal, not to hurt others. I became more and more disconnected with the online warfare as the months went on, but I could never deny the entertainment value. Most of the insults traded back and forth were done by Vince and Jessica with an unsuspecting victim. Occasionally I would join, but mostly I would watch.

After all, I had a beautiful girlfriend who was happy. Who was I to tell her what made her happy was wrong? Everything I would have normally considered inappropriate, even insulting people, seemed acceptable with her around. Convinced I was still being influenced by the Mormon religion and their ridiculous moral rules I never spoke up. Why would I? Mormonism had controlled me long enough, and I would never let it control me again. Fighting against what we had been taught made the most sense. Her personality amazed me. She inspired me.

Vince's visit was short. After a weekend spent dropping off his daughters and meeting people from our online community in person for the first time, it was time for him to leave. He stood with his suitcase in our living room, petting Jessica's two dogs. Our cat Sariah ran across the living room to hide. Our bird chirped in the background. At this moment I am certain Jessica's hamster was running on his wheel and her fish was also jumping out of the water to make noise. Vince looked at us.

"Seriously? Why do you have so many animals? Get some freaking kids already." We laughed. "Really, stop it with the animals. Get some kids."

| FIVE |
The Plan of Salvation
May 2005

Motivated by what I assume was Vince's statement about Jessica and me having children, she came home the next day from work in a panic. She was acting manic, but also sad, which was an extremely weird combination of emotion to experience from someone you love.

"Where is this relationship going?" She asked in a way that seemed almost like a statement rather than a question. It was like she had a point to make but was waiting for my response before making it.

"Forward Jessica, the relationship is moving forward." I realize my response was ambiguous, but at the same time I was not fully prepared for the marriage talk, especially while our relationship was still licking its wounds from the Bryce fiasco.

"Oh." Whatever she had planned on saying before suddenly had no place in our conversation. Jessica looked defeated. "I don't want to waste my time if we're not going to be talking about marriage." The conversation I was trying to avoid had found a way to demand to be discussed. She left the living room and went into the bedroom; I assumed to disrobe from her daily military fatigues. I waited for her to come back out. She did not.

Approaching the bedroom, I saw her in the bed under the covers. Her face was buried in the pillows. "What's wrong?" I had not forgotten the conversation we just had, and I was hoping that something else suddenly bothered her.

"You know," she said. Her face still buried in the pillows. She was pulling the oldest trick in the book. If she were a toddler, she would be holding her breath. If she was my first wife, she was pouting until she got her way. Jessica was moping and acting like a teenaged girl, hoping to elicit a response from me. She was throwing a fit in order to get her way. It was most likely something she had learned from her childhood and continued to do until that day.

Unfortunately it worked. I would rather give in and end the nonsense than have to put up with someone acting like a child for a few days. The path of least resistance was to talk about the issue bothering her. I had to tell her about some plans I had already started to prepare for.

We had a trip planned to go to Southern California for my college graduation. We were going to see my family and find some time to walk on the beach. I had planned on proposing marriage to her on the beach. The setting worked so great for me for my first marriage, and so many movies had told me a romantic setting was exactly what women love when being asked to spend the rest of their lives with someone. It seemed that waiting wasn't an option any more.

"Jessica, I was planning on proposing to you in California. That's where this relationship is going."

"*Really?*" Her interest was sparked. She then became sad again. "My first husband's proposal to me was not very romantic. We just talked about it and that was that. We were engaged."

"I was planning on the beach. I wanted to talk to your father first though."

"Why?" Her confused sadness became defensiveness.

"Out of respect. He is your father after all."

"I am a grown woman. I do not need my father's permission to get married. I think it's horribly disrespectful for you to even think I would want that." I don't know why I didn't think about that sooner. Why would Jessica, a grown, beautiful, independent woman need the blessing from her father, a *man*, to get married? I felt stupid for even considering it. "You were really going to propose?"

"Yes," I replied. Her head went back into the pillow.

"I can't believe I'm doing this." Her anger and confusion was suddenly directed at herself. Happy I was no longer the target of her childish angst I sat down on the bed to console her.

"Doing what?" Did she regret getting into a relationship with me? Was her frustration towards the makeup on the pillow case? What was she talking about now?

"I ruined it. I ruined your chance to be romantic by acting like a child." While I agreed with her feeling, I knew it was not the end of the world. I also knew that telling her I agreed with her would not make anything better.

Lying on the bed, covered in a blanket, with her head on a makeup smeared pillow was the woman I loved. She was the one I wanted to spend the rest of my life with. Considering her normally aggressive and "take charge" personality I was surprised that she had not proposed first.

"Do you want me to get on one knee?" She bit her lip.

"No Matt, that's stupid. Just ask me to marry you." I crawled onto the bed and gave her a long kiss. I looked into her eyes.

"Marry me," I said. "Be my wife." She paused for a moment, gazing back into my eyes.

"Yes!" Her demeanor went from sad and mopey to happy and excited. "I cannot wait to tell everyone!" And tell everyone she did. Our rag-tag band of former Mormons were elated for us.

We were proof that true love existed. We were an example that even after your world got turned upside down after leaving a belief system there was a way out. There was an end goal – happiness – after Mormonism.

One of the fundamental teachings of Mormonism is called *The Plan of Salvation*. The Plan of Salvation is a simple flowchart of life. The flow chart starts in the pre-existence, where we all existed as spirits before being born. Through choices we make we are born, live, and die. Where we go and what we do after death is determined on the choices we make. It was a simple, beautiful plan. I felt as though my life was on the right track again. I felt like I could look forward and see how it was all going to play out.

I held Jessica and envisioned a life together. We would grow old, have kids, and have grandchildren. We would fight the world and we would do it together.

She called her family and told them the good news. Her family was less than pleased. They all still imagined that she would go through her "non-Mormon phase" and eventually come back to the church. Marrying another former Mormon would only make the path back to righteousness so much more difficult for her. They assumed that I was the bad influence. They had no idea.

We drove to Southern California and told my family. Coming from a non-religious family, our belief system was not a factor in their acceptance of our planned nuptials. My brother was less than excited, but it had nothing to do with us. He worked two jobs in order to support his unemployed wife and two daughters. With a son on the way, his anxiety was through the roof. I hoped he was jealous of me and my hot fiancé. "Attaching the ball and chain, eh?" He was trying to be funny. His sense of humor was one that few people got. I understood it though. He might as well have said, "Run, don't do it. Your life could end up like mine." He smiled. "Congratulations you two," he said.

Telling my mother was something I dreaded, especially since my previous marriage had ended only a little over year before. I remembered when I told her about my first engagement. She was excited back then, just as she was when we broke the news to her this time. I had a real plan for my own salvation. I was not to be saved from the Devil or Evil, but rather from a life of loneliness and depression. Jessica was it. I knew it. Sitting in my mother's apartment with my new fiancé I looked at the two most important women in my life. We laughed and drank wine, happy to be together. I was happy to have a second chance at true love, a second chance at marriage and kids and everything else I had always wanted.

As a Mormon we made our decisions based on a feeling. The good *warm fuzzy* feelings, we were told, were the Holy Ghost. The Holy Ghost would confirm the truthfulness of things we heard or answer prayers. It was the same *good feeling* that had motivated me to propose to my first wife, who I had only known for three weeks. Even though Mormonism was in my past, the lessons I learned from it stuck with me. Marrying Jessica *felt* good. It *felt* right. Her transgressions with me were no longer important. Her drinking or Internet fiascos did not matter. The fact that drama followed her everywhere she went was unimportant. What mattered to me at that moment was how I felt.

And I felt great.

| SIX |
Reunited
August 2005

It was raining out and Jessica and I were both standing under a gazebo with hot coffee in our hands. We had to bring coffee because it was a cold day. We had to bring coffee;

Mormons don't drink coffee.

We were at my missionary reunion, reconnecting with everyone who had been a Mormon missionary in the area of the Philippines where I had served during my two year mission. It was the first time many of us had see each other for years. I helped organize the reunion, even as a non-believer.

Some of Jessica's tattoos were visible. Her visible ink was a sign to my still-believing friends that I had moved on from Mormonism. It was one more visible testimony that I was free. On the outside, my appearance was no different than the other former missionaries huddled in the gazebo. My appearance was clean cut, with glasses and short hair. I was even on the blonde side of brown, which made me look more All-American than some of my friends.

It was August of 2005, and we were at a local park. One of the former missionaries, Elder Sampson, showed up with a grill he had made himself out of an old beer keg. Since beer kegs were illegal in Utah, I had no idea where he acquired it or even why it was such a great idea to turn it into a grill. He was proud of it though. Perhaps creating the grill out of something that was so completely sinful was his way of showing the world he too was different. He could embrace the light and the dark, as long as it was only a method to cook meat.

President Wagstaff, as we knew him, showed up. He had been our leader during our two year mission. He was our highest leader, the leader of every missionary who had served during his tenure. In Mormonism your leaders are able to receive revelation from God on your behalf. This made President Wagstaff more than our leader; he was our conduit for receiving God's instructions while we were missionaries. He walked up to the picnic area and put down a pile of books and audio CDs. They were his newest book and CD, *on sale now* at the nearest Mormon Church owned bookstore. We were fortunate enough to get them for free.

Remembering the mission, we all talked and laughed. I introduced my beautiful fiance to the rest of them. They all knew that I no longer believed, but they talked to me anyway. At least some of them did.

Elder Dana, as I knew him, talked to my friend who had helped organize the reunion. "I just don't know what to say to Timion." As missionaries we referred to ourselves by our last names, with the title *Elder* or *Sister* in front of it, depending on gender. Even though it had been five long years since many of us had left missionary service, our last names were the most comfortable way of identifying and referring to each other.

"What do you mean?" My friend didn't understand Elder Dana's confusion. Even though my friend was a believing Mormon he had never had an issue with me. My disbelief had zero influence on him.

"What do I say to him? What do we talk about? What do we have in common any more?" Elder Dana clearly wanted to talk to me, someone he had such a great connection half a world away years before, but since our common ground was gone he didn't even know where to start.

Elder Dana looked up to me during our missionary service. I was the only American convert missionary at the time. In other words, I joined Mormonism and decided to serve a mission of my own free will. The rest of the American missionaries were born into their religion and a mission was something they had known about since they were old enough to talk.

Luckily for me Elder Dana never said more to me than common pleasantries. I was outnumbered at the reunion, and if I had been required to defend my lack of faith it could have turned ugly rather quickly. All I wanted to do was see my friends with whom I shared an amazing two years.

Elder Dana was not the only one reluctant to talk to me. Very few approached me themselves. These people that at one point I knew so intimately walked around like I might have an infectious disease, only talking with me after I struck up a conversation with them.

The awkward behavior I had received that day was no surprise to me. I had seen it before: Convicted sex offenders entrusted to be alone with children, liars allowed to teach Sunday School, thieves in charge of church finances, adulterers given permission to care for widows, and con-artists given the pulpit as a way to solicit participants in a new multi-level marketing scheme. All of these people were Mormon, and as long as they proclaimed their faith, they were welcome into the congregation without question. The moment, however, a law abiding believer started to question the faith, s/he was considered to be a bad influence, controlled by Satan, and disregarded completely.

My six years in Mormonism resulted in social isolation from anyone outside of the Mormon community. My Mormon experience caused me to reject all of my non-Mormon friends. While a Mormon all I had were my fellow believes.

Once I left, in my Mormon friends' eyes, I had become a bad influence. I was treated as a leper. Sometimes I was a pity case, and they would attempt to remind me why rejecting my faith was a bad decision. The community, the feeling of being a part of a group that I had so long sought after, was gone. They let me know I would gladly be taken me back if I rejected my disbelief. Lying to myself was something I had spent enough time doing, and I could not let happen again.

President Wagstaff took the center of attention. "Okay, who can recite the *First Vision* in Tagalog?" Tagalog was the language we spoke in the Philippines. The First Vision is the account of Mormonism's founder, Joseph Smith, when God and Jesus themselves appeared to him, telling him to form his own church. The First Vision is a crucial part of teaching prospective converts. The story was extremely important to make them *feel* just how amazing it was that a young Joseph Smith saw God

AND Jesus.

No one raised their hands. Jessica poked me in the ribs. "Hey, *you* should do it. That will show them that the atheist remembers their own religion better than they do." She was right, I still did remember it. Even today I *still* remember the First Vision in Tagalog. People used to say that my ability to pick up Tagalog so quickly, and still retain it years afterwards, was God giving me the *Gift of Tongues.* It was proof that God was working through me. I'm just good with languages.

Someone finally stepped up and did a semi-decent job remembering the translated version of Joseph Smith's words. He was given a Butterfinger bar as a reward. The questions continued. "Who has gotten married?" Butterfinger bars handed out. "Who has children?" More candy given to the faithful. I suddenly remembered how often President Wagstaff had given out Butterfingers to those who performed the best on the mission. Everything I learned in college later told me that he was simply rewarding the behavior he desired. It was very Pavlovian.

Faithful former missionaries who had wives and children had the most candy as a reward. I had none. I didn't really want any though, mostly because I told myself I didn't want their approval. I tried extra hard not to play into their mindset. I did this partially to show I was *better* than my missionary pals and also to show Jessica I wasn't one of *them* any more.

We talked and caught up some more with my former brothers in Christ, my former fellow soldiers in a war against Satan. All the while I felt eyes on me, as if I was being observed. Most of them wanted to know how a former Mormon behaved. I was a test subject to be observed, an anecdote to be relayed back to their families about the consequences of denying the faith.

A scrapbook sat on the table which all of us signed when we ended our missionary service and left the mission for our homes. We wrote our dedications to President Wagstaff and his wife.

You are the closest thing to parents I have ever had. Thank you so much. I love you two!

When I wrote that I was twenty one years old, and I was terribly sad that none of my family was Mormon like me. I wanted a good Mormon family. President Wagstaff and his wife served as role models for quite some time. "What the fuck Matt?" Jessica asked me, a little louder than I felt comfortable with. She couldn't believe that at one point I had totally believed it all. She couldn't believe that at one point I had *wanted* a perfect Mormon life. Jessica always had had her doubts. She always rebelled against the religion of her parents. I was so jealous of her conviction, or *lack* of conviction, when it came to religion.

We left soon afterwards with my new book and audio CD in tow. "Seriously Matt, that was fucked up."

"What?" I was probably being naïve; not instantly understanding what she had meant.

"Why the hell did we even go to that thing? What were we doing there?"

"Visiting with old friends of mine."

"Yeah, next time you're going by yourself. I'm not subjecting myself to that again. Everyone kept looking at us. If I wanted that kind of judgment I would go hang out at my family's house."

Her point was made. No more missionary reunions for me, especially ones I had organized. She was right though, they were all staring at us. No one had expected the former Mormon missionary to come. Let alone come willing to discuss shared memories and refuse to bring up anything negative. No one expected the former Mormon missionary to actually think their two years abroad was a positive experience.

We pulled into the driveway and she reiterated her previous statement. "Never again," she said.

"Okay, got it."

| SEVEN|
A Black Dress
October 2005

I'd never seen so many tattoos in my entire life. Walking the streets of Salt Lake City, with its old buildings, beautiful landscaping, and snow capped mountains in every direction, I was still focused more on the tattoos. They were everywhere. I am told that cities like Seattle or San Francisco have more tattoos, but I never saw more tattoos in those cities when I visited.

Salt Lake City is a city of subtle protest. With (at the time) 70% of the state being Mormon, people go to extremes to show that they were either not Mormon or that they rejected Mormonism. In some instances this would mean wearing revealing clothes; pious young Mormon girls would only wear a spaghetti strap top as long as it had a t-shirt underneath. Tattoos signaled to the world one's identity; finding a person with tattoos up and down his/her arms could be as difficult as finding a Catholic priest in Vatican City.

From what I had heard, City Weekly, the local independent newspaper, had a column at one point where the writer would walk up to the most tattooed person they could find on the street and ask them where he or she served his or her Mormon mission. Not surprisingly, every single person had a story about his or her mission. In a culture where having two SUVs meant you were righteous and in God's favor, having tattoos meant you were not Mormon. The two sides played by the same rule book.

Our wedding planning was also a subtle protest. While we didn't get tattoos for our wedding, we made a conscious decision to do everything opposite of what *they* would think we should have done. Our decisions were well thought out and meticulously planned. Some were a slap in the face of Mormonism, motivated by Jessica's insistence that her family was to be constantly reminded she was no longer Mormon. Other choices were subtle and I doubt anyone besides us recognized them for what they were.

Our wedding was organized around a black dress. White symbolizes purity, and we refused to repeat traditions from a Christian wedding. The sleeveless black wedding gown with small white flowers flowed when Jessica walked. It was perfect, simple, and elegant. She looked like a rock star when she wore it. Jessica confessed that she secretly hoped her appearance would offend her Mormon family.

We drove down to Las Vegas, where our wedding was to take place. After we arrived at our hotel room, we spent the night getting ready for the next day. Jessica made our wedding cake, pursuant to her new fascination with baking. It was a lopsided chocolate cake that looked like it had been made by a teenaged boy in a high school home economics class, but it tasted wonderful. Her friends showed up and helped with her makeup. We ignored the rule of not seeing each other that morning. Beliefs like that were built on superstition, and superstition had no place in our marriage.

We took photos as part of the casino's wedding package. The door to the chapel opened and everyone turned their heads in anticipation of us walking in. Jessica asked a quick question before we stepped through the door. "Hey, which side does the bride's family normally stand on?"

"I honestly have no idea." My first marriage was in a Mormon temple without aisles, tuxedos, or many family members. Since my first marriage ended by exchanging a secret handshake over an altar, my knowledge of traditional marriages was lacking.

"The left!" The casino worker told us. She was thrilled

to be a part of this wedding, which according to her was the most unique she had ever seen. That says a lot when your job was holding twenty weddings a day.

"Okay, let's switch sides. I don't want to be part of this patriarchal bullshit." And we switched sides.

We walked down the aisle together, arm in arm. In a room full of people, only her father stood up to see her. The rest of the room remained seated.

Jessica's sleeveless dress showed off her tattoo of the letter "M" with wings on it. It was her mother's first initial. At the end of the aisle stood Lester, the ex-Mormon spiritual guru. He stood there in flip flops, slightly tattered jeans, and a see-through silk shirt. Tattoos covering his torso were visible to everyone. Of course we wanted to be married by a flamboyant gay man. It was one more way to be different. It was just one more way to show everyone how "recovered" from Mormonism we were.

When we first asked him, Lester was reluctant to officiate the wedding, but he agreed to do it anyway. He had initially said that he would never attend another wedding until he had the right to be married himself. Offer an attention-hungry person center stage, and, like Lester, he or she will rarely turn the opportunity down.

Family and friends were all around us. Although some people boycotted our wedding due to our perceived involvement in yet another online harassment brouhaha, many members of the ex-Mormon community traveled from all over to attend. Our wedding was a momentous event for our group of former Mormons. It brought together years of friendships; it was a reason for everyone to celebrate.

Lester spoke and everyone listened. He talked about true love. He talked about how he saw an example of true love conquering all in Jessica and me. It was a very touching ceremony. "I don't talk about this much, but I occasionally perform services for people where I give them a blessing. This is not like the Mormon version of a blessing, but a very spiritual one." I was surprised it took so long for someone to mention Mormonism. He held our hands and blessed us with a long marriage, children, and a long life together.

"As some of you may know," Lester continued, "I crochet. I import yarns from all over the world and make hats for people." He reached into his satchel and pulled out two long coils of yarn. One was brown, the other was white. He put one coil of yarn around Jessica's neck and one around mine. "Okay, that's it."

There was no "I now pronounce you man and wife." There was no "In the name of Jesus Christ, Amen," as we would expect in Mormonism. "That's it" ended our wedding ceremony. It was October 16, 2005, and we were married. Music played and people clapped.

We rushed up to our hotel room where the reception was held. Free alcohol and cigars were readily available. These items, which possibly made her Mormon relatives uncomfortable, were free for the taking. "If they are uncomfortable with who I am Matt, fuck 'em. I don't want them at my wedding."

Fifty people crammed into a small hotel room. We used the opportunity to mingle. Jessica's family met my family. Our ex-Mormon friends split between occupying one of the beds or huddling around the bathroom where the Mojitos were being produced at a record rate. Jessica's Mormon family mostly stayed in one corner of the room. Her step-mother kept complaining about the heat. "That fucking bitch, this is my day, and all she does it bitch about the heat," Jessica snapped. If I had learned anything from years of television, you *never* tell a bride to settle down on her wedding day. I said nothing in return.

Her family began leaving to drive home so that they could attend Sunday church services the next morning. My brother and his wife left too, but that was only because they had three children and the reception was turning into a drinking fest, which was inappropriate for children.

Those of us who remained went to the top floor of the hotel and ate dinner. Directly outside the restaurant was a rooftop club. There was a bar and dancing. The air was still warm, and there was only a slight wind. We all went outside and started to dance. Well, everyone else danced. Although it was my wedding day, I refused to embarrass myself by looking like I was having a seizure while "dancing."

I looked over and saw my mother dancing with James, a recently *out of the closet* ex-Mormon. Next to him Lester was dancing with a man, a straight man. Soon Lester's dancing partner switched to another straight man. In what I can only imagine was an attempt to show just how *free* and how *unaffected* he was by Mormonism, Lester's straight dance partner started french kissing Lester. And then it was another man, and another.

Straight married men, and women, started lining up to make out with the gay men. "Oh my God!" Jessica yelled. "That's hilarious! Matt, you should kiss Lester!"

"Nah, there is only one person I want to kiss tonight." Not only did kissing another man seem like a weird idea to me, but *Jessica* suggesting it made it seem that much more bizarre. The dancing continued. The kissing continued. People started leaving the rooftop bar, and eventually we left too.

We walked down to the lobby of the casino with my boss and his wife. They were both Mormons, but very liberal Mormons, an uncommon trait. They had tattoos and piercings. They drank alcohol and smoked pot. They participated in a gay bowling league on Friday nights. Although they believed in Mormonism, they spent their lives in a not-so-subtle protest. They were both drinking, and my boss's hands were all over his wife's body.

"I got a new piercing," my boss's wife told Jessica and

me.

"Oh yeah?" Jessica was half drunk and giddy.

"Do you want to see it?" my boss's wife asked again. My boss was right there, encouraging us to take a look.

We nodded and my boss's wife pulled down her shirt in the lobby of the casino, fully exposing her breast. She had a nipple piercing. My boss loved if when people admired his wife's breasts. Her implanted DD breasts crowned a petite 5'3" frame as a trophy for him. His actions bragged, "I get to have sex with this, and you do not."

We stared at her exposed breast in the hotel lobby. I half expected security to kick us out of the hotel, but no one came. Nothing happened. It was Las Vegas after all.

We retired to our hotel room happily married. The future was unwritten for us, but if our wedding ceremony was any indicator, we were going to have a very interesting life together.

PART 2

| EIGHT |

Our Gay Child
October 17th, 2005

We drove home from the wedding elated. Our bond was official. Actually, it had been official for over a week. We had secretly married in the Salt Lake City courthouse ten days prior, but we had never told anyone about it. Getting our silk-shirt-wearing yarn-enthusiast minister registered in the state of Nevada was too much of a headache. We had done it the old fashioned way: in front of a justice of the peace. No one knew this, not even our families.

We arrived home to find our friend Tyson living in our house. He was from out of town, someone we had met as a result of our association with the ex-Mormons. However, Tyson had never been a Mormon. He was interested in Mormons, and he was going to spend two months living with us so that he could complete research on his doctoral dissertation.

Life went back to normal quickly with the addition of a wedding band. Jessica started knitting the yarn draped over us at our wedding into two hats that combined the two colors of yarn together. She also knitted a smaller version of the caps for a potential child. Our first baby would one day have a cap made from that same exotic yarn. Tyson spent his days traveling to libraries and universities. When he came home we would all talk.

"The most amazing thing happened to me today," Tyson would begin. His words were slightly muffled from the small *meows* coming from the bathroom. Jessica had insisted on getting another cat, we named him Tom Jones. The cat was in the bathroom so that he could adjust and survive without being eaten by the two large dogs we had patrolling the house.

"I went to BYU today and felt like I could have as much gay sex as I wanted."

"What!?!?!" Jessica's contagious laughter encouraged Tyson to continue with his story.

"I swear, I have a great *gaydar,* and it seemed that every other male on that campus was gay. I am positive the guy at the library was hitting on me." Tyson was gay, but not in the same way that Lester and James were gay. Tyson had *always* been gay, and he had never lived in a sheltered religion where gay people went to support groups and received electroshock therapy in an attempt to *cure* homosexuality.

Tyson's being gay excited Jessica. She used his presence in our home to gain attention for herself. His presence gave her a good excuse to do what all progressive people do: hang out at gay bars and invite everyone to go with us.

Our gay bar adventures started at a bar with a younger crowd that was our age.

Most of them were good looking without shirts or chest hair. They obviously worked out a lot. I felt like a total frump in that crowd. I wanted to take our group of friends to a video arcade so that I could be the best looking guy around. Interestingly enough Tyson was not dancing with other men. He had a boyfriend back in New York. The ex-Mormons who came with us though danced with each other and other random men. Since male-on-male makeouts were now okay, having received such great feedback at our wedding, the same behavior occurred in the gay bar.

But one gay bar wasn't enough. We had to experience more than one bar with a tame crowd. We had to be different and explore everything we could while we had Tyson with us. As usual Jessica took the lead.

"We need to go to the lesbian bar!"

The lesbian bar? Admittedly I did not know many lesbians, but everything I had heard of *The Paper Moon* made it sound like a place we would not fit in. No one in our party was a lesbian. My straight wife, my straight self, and our gay roommate, Tyson, would not fit in at a lesbian bar.

But Jessica persisted. "C'mon! It'll be fun! Imagine what we might see!"

She was right. I had no idea what we might see there. What secret treasures could a lesbian bar hold? What stories would we be able to tell? Besides, we had to show everyone, and mostly ourselves, that we were accepting of everyone despite their lifestyles. We had to prove that the behavior Mormonism deemed as inappropriate was okay with us.

While at the Paper Moon I went into the male bathroom, half surprised such an establishment would even have accommodations for men. I walked up to the urinal and unzipped my pants. "Hey," a voice came from behind me. I looked around and a butch woman was in my bathroom walking to the stall.

"Oh, hey," I said back. Was I in the wrong bathroom? Certainly I was in the right place. Women's restrooms do not have urinals, do they?

"Having a good night?" She spoke to me from the stall adjacent to my urinal. There was no door and we were essentially talking face to face.

"Yeah, you?" I finished my business and zipped up my pants. She responded while I was washing my hands. I didn't want to be rude, but I don't even normally talk to *men* in the restroom, let alone a random women doing her bathroom business in front of me. I was more concerned with getting out of the bathroom and telling everyone what I had just experienced.

I walked out of the bathroom, did a double check that it was in fact the bathroom for the boys, and found my group at the bar. I heard Jessica's loud laughter from across the room. "Watch this," she said to the group. "Bartender, I want a *wet pussy!*" She laughed again. She easily thought she was the funniest person in the room, having asked for a drink she was certain never existed. It was all for shock value.

"Okay," the bartender said, and then proceeded to pour the drink.

"What!? You have a drink called the wet pussy!? Hey everyone," she announced to our group of friends, "the bartender just gave me a wet pussy!" Tyson and I looked at each other. We were the only real *outsiders* in that group. He was never a Mormon and from out of state. Even though at that point I had been in Utah for almost a year I was also from out of state and I had only had a short lived Mormon phase.

"Yeah, I remember when I had my first beer too," he said to me quietly. We both snickered.

Eventually we had to go to the last gay bar in the area, named *Try Angles.* Tyson told me that in New York there were *bear bars,* where big hairy men go, *twink bars,* where our *Abercrombie Gays* would end up, and other bars dedicated to every different flavor of homosexual. In Salt Lake City, however, there were only a few. *Try Angles* was a melting pot of all different genres of gay. Bears dancing next to twinks. Old men and young men. It was a Noah's Ark of homosexuality with at least two of each kind in the room in case we ever needed to repopulate the earth with gay men.

"I feel like I'm learning about gays for the first time," Tyson said. His eyes were wide and his jaw gaped, almost falling to the floor. "These homosexuals fascinate me!" He said it in his best academic voice.

Even though Tyson had *always* been gay, he had never before seen such behavior. Gay men with families of their own (some still married to their Mormon wives and some completely out of the closet) were at the club acting out on decades of Mormon induced sexual repression. "Wow," were the only words Tyson could muster after watching a big hairy man in leather start grinding his crotch against one of our straight ex-Mormon friends. "Just wow, I feel like I want to come back here and study these people." I'm glad he said that. While I had known gay people my entire life, I had never been to a gay bar before I had lived in Salt Lake City. I thought that the gay bars I had attended were normal. I thought it was how gay men acted. "I don't know what I'm looking at Matt, but I cannot take my eyes away."

And that's how the short lived gay bar experiment happened. Jessica owned the room usually, and I felt like a prude for not kissing men. At least we were married and I still got to go home with her.

Before Tyson had to leave for the next stop on his research, all three of us visited the Church History Museum in downtown Salt Lake City. Tyson was, after all, writing his dissertation in American History. We looked at relics of Mormon past including clothes worn by the actual prophets (modern Mormon prophets, not ancient Jewish prophets), personal property of Brigham Young, Joseph Smith's death mask, and an entire section dedicated to Emma Smith, Joseph Smith's wife.

Jessica, full of protest, questioned over and over again with increasing belligerence "Where is the section dedicated to Joseph Smith's *other* wives?"

In his book *In Sacred Loneliness* Todd Compton estimated that Joseph Smith had had at least thirty-four wives ranging from age fourteen to fifty eight. While Jessica had made a valid point, it was really just an attempt to try to be edgy. She was standing up to the church of her father while trying to make us laugh.

Her behavior came across as initially funny, but ultimately annoying. I hated people staring at us because of her increasing loudness. My nine-year-old son does the same thing. He does something hilarious, and as soon as he gets a response, including a positive reaction, he drives that behavior into the ground. Jessica's call for attention worked as we noticed Mormon security guards following us around for the rest of our visit at the Museum.

"Screw this place, I'm bored," she said. We left.

The rest of Tyson's visit with us was great. Jessica taught him to knit. We all cooked together. We watched television together. He was the perfect houseguest and served a valid purpose, reminding me that some of the behavior we saw was not normal. Had he not been with us during that time period, I am certain there were occasions I would not have known if what I was experiencing was part of normal life or completely insane. Tyson grounded me at times, and he continued to do so for as long as I knew him.

"This is our friend Tyson; he's living with us," is how Jessica would always introduce Tyson to people. "And he's gaaaaaay!" She had to throw that in. Once Tyson was gone we would no longer be able to introduce him as our gay live-in friend. Fighting the system by being so openly *okay* with homosexuality would lose its appeal with her. For a few months however, having a gay man in our home made her happy. She told me one night, "it's like we have a gay child!"

Jessica laughed at herself again; thinking she was hilarious. Her laughter made me smile.

| NINE |
Stability
Winter 2005

We sat in the cafe for our weekly brunch with the ex-Mormons. It had become a tradition for us. Our favorite place to go was Orbitz cafe, right next to the new mall built for the 2002 Winter Olympics. A sign outside the cafe described that area as a former brothel, and the existence of that brothel (among others) had been completely sanctioned by the Mormon Church. Our brunch location was one of historic value, even if the only *hunger* it fed was no longer sexual.

What started as weekly brunches turned into weekly exercises. Jessica and I had taken our goal to become more healthy seriously, and we were exercising regularly. She had begun riding her bicycle to work, and on the weekends we would often take long bike rides on the Jordan River Parkway, a paved path running all along the Jordan River in Utah.

Not everyone in the ex-Mormon group had a decent bicycle, but everyone did have rollerblades. We started rollerblading every Sunday. Occasionally someone in the group would stop and smoke pot. I had no idea how they did it. Rollerblading and pot was out of the question because every time I had ever smoked pot, I could barely sit on the couch. These people were either extremely gifted rollerbladers or gifted pot smokers. Either way I was impressed.

And that is how our lives went on for a year. We rollerbladed with friends, had house parties once a month or so, and Jessica and I fell more in love. We began gardening together that spring. We spent our time with each other always, and it was spectacular. I was always reminded of what a great choice I had made when I married her. My first wife did not hold a candle to Jessica.

One weekend, in an effort to become a bigger part of the ex-Mormons group, our friend Nadia was throwing a party at her house in Tooele, about a forty five minute drive away. We showed up, and then it was clear to me why Nadia lived in the middle of nowhere. Her house was huge and her monthly bills were less than we paid.

At every party there was always someone new. The new members of the group were either people we all knew from online or someone who tagged along with a friend.

A young eighteen-year-old girl made her first appearance at this party. I will be the first to admit that she was cute, in a weird *if I were still in high school* kind of way. A drunk forty-year-old man approached her with his wife seated only a few feet away. He began heavy-handedly flirting with the eighteen year old, who appeared to be too overwhelmed by the number of people to really acknowledge that the forty year old was undressing her with his eyes. Perhaps she did notice and just didn't react. I can tell you however that she never came to one of those parties again.

The drunken man and his wife had had an agreement. They could have sex with whoever they wanted. This idea of an "open marriage" was common to me at this point. Instead of being confused by such a relationship, I instead admired them for their openness and trust. They loved each other so much that sex wasn't a part of it anymore. Their relationship was at a level of commitment I doubted I could ever get to, a point I could never reach. In our group many saw a stable, happy, open marriage as the ex-Mormon version of Nirvana. It was something we all strived for. If you could get to that point in your marriage then you were doing something right.

During a weekly trip up the Jordan River Parkway, Brian, a regular rollerblader, began talking to me. Brian lived in a giant home all by himself. It used to be his father's home, but his father had died a long time ago from old age. I think that Brian's father had been well into his sixties when Brian was born. "What you eat doesn't matter," he proclaimed.

"Why not?" I was eating very healthily back then. I had stopped consuming soda and sugar. I had lost a bit of weight with diet and exercise. Brian was the same height as me but weighed easily twenty or thirty pounds lighter.

"Take my brother for example, he only eats cashews and he's as healthy as anyone I know." I was no doctor but eating only cashews did not seem like a good way to stay healthy and fit.

These diet ideas were common among our group. Some would go for the cashew diet while others would go for the raw food diet. I will never stop being amazed at how a group of people smart enough to see the flaws in their indoctrinated belief system were unable to see the fallacy in their new diets or new chosen faiths. Their new beliefs usually involved lots of talk of sending "good energy." This shouldn't have surprised me considering how many of these people were high all of the time.

Along with rollerblading, one of the newest fads in the group involved belly dancing and Jessica jumped right on board. She started buying outfits, bells, and scarfs. Her private weekly ritual altered to include belly dancing classes. According to Jessica, her instructor told her that she was the best student; she had real talent, and she should be in the advanced class. She opted not to join the advanced class, however, as she wanted to make sure she had the fundamentals down. She also did not want to embarrass the other students with her natural talent.

Jessica went belly dancing, and I stayed home working on the computer or on my car. Before her belly dancing phase, she had had a craft phase followed by a baking phase. Since her phases only lasted a month or so, when the belly dancing phase was over, she took up smoking hookah daily. She then decorated the guest bedroom in very middle eastern decorations. She really embraced her new hobbies, as short lived as they were.

Her new hobbies gave me time to start some of my own. There were so many things I had always wanted to learn how to do, and I was going to do them. I had the perfect life with amazing friends. I had never felt so popular. Life was mine for the taking, and I intended on doing exactly that. Nothing but good things could happen.

| TEN |

My Second Adolescence
Spring 2006

Jessica and I soon relaxed enough to really let our hair down. We went through a small phase of going to clubs all of the time. I guess it might be better to say that it was a phase that *I* went through, not her. In the past Jessica had spent a good portion of her military career going to clubs and partying. It was really no surprise considering how much she drank, how great of a party she could always throw, and how well she could dance. She would always relate these stories to me about "clubbing," and how she would always be the queen of the room. I always saw it as going hand-in-hand with her popularity.

Jessica was okay without clubbing for a while, but, like an alcoholic clean for years, she eventually had cravings. The nightlife was a part of her, and something she needed to experience every so often to get her fix. I happily tagged along with her in order to find out what the scene was all about. The only bar I had ever visited with any frequency was as a child tagging along with my father every day after work.

As a married couple, we went to the club together. The only two clubs we really went to were both gothic clubs. For whatever reason there is still a huge gothic scene in Utah. "Goths" are people with white makeup, tall boots, eyeliner, and black clothes. Some trends never left Utah, which explained why I would occasionally see leg warmers while walking around. It would also explain why in May of 2012 Travel and Leisure Magazine ranked Salt Lake City as the second worst dressed city in the country, right behind Anchorage, Alaska.

The clubbing would involve us going to a bar, drinking, dancing, and later coming home to be an intimate alcohol-filled married couple. This exposure to becoming a regular club attendee was something I absolutely loved. For a few months, we went clubbing every weekend.

When I turned twenty-one, the age at which most Americans get drunk in celebration, I was a Mormon missionary in the Philippines. Mormons don't drink alcohol and do not go to clubs. Even if I hadn't been a missionary, I still had my own set of prohibitions that prevented me from stepping into a club. My dedication to God and his commandments was too important.

After leaving the Mormon Church I legitimately had no idea what was normal. I did not know how to interact with people unless it was in a church setting. The club "scene" was so new to me and so exciting that I looked forward to going every time we went. I enjoyed dancing with my wife and getting jealous looks from other guys. I enjoyed watching skinny guys wearing glow sticks, who were clearly high on something, dance around the room like they were on a different planet. I loved the energy and the freedom, regardless of the damage the music did to my hearing.

We had a few drinks with friends, and then we spent the rest of the night at the club. We danced, groped, drank, laughed, and drank some more. We all had a great time. We took turns dancing in a cage located on the stage as well as buying rounds of drinks. *This is what real adults do,* I thought. I had no idea this world existed, and while I wasn't too fond of dancing, I embraced the drinking and the eye candy all around me.

One night a number of us went out to the club. Jessica ordered the first round of drinks, which I was told is customary. She said that everyone over the night was supposed to take turns ordering drinks for everyone. I was learning so much about how to be normal. We sat around and drank, making fun of the pathetic guys with their fake tans and flipped up collars. "Douchebags," she would say. Sometimes she would yell it right in their face and then come back to us laughing hysterically. She could get away with anything.

We danced that night. The lights were low and some sort of disco ball provided just enough light for us to see. She danced in her tight jeans, accentuating her supple thighs. I was tipsy, and I can only imagine I looked just like all of the other white guys dancing on the floor. I was never a good dancer. At that moment I didn't care though. I looked at Jessica dancing to the beat, and for an instant I saw no one else. She was the only woman in the room. I wanted to take her home and make love to her all night. I wanted to feel what it felt like to be a part of her world. I wanted to have so much confidence that I could walk up to a frat boy and call him a douchebag. I wondered what it was like to be wanted like she was.

These evenings usually ended with all of us going to a greasy restaurant to dilute the alcohol in our stomachs. The post-bar greasy food had become part of our ritual. In the year I had lived in Utah, I had more fun and more friends than I had ever had in my life. If my life were to have ended at that moment I would have died feeling complete. I would have died happy knowing that the woman in the nightclub was also the woman with whom I shared my life.

| ELEVEN |
Don Quixote
Summer 2006

Ever since I had seen the play "Man of La Mancha" on stage I was hooked. I loved the story of Don Quixote. Even though his character was clearly fictional, and a bit, well, insane, the message rang loud and clear.

The character of Don Quixote was living life the way it was supposed to be, not the way it was. He fought for what was right even if he knew he could never win. That is exactly how life is supposed to be lived.

Jessica and I both resonated with the message and with the character who lived life the way it *should be*. I looked out our window and saw my small 1989 Honda Civic. It was my small contribution to the world.

When I moved to Utah I drove a giant Jeep Wrangler. It guzzled gas and was expensive. I loved the *idea* of getting great gas mileage and living without a car payment. Jessica loved that I was so passionate about it. So when I decided to sell the Jeep and buy a small car for all of the above mentioned reasons, she followed suit.

She sold her much more modern car for an even smaller older Honda. Her two-door hatchback drove like a go-cart. My four door sedan seemed giant in comparison.

But just owning the car was not enough. I wanted to make it better. It had to be more fuel efficient. It needed a paint job and new tires! So I set out traveling to the junkyard on a regular basis to find discarded car parts. I was going to convert my car into something it was never designed to be.

I ordered an engine online and over many months installed it myself. I redid the wiring for the car and put in a new computer. I painted it just the right shade of black to complement the right wheels. By the time I was done with it, I had taken one old car and turned it into something amazing. It was the perfect car. I could drive and easily get fifty miles per gallon.

Jessica took it up a notch and started riding her bicycle to work. Together we were like Don Quixote with a monkey wrench and bicycle shorts.

We were living life the way it was supposed to be lived. We recycled, put blood and sweat into projects that would help the environment, and loved with all of our hearts. It was some of the best times of my life.

Just like I was trying to build my perfect car, Jessica and I were trying to build our perfect family. We spent all of our time together and also tried to have kids for a little over a year. Our attempts to get pregnant never worked. I had always been afraid that Jessica wouldn't be able to have children because in her first marriage she had had two stillborn babies. Her stillbirths were six and nine months along, which understandably made it extremely difficult for her to discuss the matter.

"I went to church a week after my first stillbirth. Before I lost the baby I was nine months along," she told me. I had no experience with anything like this so the story was hers to tell.

"A woman approached me and my husband. She had a big shit-eating grin on her face and asked us when we were going to have kids!" The story seemed so unbelievable, not because I didn't believe her, but for someone to be so oblivious to her situation blew my mind.

The only people "allowed" to talk about the stillbirths in her family were her brother and sister-in-law who also had two stillborn babies, approximately six and nine months along as well. It appeared to me that there might be a genetic issue with her family, and this would easily explain why we were having such a difficult time conceiving. I knew it couldn't have been me, because my brother is so virile he could get women pregnant by shaking their hands. So we kept trying, but we also looked for a backup plan.

After hearing a segment on the radio called "Wednesday's Child," a segment where they feature a foster child once a week, Jessica came home with an idea. We were going to become foster parents and adopt a child. The more I thought about it, the more I liked the idea.

We wanted a child, and we lived our lives in a socially responsible manner. Adopting helped us build a family, and it reflected our values. It was exactly what Don Quixote would have done. He would have rescued and helped children who needed a home. We began researching and quickly registered to take the classes needed to be licensed foster parents. This process involved completing a background check, drug test, and a home visit (called a "home study") where the state not only would inspect the safety of our home but also interview us to obtain a mini-biography.

The foster training was complete and the home study was upon us. We sat with the interviewer in our living room waiting for the questions to begin. The interviewer wasted no time, pulled out her notebook, and began.

"Have you ever done drugs?" was the first question

proposed.

"Yes, but years ago, and just pot," was my honest answer. I had the feeling the questions being asked by the interviewer were routine questions.

When the same question was asked of Jessica, her answer baffled me. I just had admitted freely that yes, when I was a teenager I had smoked pot. My admission should have been no more shocking than a young man admitting he had once looked at Playboy magazines.

"What about you Jessica? Have you ever done drugs?"

"Nope," she said.

I distinctly remembered Jessica calling me when I was still in California. She was scared because she had smoked pot that night. The military does random drug tests and if you "piss hot" (test positive) you were immediately kicked out of the military. She was scared for her job. I also heard numerous stories about her life as a rebellious teenager where she would have wild parties in her house when her father was away for work. These parties involved sex and, you guessed it, drugs. Why did she feel the need to lie about it all? It wasn't like she was still the same person that she had been years before. I was convinced she was either nervous or always afraid anything she said would go on record and could somehow come back to hurt her with her job in the military. She was playing it safe. That had to be it.

After a barrage of questions, we both concluded that the home study went well, even though they never went through the checklist to ensure we had everything done properly. They didn't ask to see where we kept alcohol and cleaning supplies to ensure that they were in a locking cabinet. The interviewer didn't ask to see the fire extinguisher in the kitchen and the fire extinguishers in each car. We were not ask to show how we childprooted the doors and the cabinets. I felt like a kid who had just made a masterpiece with my play-doh only to show a parent who clearly didn't care. I wanted to show off! The interviewer really wanted to ask us about drugs, previous marriages, and why we wanted to foster a child.

Being married opened the door for us to foster a child. In Utah at the time there was a law that said one could not foster children if he or she had other adults in their home that were not part of the immediate family (unless they were married to that person). This law was just the Utah State Legislature's way of preventing gay couples from fostering children; everyone I talked with at the Utah Foster Agency confirmed so. Another by-product of this law passed by the 80% Mormon legislature was that live-in straight couples couldn't foster children either. The only people who could foster kids in Utah had to be straight and married or single and living alone. This was just one more way morality was legislated in the Beehive State.

We awaited our response from the state, checking our mail box every day. By this time it had been almost a year since our wedding and the idea of a family was something we both wanted. We had both worked hard towards our shared dream of a family. It was though the results of a lifetime of planning and heartfelt emotion was finally taking place. Everything seemed to be finally looking up. Our mistakes from the past were forgotten. We were living in the moment. One day while checking the mail, Jessica came into the house looking as white as a ghost. Was it the response we were waiting for from the state? Could we be foster parents? Perhaps they rejected us. What was it?

"It's the CIA." She spit out the words like they were poison.

"The CIA?" I was certain I misunderstood her.

"Yeah, they want me to work for them again." Her statement was so *matter of fact* I was thrown completely off guard.

"What?" Seriously, what?

"They sent me a letter, written in a way that only I

would be able to understand. You wouldn't have even known it was from them."

"So they sent you an encoded message in a letter telling you they want you to be a CIA agent?"

"Yes. It's something I used to do."

"What?"

| TWELVE |

My Wife the Spy
Late Summer 2006

I should have seen this coming. She had been dropping hints about her "other job" for years. Truthfully, I don't come from a military family. I don't understand how the military really works. In my mind members of the military go to boot camp, shoot at the enemy, and then get to wear camouflage. Due to my admitted ignorance of the workings of the military, Jessica was my guide and my teacher into this unfamiliar American subculture.

She had told stories for a while, all small stories, about her experiences in the military. She was a member of an intelligence squadron in the Air Force before her and I met. Their job was to fly in planes and eavesdrop on people's phone calls, radio signals, etc. They gathered intelligence. I knew for a fact that she was a part of that elite military unit because I met a number of her coworkers who were still a part of her former job.

Jessica eventually left her job in intelligence because she was sick of traveling ten months a year for work. She also let slip once that she shot a man while on a work trip in Colombia. Her racially ambiguous features and fluency in Spanish made her a perfect candidate for her covert operations.

She recounted while in Colombia she was undercover and a suspect started to run. Pulling out her 9mm pistol, she shot the runaway suspect in the leg. Her accuracy in shooting was no surprise to me since she had described her recent munitions requalification for her Air Force job. During her test, she showed off by shooting a heart in the target. Her boss was so impressed with her she was asked to join the Air Force shooting team. She declined.

I didn't doubt her past. It kind of all fit together, and besides, when your wife tells you that in the past she worked for the CIA doing clandestine missions, it's kind of cool. We had been watching the television show *Alias* and she told me that it was the most realistic version of how the CIA really operates. I wondered how she knew, but after learning about her past, I understood.

Her revelation to me also answered another question I had concerning a story she told me. She never gave me details but she said once she was on a work trip ("work trip" means an undercover operation) in Miami. While on this trip to Miami she saw her brother, who was also on a "work trip." "It's something we don't talk about Matt, but my entire family is involved in the intelligence community." She told me under an oath of secrecy that her brother and her father were also CIA agents. Her father was so high up in the ranks that he had as much influence as a United States Senator.

She told me one story, straight out of *Meet the Parents*, where she overheard her father talking on the phone in some Asian language. "I am certain he speaks five or six languages, but he won't admit it." His job as a currency broker for the Mormon Church was apparently just a cover job that allowed him to travel the world and do his *real* job. Her brother was the same way. His frequent business trip to Miami had nothing to do with work. He was clearly involved in something bigger.

I was floored.

I looked at her with a new sense of awe. She had done something dangerous and fascinating. My new family was also involved. I was told that if I ever discussed what she had told me we could be arrested. The only reason she was telling me this other side of her was because I was her husband, and I needed to know so I wouldn't worry. It all made perfect sense.

If anyone else had told me this exact same story I would have called them a liar, but knowing her and remembering the stories she told before clamming up (realizing she had said too much) it kind of all fit together. I had become part of a spy family, and my wife chose to disregard espionage for a chance to have a family with me. I had never felt as important as I did at that moment.

We shared conversations about her history for a while. Apparently she was *on the ground* during George W. Bush's infamous "Shock and Awe." She was on the ground collecting intelligence to relay it back to the bombers. Her father apparently had so much money and influence that just being related to him would make our lives dramatically easier. Jessica worked for six months on Capitol Hill and almost every senator she met had asked if she was related to her father. It was like I was married to some underground secret royalty.

Finally getting to know the *real* Jessica also put her martial arts training into perspective. I remembered her stories of being a professional fighter and having a third degree black belt in Brazilian Ju-Jitsu. A skilled and trained CIA agent would naturally have extensive martial arts training. A government operative *would* have spent six months learning Greco-Roman takedowns, as she later told me. It was like she had been giving me pieces of who she really was for so long, and now, finally, I could put the pieces together.

I suddenly realized this new information explained why she had lied to the foster agency about her teenage drug use. Of course she would lie about that. Of course the CIA would have access to that information. She was intentionally avoiding having that information recorded anywhere. The CIA could never know she smoked pot, no matter how long ago it happened.

Knowledge of her past transgressions would affect her, her brother, and her father. The much larger picture of who she was became crystal clear.

I will admit that I felt rather clueless around her again. She had had all of these experiences. She had seen and done so many things. I left Mormonism, and she was there to show me how the *real world* worked. She did. She showed me that there is secrecy and espionage. Her life and presence showed me just how grand the world was and how it, together, built a bigger picture. It was a beautiful picture, one I was thrilled to be a part of. Especially with her.

| THIRTEEN |

Harassment
Summer 2006

Armed with this new knowledge, my enthusiasm for being with Jessica magnified. Being fun and beautiful was one thing. Knowing she was trained in intelligence operations, however, made it easy to follow her lead on life's adventures. Perhaps she would rub off on me? In following her lead, we began harassing people on the Internet again. This time we had a new accomplice: Vince,our strikingly attractive friend from out of town. The new target was a man named Chris, who was raised in a fundamentalist polygamist offshoot of the Mormon church. Chris had numerous mothers all married to his father. In some ways this made him an easy target.

Chris's unique upbringing set him apart from the rest of the former Mormons, making him the only resource we had if we wanted to ask a question about polygamy. What made him frustrating, however, was his insistence that he was a philosopher. He would post on the Internet long drawn out philosophical tomes about the most random things. He also once confessed to me that he had a fetish for hairy women, information I had a difficult time keeping to myself, especially during heated Internet "debates."

The formula for our harassment went like this: Chris would post some philosophical rant about some topic reminiscent of something a stoned hippie might say. Promptly Vince, Jessica, and myself would read his posts, find a few things he said incorrectly or misstated, and then proceed to tell him why he was wrong. Chris would then have a meltdown for all of us to see. Personal attacks would go back and forth and then the three of us would laugh and give each other high fives. We thought we were the funniest people in the world. Some people loved us for it, others hated us. After all, Chris was just trying to share something beautiful. Why did we need to tear him down? I can admit I did it simply to receive validation from Jessica and Vince. I was no different than the scrawny kid who pushes the other kid off of the slide in order to win favor with the cool crowd.

Months later Chris was in a car accident and suffered brain damage. He kept posting and Vince kept baiting him. It was sad; Chris's brain damage made his long rants completely incomprehensible, even more than before. Chris's accident eventually resulted in his wife kicking him out, and Chris was sometimes seen on the street, homeless. The thought of a homeless, brain damaged Chris posting on the Internet from a public library was enough to make me back off. Vince and Jessica did not share my sympathy though. To them nothing was sacred and sometimes the easiest target was the damaged one.

***

Getting sucked into Jessica's world was often times exhilarating and frightening at the same time. We did things that should have ended numerous relationships. Why was it so easy to do these things with her? I am certain that there was an issue with impulse control on her part. She was doing stuff that we all want to do but restrained ourselves from doing. Clearly there was an issue with impulse control on my part too. Why wouldn't I just stand up to my wife and tell her she was being cruel? Well, telling someone you love them is always so much easier than telling someone they are behaving like a douchebag. And people you call douchebags usually won't have sex with you.

Jessica was my wife and my soulmate. I trusted her without question. She trusted me without question. We did not have to worry about infidelities, lies, distortions, or the need to fact check each other in our marriage. I had had enough of that the year before with the whole Bryce incident. When she told me that she was in the CIA previously I believed her. Why would she lie? She probably could have told me anything, any story, and I would have believed it. I refused to live a life with her riddled with doubt or distrust. Dishonesty and distrust had no place in our marriage. Our perfect marriage was filled with hopes, dreams, and endless possibilities.

***

A few weeks after Jessica had told me of her CIA background, we heard from the Utah Foster Agency. They told us we were indeed approved to be foster parents. The news was fantastic. It was even slightly more exciting than hearing my wife was a former spy. I was going to be a father, and I was elated.

When I was a child, I was asked what I wanted to be when I grew up. They were expecting an answer like "astronaut" or "fireman." I always replied, "I want to be a father." This had a lot to do with my alcoholic father, who I know loved me, but was always emotionally distant. He said he would put the energy into getting to know my brother and me when we were teenagers. According to my father, the teenage years were when children needed their fathers the most. Unfortunately this never happened as my father died when I was sixteen. My wildest dreams have never been about fame and fortune, but rather about being a father. Our attempts to have our own baby were not working and fostering with the intent to adopt made perfect sense.

By this point Jessica had stopped harassing homeless Chris and turned her attention to an online community where a number of Mormon housewives would gather and post pictures of their biblically named animals and discuss quilting and cake recipes. She took on a new alter-ego to gain their trust and then started questioning the Mormon Church's teachings. She wanted to make her character's loss of faith seem legitimate so she could see how many other people she could make question their own religion.

Jessica tried to convert people away from Mormonism under her new alter-ego, but it was ultimately fruitless.

While busy harassing people online and waiting for a possible placement from the state's foster agency, it was time for the annual ex-Mormon Conference again. It was the middle of October 2006, and friends of ours from all over the country were coming into town to listen to other former Mormons talk about why Mormonism is a farce. This is not unlike the time Jessica and I attended a local Atheist meetup. The Atheist meetup went like this: We all met at the Sizzler in a back room. Someone got up and told us the happenings of the National Atheist Conference. They then literally passed around a collection plate. We watched *Guns, Germs, and Steel,* and then someone else got up to talk about why religion is stupid. It was as if we were in an Atheist Church (complete with a collection plate). At least at this church I was allowed to eat lobster.

The ex-Mormon Conference happened once a year, usually scheduled near the same time as the Mormon Church's semi-annual "General Conference." While the content of the two are vastly different, they otherwise mirror each other. The General Conference is where Mormon leaders talk to the entire church body. They discuss spirituality, lifestyle choices, and try to instill a faith promoting message in their flock. The ex-Mormon Conference (run by the ex-Mormon Foundation) is where people who are all *former* Mormons gather and listen to authors, celebrities (Tal Bachman, a former Mormon, was a keynote speaker a few years back), journalists, and otherwise inspiring people who will inspire you to dislike Mormonism. Their goal is also to uplift, but to uplift disbelief. They would discuss their personal experiences leaving Mormonism, have entire lectures about the absurdity of the Book of Mormon being factual (backed up with historical evidence and science), discuss the possible secret political agenda of the Mormon Church and other topics against the Mormon Church.

When conference time arrived that year, our friend Tyson came back into town and stayed with us along with two other friends from out of state. In lieu of attending the conference, which would turn into a drunken orgy afterwards, we went to a friend's house a few blocks away. Everyone we knew was there, so it was kind of like our mini-drunken orgy, without the sex part.

We showed up and began socializing. There was an out-of-town guest who brought gay pornography to the party, which still puzzles me. Staying true to embodying everything Mormonism was not these former Mormons agreed to watch the video of two men in a field having carnal sex. Watching the videos was a room full of straight men and woman, all with what appeared to be legitimate intellectual interest in what was on the screen. My friend Tyson once again was fascinated with the group. "People just don't do this," he said.

Was he right? As I have previously mentioned my exposure to adult behavior up until that point had been largely influenced by Mormonism (both as a Mormon and as a former

Mormon). After performing a quick mental search of my life I realized that I had never, in fact, sat around and watched pornography (gay or straight) with anyone else. Tyson was right: this behavior was not normal. I looked around and saw my wife watching the video with everyone else. A few minutes later she was gone and was nowhere to be found.

"Matt!" I heard someone yell. "Come get your wife. She's on the floor."

Just as described, Jessica was on the floor. Most people have "one too many" drinks. She easily had five or six too many. It was time to go home. I held her while she stumbled down the street. When we arrived home she christened our front porch with vomit before going inside and passing out. Her CIA background could easily explain her heavy drinking. She had probably seen, and *done* so much that the only way she could cope was by drinking.

The next morning we mixed hangovers and mimosas and met some friends for brunch, reviving our old tradition at Orbitz cafe. When we arrived back at to the house the phone rang. It was the foster agency, and they had a perfect placement for us. Three kids, aged thirteen, eight, and three. Since we had told the agency that we preferred Hispanics because Jessica spoke fluent Spanish and I spoke enough Spanish to navigate myself through Santa Ana, California, they found us exactly what we asked for. These three kids' parents were going to have their parental rights terminated within a few months, which meant that we would be able to adopt them soon afterwards. Jessica gave me the look a child would give her parent when they want a puppy. "What do you think?" she asked. Three seemed like a lot, especially since one of them was a teenager. I was skeptical, but also supportive. My friends from out of town sat there in total shock, saying nothing.

I knew better than to take three kids without parenting experience, but the part of me that got sucked into Jessica's personality somehow made it seem like anything was possible. We could do *anything!*

"Let's do it," I said.

| FOURTEEN |
Part of the Problem
October 2006

We eagerly called the Foster Agency and told them we wanted to take their placement. Three kids. I couldn't believe it. Before we could move the kids in, we had to meet them. We drove down to the Christmas Box House, a non-profit in Utah to help kids, foster or not, in order to meet them. We talked with them, played games, and otherwise tried to get to know them. The caseworker told us that they sort of spoke in a different "dialect" that most people were not used to. She said it was half Spanish and half English. The truth is that it was all English, but it was mumbled and featured extreme slang. We met Peter (the oldest), Ariel, and Manuel (the youngest). Manuel preferred to go by the name "Manny." They were all ridiculously cute kids and despite their Hispanic background, they all appeared very Caucasian looking.

These kids faced two major problems in the adoption culture of Utah at the time. First they were older. Even Manny, a three-year-old, was considered "too old" to be considered by most to be adopted. It was a common problem where people only wanted to adopt babies and not children who were seen as damaged goods.

Their ethnicity was their second obstacle. Even though they appeared very Caucasian, our caseworker from the state foster agency told us Hispanic children had a difficult time being placed in Utah. There is a racist undertone in the Western United States against Hispanics, and this was especially true in the cowboy culture of Utah. This is not true of everyone in Utah, but our experiences (and the experiences of the caseworker) proved it to be a real problem for minority children who just wanted a home and a family.

We both decided that we would take the kids after talking it over regardless of my justifiable hesitation of taking three children. When I expressed concern over the amount of work required, Jessica quickly reminded me that we had the money and space, and that those kids needed a home. Turning them away would not only be wrong, but cruel.

I sometimes felt like I did not know how to function as a person when I was around Jessica. I would express concern, or in this case hesitation, and she would give me of those looks. One of those *are you serious* looks. It was as if I didn't know how to do anything. I had to trust her again, the worldly well-traveled beautiful woman with so much experience in life. She would continue to show me the way. She would always give me that look when I underestimated myself or shirked away from doing the noble thing. Having her there to remind me to always do the right thing made me just want to trust her even more.

And you know what? It didn't make sense to take three kids. But with Jessica by my side, and seemingly so filled with righteous fervor for helping those helpless kids, anything seemed possible. We could do it! We would save the world one person at a time!

But things didn't have to make sense with Jessica around. They just had to feel good and I knew doing what *felt good* would always pay off. It had paid off so far with us.

It became evident that Jessica's motivation for wanting the kids seemed to be a mixture of helping people in need and also showing her family and friends that she was a good mother. Much of the Mormon identity is tied around the "family." The family is the central unit of the Mormon Church, so much so that the ultimate ceremony performed within the walls of the Mormon temples is to unite the family for "time and all eternity." Family is the ultimate goal.

While we were no longer Mormon, there was a part of her that needed to prove to her family that she was still a good person and that being an ex-Mormon did not prevent her from putting family first. Being an atheist did not stop a person from doing good. She didn't need a private temple ceremony to have a family. She needed to make a public spectacle of it so that everyone could see. At the time it made sense to me too. In our minds we were persecuted by Mormons for our *lack* of belief. We had something to prove.

Most of our friends were skeptical and tried to warn us of what we were getting into. We took what they said as friendly advice because our friends wouldn't speak bluntly. My friend Nadia said, "I don't know Matt, three kids is a lot to suddenly have to deal with. It will be a lot of work." In hindsight she was saying, "don't do it," but all I heard was, "this is a challenge so be prepared."

If someone had been blunt, Jessica would have probably removed that person from our lives. She never took criticism well, and I learned later that the fear of social isolation was the reason so many people stayed loyal to her. No one wanted to be outcast from the group of friends that revolved around Jessica.

With friends feigning support and excitement, I have no idea why the Utah Foster Agency gave us, first time foster parents without any real experience raising children, three children ranging in age from three to thirteen to care for. At the time I was glad that they didn't disqualify us outright. Jessica and I were on a mission to be part of the most amazing family ever. Everyone would know how giving and helping we were. Everyone would want to be us.

It was October 26, 2006, and Jessica and I picked up our new foster children from a temporary foster home. We climbed into our cars and drove home. They brought with them garbage bags, filled with their only earthly possessions. Suddenly my new Honda Fit was full. Every time we went somewhere it would never be empty again. We set up the kids in their rooms. Peter, the oldest, took a room in the basement. He insisted on the room being cold. Calling it cold was an understatement as he made sure to leave the windows open in the middle of October. It was freezing, but if he needed that to feel "at home" in our house it was the least we could do.

We expected the kids to have a difficult time adjusting, but all of the foster training classes in the world couldn't prepare us for everything. We were not affected when Peter wet the bed because wetting the bed was a very common thing for foster kids to do. If my entire life were uprooted and I were taken away from my family I would probably wet the bed too.

Manny had a difficult time adjusting as well, but this was mainly due to the fact that he was almost four years old and had a vocabulary of roughly fifty words. His communication skills were almost non-existent, he was not yet potty trained, and his ability to manage his anger was poor at best. In college I learned that the best way to extinguish a behavior was to ignore it. If the child gets no response then eventually the behavior will stop. Manny, at three years old, did his very best to prove that everything I learned in college was wrong.

If Manny were upset (he didn't get a toy, didn't like his food, had to go to bed, had to wake up, etc.) a tantrum would start. The tantrums usually involved him screaming at the top of his lungs and then falling on the floor. When the wailing wasn't acknowledged (even after forty-five minutes of it, up to four times a day) he would escalate the behavior by banging his head against the floor. And he banged it hard. We couldn't allow that and had to pick him up, holding him while he flailed and kicked. I guess in some way we reinforced the behavior by giving him the attention he wanted. All we were trying to do, however, was protect him.

And then there was Ariel, who adjusted right away,

started calling us mom and dad, and was generally happy. When Ariel got upset, however, he would wrap a belt around his neck, choking himself. He learned this behavior from Peter, and years later I would catch Manny doing the same thing. As much as I believed human behaviors are biologically driven some behaviors have to be learned. I refused to believe that there is a *wrap a belt around my neck and choke myself* gene. Choking themselves was clearly a learned behavior and probably the only way they ever received attention at home with their biological family.

We slipped into a routine fairly quickly. Jessica picked up some of the domestic routines (cooking dinner) and I, working at home, was the designated taxi. In the morning I would get Manny on the bus for his therapeutic preschool, take Ariel to elementary school, and then take Peter to junior high. By the time I got back it was around nine in the morning, so I would get as much work done as humanly possibly considering just a few hours later Manny would be dropped off from preschool. I know people love the idea of working from home, which has its perks, but the truth is there is no way you can do something that requires any substantial amount of brain power if as a parent you cannot read a book with a three year old in the next room.

At two in the afternoon Ariel would come home from school, and then we would go pick up Peter. Getting Manny in the car was a nightmare. He couldn't be budged from the television. He loved watching "Sponge-a-bob" as he called it. Ripping him away from his Bikini Bottom lifeline usually involved screaming and crying. He couldn't tie his shoes yet but he managed to figure out how to undo his seat belt while I was driving. This resulted in a screaming, flopping three year old on the floor of the backseat. Since I was driving I couldn't do much about it. A few hours later Jessica would come home and we would eat dinner, do homework, and start the cycle all over again.

That routine quickly became my life: somehow passing off two hours of work a day as eight, and dealing with two dogs, two cats, a gerbil, and now three kids. I totally understood why stay-at-home-moms often feel unappreciated by their spouses. I felt like a chauffeur and my own needs (emotional and physical) were not being met even on the most basic level. The toll it started to take on me was that I was losing weight, and the only way I could cope was by starting to smoke again.

Our social life was non-existent. The clubbing phase was over. The parties at our house were over. Weekly brunches and roller-blading with our friends no longer happened. The only interaction I had with friends for the next while only happened through email or phone calls.

Since the kids became a part of our household just five days before Halloween, it was a chance to go trick-or-treating as a family. Peter dressed as some sort of monster, Ariel was a ninja, and Manny was a lion. They already had their costumes. Jessica walked hand in hand with Manny around the neighborhood. I walked with Ariel. Peter just walked around trying to look tough and scary. Peter would split the candy he acquired with his two brothers. I saw in Peter a thirteen year old who was forced to raise and protect his brothers for his entire life. His own childhood was sacrificed for the greater good of his brothers. It was very noble, but also very sad.

Foster children can come with a slew of behavioral and emotional problems. Some are caused by neglect, abuse, or just the very fact that they have no real "home" and their family was ripped away from them. We received training on how to deal with most of these issues but we did not receive training on how much our lives would change. The constant chaos and stress was starting to take a toll on me. Jessica and I started to have almost no time to ourselves as I put everything I had into raising the kids as best I could. When we did have time it was usually me being told how I was falling short, or her being frustrated and tired. What was originally a truly selfless act turned into something that was starting to wear us down and tear us apart.

We were in over our heads. I knew it. Jessica did not agree, saying *I* was the one who could not handle it. Maybe she was right. Of course she was right. She was right about almost everything.

One day while working at my dining room table in the afternoon I received a phone call from Peter's school. He got angry and punched a kid in the bathroom. Anger management and impulse control seemed to be issues for all three of these boys. He was suspended from school for a week. I picked him up, talked with the principal, and went home. It was becoming clear to me the level of attention those kids needed was more than both of us could offer.

Foster kids were classified in different tiers, and their associated foster parents receive more or less training to account for different needs. After talking with the caseworker, we agreed that Peter needed more help than Jessica and I could offer. The same was true for Ariel who had just turned eight and was still in the first grade. Peter, Ariel, and their older brother Terrance who was at the time in a boot-camp alternative to juvenile detention were all held back in school one year. School officials had labeled Ariel "borderline retarded," something I disagree with to this day. What I saw in Ariel, however, was someone who needed full time attention. There was no way we were adequate for that.

Peter was first. We explained the situation to him and that he needed to move. He was devastated. This was only weeks after Jessica told all three boys "We're going to adopt you all and be a big family," which we were told over and over again never to do in training. She clearly didn't pay attention, or didn't care. Two weeks later it was Ariel's turn, who was oddly enthusiastic about the thought of another home. His emotional attachments seemed to be with whomever was immediately around him. It made his moving much easier.

We became part of the problem. Foster kids are shuffled around over and over and it affects them for the rest of their lives. They feel unwanted and rejected. In our attempt to really make a difference in these kids' lives, we became part of the system that makes it extremely difficult for them to ever be at peace with their childhoods.

After Ariel happily and excitedly left, all that was left was just the three of us, which was maybe how it should have been in the first place. Jessica made up a story to tell our friends and her family. Since Peter and Ariel shared the same biological father she told everyone we knew the court gave custody to their biological father. Because of this Peter and Ariel had to move to California. Jessica didn't want to admit defeat. I have always been under the impression that being honest about your shortcomings and limitations is a lot more admirable and helpful than pretending to have it all together all of the time. By telling everyone it was out of our hands she showed me her opinion was different.

I finally had enough time in the day to start being productive again. I was finally able to work a full day's work, and Jessica was also not as stressed as she had been before. Manny had the attention of both parents so I viewed everyone as being winners in our situation. When Manny went to sleep we were able to be a young couple again, but now we had a little boy in our lives who would one day be our son.

Taking care of Manny proved to be a little difficult with his behavioral issues. The potty training was one thing, and the tantrums were another. As I mentioned before, Manny attended a therapeutic preschool for children with emotional problems. Many of Manny's schoolmates came from homes with abuse, neglect, or other equally damaging factors.

Part of Manny's attendance in his preschool required us to meet with an on-site therapist every week to talk about how

Manny was doing. Susan, the therapist assigned to Manny appeared to be very good. Jessica showed up for probably four of the weekly sessions over the course of eight months that we had Manny. She always blamed work for not attending, but it was becoming very clear to myself and the caseworker at the foster agency that *I* was the primary caretaker of Manny.

With the help of some therapy, Manny's behavioral issues slowly changed. His vocabulary was getting better, and the tantrums were lessening in frequency and duration. Who knew it could work?

As the primary caretaker for a three year old, I was also the one who coordinated visits with his brothers. The three kids were living in three different homes. I would take Manny to pick up Ariel. We would all then drive to pick up Peter. I saw no harm in facilitating this interaction. We did this a few times, including the time I took them Christmas shopping. Peter was adamant that he buy a particular thing so we searched the entire mall for it. Truthfully I think he just wanted to hang out and be out of the house because Peter's "foster brothers" would regularly beat him up. Eventually he was moved out of that house for his safety.

Jessica was terribly excited to be a mother, and she wanted everyone to know. She organized her own baby shower for her new three year old son. It would be organized and thrown at her work. Some people scratched their heads at this act, but they understood that it was important to Jessica. Her co-workers showed up, as did my mother, who flew in from Southern California for the event. My mother didn't quite understand the need for the event either, but she wanted to be a supportive grandmother and mother-in-law. None of our other friends were invited, however, and none of Jessica's family felt this event warranted their presence.

Jessica's family's lack of interest in a self-thrown party made Jessica extremely upset. "It's like my family doesn't care about me. Fuck them."

"My mom showed up, Jessica."

"I know Matt. She's the only one who cares about us getting a kid. I think I might be ready to call your mother 'mom.'"

My mother had become Jessica's new favorite relative.

That year for Christmas we drove down to Southern California to visit my mother. Jessica's greatest accomplishment on that trip was teaching Manny how to flip people off, which he would do whenever Jessica requested it. She showed off this trick to a number of people and a number of cars driving by on the freeway. She was a proud mother.

During this trip Manny was in my mother's care for a few hours during which he tripped and hurt himself. "How can your mom be so irresponsible Matt? She can't let him run around like that! I don't know if I can trust her with Manny again!" My mother suddenly lost the "favorite relative" role and instantly became someone who could not be trusted with a three year old although she had raised two children herself.

The responsibilities of being thrust into parenthood forced Jessica and me to see each other in a new light. The time for the carefree life was over. We couldn't take a bike ride whenever we wanted, go out to clubs, sleep in late on the weekends, and our weekly ex-Mormon roller-blading events were over. We rapidly had to adjust from being parents of three children to two and eventually to one.

I was no longer Matt the cute husband, but Matt the overstressed father. She was no longer Jessica the sexy fun wife, but Jessica the mother who didn't help much with Manny's emotional development. The role she took was to take care of his physical well-being (clothes, food, and bathing, mostly). I viewed the emotional development as so much more important considering his background. Her focus was on him not being the "weird kid" and ensuring that he always wore designer clothing.

Our end goals might have been the same, but the path to achieve them was clearly night and day.

The sudden change in lifestyle started to take a toll on our relationship, and we both needed something to fix that. After receiving her coded letter from the CIA a few months back she had been thinking a lot about getting back into the intelligence community. It was going to be her "escape" and give her a bigger sense of importance. In order for her to bring her best to the relationship she needed to make herself the best she possibly could.

I reluctantly agreed, knowing that this choice would take her away from the house more and possibly put her in harm's way. It wasn't my choice to make, though, even if I felt it was irresponsible for a parent to risk her life with a child at home. With this discussion she reached out to her contact in the CIA and an interview was set up. She was going to be a spy again, and it looked like I was in for the long haul as a stay-at-home dad, or at least the primary caregiver, of Manny.

| FIFTEEN |
Variety
March 2007

"Are you a princess? Are you a princess?" I sat on the couch watching Jessica videotape Manny. Manny's obsession with princesses was very age appropriate. Sometimes Jessica pushed it a little far though. She told me she secretly hoped Manny would be gay when he was older. I think she just wanted the wear the badge of honor of not only fostering and adopting a kid, but fostering and adopting a gay kid. People would line up to receive her sage advice. She would be idolized.

"I'm a princess." He danced and twirled. He was wearing his green skin tight pajamas from Old Navy and a paper crown given to him by his preschool. Manny twirled and twirled.

He stopped and almost lost his footing.

"What day is it today Manny?" Jessica asked with an enthusiastic voice.

"My birfday!" He said it in a way only a child could, with the *F* sound instead of the *TH* sound.

"How old are you?"

"Four!" It was our first birthday with Manny. Instead of inviting over family or friends with kids of their own we celebrated the special day as a small, new family. Manny ate cake, ice cream, and opened gifts. Jessica's dad sent him a baseball glove. My mother sent him a Spongebob basketball hoop.

Suddenly the camera was turned on me. "I'm being filmed," I said sheepishly.

"Yes you are Matt because you're cute!" She always knew the right thing to say, at least when she wanted to.

"I want to see!" Manny's excitement couldn't be contained. He ran behind his mom and viewed me through the tiny LCD screen on the camcorder. "I'm a princess!" We went back to twirling, and the camera was off of me.

That was a good day. Overall, we were doing the best we could with what we had. We were new parents and trying to figure out how to balance everything. Despite everything being so difficult at the time I was completely certain that we were going to discover a way to find our Zen in the whole situation. We had two big issues going on: marriage and parenting. They were both so new to us still, and we needed to discuss the issues before they got worse. So we talked about it.

"I feel like things are really strained between us," I declared, pointing out the obvious.

"Yes, they are Matt." She answered in the same way a teenager would talk to you before saying, "Well duh!"

"How do we fix them?" Her attitude led me to believe she had the answer.

"We just need to keep working on it. We need to be parents and also give each other the space we need to be healthy." She said this with the tone of "I've already said this before, you clearly were not listening."

I have never believed in the "Wait and See" philosophy of dating or marriage. Any relationship is an ongoing, growing, changing, organic situation that needs to be constantly observed and acknowledged or else it can turn into something completely different. Her philosophy was to just wait and see. Give each other space. Allow us to be individuals again.

Anything was worth a shot.

During our nightly ritual after Manny was asleep, we sat watching television. At the time we were obsessed with Kat Von D's television show. Jessica had multiple tattoos, and I had one that I acquired on Valentine's Day. I had every intention of getting more, as did she. We then concocted a plan to apply to be on this reality television show.

"If you got on the show Matt I wouldn't go with you," Jessica expressed.

"Why not?" I was genuinely interested although applying for the show was mainly her idea.

"I would want you to be able to be alone and flirt with her." She knew how attractive I found Kat Von D to be. "I would trust you that nothing would happen, but I think flirting with her would be fun."

Looking back I can say that this conversation was the catalyst for some major events that happened over the next few months. It started with discussing flirting, and then suddenly we were playing a "what if" game on swapping sexual partners. That night, filled with the possibility of something so..... naughty... we had probably the most passionate sex we had ever had. We were motivated and inspired by the idea. I really enjoyed the fantasy and the fact that we were talking about it. Deep down it was something she actually wanted.

"I want to also try out a girl," she said. Thinking that a possible hidden bi-sexual desire might be partly to blame for the marital friction we have been experiencing, I entertained the idea, if it was something we would do together. She declined the proposition. According to her, seeing me with someone else would be too difficult for her to bear. She continued the conversation by telling me that one of her friends at work kept inviting her and I over to enjoy an evening in their hot tub with them.

"They want to *do* us both," she said.

"Why haven't you told me about this before?"

"I wasn't okay with it so I never brought it up. I am bringing it up now."

I wasn't okay with it either. I wasn't okay with the idea of my wife having sex with another person. I made it clear I was not okay with it. She persisted, in line with former Mormons disregarding all social mores, especially rules imposed by their former church. I had seen a number of marriages completely crumble in our ex-Mormon community due to the idea we should be allowed to have sex with whomever we wanted. To them, marriage had nothing to do with monogamy like we were taught in Sunday School. To them marriage was a commitment that could include an open sexual relationship.

In our little community of former Mormons I saw three marriages end due to couples engaging in "swinging." Eventually one of the partners in the open sexual marriage found someone they liked better than his or her spouse. I witnessed one couple who was polyamorous, meaning that the husband and wife shared a girlfriend. The girlfriend lived in the house and everyone would take turns sleeping in the master bedroom. Eventually the girlfriend would find someone else and leave, and the married couple would acquire a new live-in girlfriend. Every time a new girlfriend was introduced into the marriage, the wife was always jealous. Her husband always preferred the girlfriend to his wife.

In my entire experience with people who engaged in swinging and open marriages, I only saw one couple make an it work, and they had been "swingers" for more than twenty years. Perhaps they were enlightened and evolved, but I didn't consider myself capable of ever being like them.

"I can't do that Jessica. It's too much. I cannot be okay with the idea of you with other people."

"Fine," she replied, in the same way a young child would react when they found out the family trip to Disneyland was not going to happen immediately. My reasons for not wanting to participate in a real life wife swap didn't matter to her. She had her heart set on it and this would be one more thing I was doing wrong in the marriage.

"Why is this so important to you? I don't get it." I was trying to understand why her heart was so set on this.

"I just want some, I don't know, variety!" I felt like I was no longer adequate. What I offered her, at least sexually, wasn't enough. Regardless of her reasoning, her desire for variety was off limits. If she wanted to spice up our sex life then we would have to find a way *together* to do it. What she wanted could not happen *apart* from each other. It could not happen in a hotel room with someone new. I was not going to budge. She seemed oddly accepting of my rules, and we never argued about it again.

I hoped that my dedication to her would help her realize how much I wanted to be with her. Maybe she would see how much I loved her. While a number of married men would jump at the chance to have permission to have multiple sexual partners, I wasn't going to have it. Keeping our family together was extremely important to me.

| SIXTEEN |
Recycling
Spring 2007

Gas prices in the United States were approaching $4 per gallon. This sudden surge in the cost of fuel suddenly started making people want to save money on gas. It never occurred to them when they purchased their giant sports utility vehicles that gas would be a factor in their monthly bills.

I contacted a local television station and told them my story and about my website promoting fuel economy. The amount of visitors I was receiving to my website was increasing and new members were joining every day. KUTV News, in Salt Lake City, sent a camera crew and a reporter out to my house to interview me. I was going to be on TV!

The interview went well, although I did need a drink before we started just to calm my nerves. Jessica suggested before the camera crew started filming that we tell them we had an adopted kid. She really wanted everyone to know that we were the kind of people who not only cared about the earth by recycling paper and cardboard, but also by recycling unwanted children. Not that I'm Christian, but this is probably exactly what Jesus warned against when he said not to do your good deeds in front of others. Was Manny just a way for Jessica to get people to think how great she was?

Of course the interviewer showed off my newly purchased 1971 Honda n600, Honda's first car sold in the United States. I had purchased this a few weeks prior when I wanted to fulfill my long time goal of restoring a car. I wanted it to be a Honda, and there were only a few hundred of these little cars still around in the United States. The closest one I found was in Colorado Springs. On a whim my friend Archie and I got in his truck and drove for 20 hours (10 hours each way) to buy this car.

It was a two cylinder miniature car that could fit two comfortably. It was so small and light that two people could lift up the back of it off of the ground easily.

It was unique, rare, and I loved it. Since my Honda Civic project had been done for a long time, this would be my new project. Perhaps this car, when finished, would be able to provide me with a sense of accomplishment.

It was April of 2007, and one of our friends was having a dress up party. I didn't know adult costume parties happened in real life. They had always been something I saw on television, and always around Halloween. They never happened in April. The theme for the party was the 1980s. I remember that I dressed up as Henry Rollins. I dyed my hair black and wore a Suicide Girls t-shirt. I was looking thin, largely due to the stress of parenting and our weekly bicycle rides as a family. We tried to ride our bikes everywhere. For the life of me I have no idea what Jessica dressed as that night.

We dropped Manny off at another foster parent's house for the night. Manny cried and pleaded for us to not go. He was becoming very attached to us, and we left the house to the sound of a wailing child. It broke our hearts, but we needed some time for *us*. We needed to remind each other why we were together and what it all meant. We needed to be allowed to be fun adults *and* parents. This party was the first time we had such an opportunity.

The house where the party was held was massive, as if Orange County had relocated to a suburb of Utah. When I see houses like that all I can think of is how much work it must be to clean it. I can barely keep my car clean, let alone a giant house. We walked in, grabbed drinks, and began socializing.

At one point Jessica started bragging about how well my muscles had developed. She encouraged a number of gay men to feel my ass and my legs. She sat there giggling and egging them on because the guys liked what they felt. I felt proud, not because I enjoyed random men feeling me up, but because my wife seemed to be happy that someone else found me desirable. Looking back I would have taken any sign of approval from her, trying to figure out if I was what she really wanted, as a sign that we were going to be *okay*. Somehow her encouraging men to feel me up and her enjoying the experience made me feel special.

After the male on male groping, some of us played poker while others danced in the living room. Between hands of poker I retired to the front porch to smoke with the fellow nicotine addicts. I realized that my wife was nowhere to be found. Afraid this was another case of her drinking a bottle of vodka and passing out, I began the hunt.

"Have you seen Jessica?"

"She's out back on the phone," Evelyn, the host of the party, told me.

I snuck out back and sure enough, there was Jessica, in the gazebo, on her cell phone. She acknowledged me and held up one finger indicating "just one minute." I walked away not wanting to violate her privacy.

"Who was that?"

"It's work related," she replied.

"Work related, or *work related?*" She knew what I was asking. Was this her normal military job, or her "other job?"

"It's my other job. We will talk about it later." I was silenced, but it was understandable considering we were surrounded by twenty or thirty people who didn't know that my wife was a spy.

On the drive home she informed me that the CIA had her first assignment. It was to be in disguise of a normal military deployment. Her assignment would be in South Carolina.

"What will you be doing?" I asked. I still wanted information on her secret, elusive world.

"I don't know. I could be given something to do, but most likely I'm just going to be observed and I will never know who is watching me."

It was really happening. She was getting back into the CIA. All of this meant more time apart, but it also meant she would be making more money. The extra money would benefit both of us. She was also finally doing something she really loved, a part of her family legacy. It was going to help her feel complete and whole again. I had no choice but to be supportive.

We arrived home to the odd silence of our house, with our child away for the night. We both showered, had some wine, and went to sleep early. It was such a boring, uneventful evening at home. It reminded me that yes, we were still strong. We were taking the night off from being parents and enjoying being a couple.

Soon after this, as an act of solidarity towards our new child and family, we both received matching tattoos. Since Manny is Mexican we both felt it would be great to get something themed to match. One day we both took off of work early and met at the tattoo studio to receive tattoos of an Aztec sun on our left wrists. We sat in opposite chairs at the tattoo parlor receiving our permanent sign that we were in it together. We were making an unerasable statement to everyone that we were a family.

| SEVENTEEN |

Get a Grip
Spring 2007

Some time between receiving our new tattoos and her audition for the CIA, Jessica came home and told me that she had met with her CIA contact during lunch. His purpose was to prepare her for being in the CIA once again. His advice was simple: dye your hair and lose some weight. All of the months she had been complaining about how overweight she was and some stranger was the thing that motivated her to do it. She explained why these things were so important.

"There are CIA agents of every walk of life. Hot blondes, tattooed girls, black girls, everything."

"Why does that matter?" I didn't see the relevancy.

"These people have to use whatever weapon they can to get the information they need. Often times that involves using sex or sex appeal. I need to look better in order to do my job."

"Have you ever slept with someone to get information?"

"No, that was a big part of why I quit before. I would never compromise on that one."

She dyed her hair to match my newly black hair.

I felt something amazing over those few days, and a real sense of trust. She was once again letting me into her world, which I took as a sign that we were fundamentally okay. The strain on the relationship was melting away. I realized that I had blown everything out of proportion and really had nothing to worry about with us. I looked up to her for what she did for our country, and saw a piece of her that was really working on our relationship by working on herself. I was okay with being the stay at home father while she was off saving the world. It would be a story we could tell our kids one day, or not, because everything was very secret.

"In my perfect world, Matt we would move away from here, away from everyone we knew and start over." We sat on the porch talking.

"Why?" Her new fantasy seemed to be the complete opposite of the life we had been building.

"I just want to live a different life sometimes. I would love for us to stay married but to move to a new part of the country and just tell people that we never were married. That our love was so strong that we didn't see a need to make it a legal matter."

"Then let's do it." If it meant a life with her I had no problem with what she was asking.

"Nah, I don't know. I'm just sick of being labeled and having assumptions made about me because of the life we live."

Jessica was done with the conversation at that point and dismissed it all as silly talk. She loved our life together. This conversation made me start thinking she wasn't happy, or perhaps didn't know what she wanted. She wanted to either reinvent herself or reinvent us. She wanted a change.

All of the trust I was feeling as a result of our late night front porch conversations did not change that I knew something was off. Sometimes I didn't know if I was being unreasonable or if she was intentionally trying to make me feel insecure. Jessica felt that we had both given up so much of ourselves due to fostering and parenting thing that we needed to reconnect with friends. We couldn't go out clubbing again, so perhaps reconnecting in any way possible was the next best thing. Our lives changed drastically when we became parents. Her solution to fix this problem was to talk to her friends every night on the phone. She would call her friend Ann nightly and they would gossip. She would laugh and it would make her feel better. I usually tended to Manny during this time period, or poked around on the computer.

I saw that Jessica wasn't focused me or Manny any longer. Her attention was towards herself and her friends. Considering the delicate nature of our relationship I felt talking on the phone for hours each night was not the best use of her time. Honestly I was jealous of whoever was on the phone with her. This jealousy caused me to do something I never thought I would do. I eavesdropped. She talked so loudly, and left the door unlocked. I snuck into the bathroom and put my ear against the vent. Who could she really be talking to every night for so long, especially if she saw her friend Ann everyday at work? I was paranoid, and I thought the worst possible thing. I thought she might be cheating.

I listened closely. She wasn't talking to Ann, I knew it.

She was talking *about* a number of our ex-Mormon friends, making fun of them, calling them ridiculous, etc. Ann didn't know any of these people and especially didn't know them on the level Jessica was discussing them.

I confronted her.

"Who were you talking to?"

"Ann, you know that."

"Then why did you mention Gail? Ann doesn't know Gail."

"I talk about these people all of the time to Ann. She knows who they are."

The excuse was honestly very rational. It was good enough for me. Why was I being so paranoid?

"I don't know what you're accusing me of, but you need to get a grip."

"You're right, I do. I don't know why those thoughts even entered my mind. Maybe I need to talk to a therapist."

"Maybe you do." She stormed off, as if I had just accused her of voting for George W. Bush.

A few days later she left for the airport for her audition for the CIA. She drove herself, because she always had to check in at the CIA office prior to starting her mission and I wasn't allowed to know where the office was. "Let's just say it's somewhere near the airport," is as much detail as she would give me.

"I won't be able to answer my phone for a while Matt, due to the nature of what I'm doing."

"If there is an emergency I will let you know, but please try to contact me when you get the chance. I worry about you," wanting her to know how much I loved her and how sorry I was for even assuming she was unfaithful. I had an appointment set up for the doctor to see if some sort of medication could help.

And she was gone, off to be a CIA agent. The house seemed empty without her laughter, without her quirky comebacks. Manny sat next to me on the couch, a space normally taken by Jessica. The couch seemed so empty with his tiny body there instead of hers. I hoped everything would be okay.

PART 3

| EIGHTEEN |

The Phone Call that Changed My Life
Summer 2007

Something was clearly wrong. It had to be me. Everything she was saying and doing was not unreasonable. Why was her attempt towards gaining our individual independence such a problem for me? I decided at that moment that I would do what I could to make things better, no matter what it meant. Perhaps her trip away for the weekend was what we needed. While away she was going to be picked up by Vince, who lived only a state away from her assignment, and meet up with some of our other friends for lunch. I am the first to admit that the idea of her meeting up with handsome Vince made me insecure. Despite my insecurities I vowed to trust her years ago when I found out about her transgression with Bryce. Now that we were married why would I ever take that back? I wouldn't.

She came home and was surprised to find that I had cleaned the entire house and also reorganized her closet and dresser. It needed reorganization badly. She thanked me profusely. She had no answer about how her CIA audition went, as she would find out eventually. What she did have to tell me, however, was that she was repulsed by Vince.

"He's kind of funny looking, and his car smelled like a gym bag."

"Really? That's hilarious," secretly relieved that she didn't comment on his good looks.

"I was afraid that he would try to make a move on me, and I was prepared to tell him to fuck off."

More relief came over me. I was insecure due to her never calling me the entire weekend.

"Why didn't you call? I missed you," I pleaded.

"You could have called me too Matt." She was right. I could have called too. I was just as guilty as she was.

That night we slipped right back into the same routine of her sitting in the bedroom and talking on the phone for hours. This time though, knowing that I overheard her before, she turned on the TV in the bedroom and locked the door. If her goal was to heighten my paranoia, she succeeded. I had an appointment the next day to see a doctor. All I could think of was how she might be cheating on me.

The next day I filled out a questionnaire at the doctors office to determine a possible issue. The doctor examined my results and prescribed Paxil to ease my extreme anxiety. The doctor, who later accidentally prescribed me an alternative to morphine for another issue, clearly didn't know what he was doing. He neglected to tell me that Paxil would often times increase the symptoms for a few weeks. Over the next few days I was so paranoid and anxious that I was physically shaking. My mind raced with every single possible thing that Jessica could be saying on the phone, and to whom she was saying it.

One night while Jessica was on the phone I found Vince online and started chatting with him about Chris, the man we targeted online months before. We enjoyed talking about how nuts Chris was and our recent attempts to bait him. Fueled with Paxil-induced paranoia I said, "So are you enjoying talking with Jessica right now?"

There was no response. Was I right? Did I overstep some boundaries?

Jessica didn't say a word about it that night. Maybe Vince didn't see it and just went to sleep. I had no idea, until the next day.

"You really need to get a grip. Why did you accuse Vince of talking with me?"

"Because I thought you were."

"He doesn't even want to talk to you any more. He's your friend and you crossed a line. He doesn't like being accused of sleeping with someone's wife. You really screwed it up."

Vince removed me from our chat program. My paranoia was making things worse, and it was probably the driving force behind Jessica's need to talk with other people on the phone every night, which she started doing in a hammock high up in a tree in our backyard. I had zero way of eavesdropping after her change of venue. I realized that if I kept trying to prove something secret was going on with her, I would keep looking until I proved it to myself. I was the one with the problem, not her. I was acting like a paranoid crazy person. I needed to back off and let her do what she needed to do.

Recognizing my unease, she recommended that I smoke some pot. I had not smoked pot in years and have never been much of a fan, but perhaps Jessica was right and this would help calm me down. It didn't help. The details of that evening are still pretty foggy to me, but I remember somehow ending up in the bathroom throwing up. Crouched in front of the toilet I knew I couldn't move and needed help. I sent Jessica a text message from the bathroom, an endeavor which felt like it took an hour. "HELP" I sent. An eternity later she rushed into the house. She found me hunched over the toilet and her gag reflex kicked in. She told whoever she was on the phone with what was going on. She sounded annoyed, but they still laughed before she got off the phone.

She took me into bed and laid me down. She joined me soon after. I was twitching and couldn't lay still. The next morning she told me, "If I have to deal with another night like last night, we're done. I cannot do that again." I didn't get it. She encouraged me to take Paxil because I needed to "get a grip" and she encouraged me to smoke pot to calm down. This was as much her fault as mine. Why did she just jump to threatening divorce? We had a child after all. Why wasn't she being the supportive wife willing to help me out? Why was she distancing herself from me and escaping to her tree hideout? I was done with pot, and I was especially done with Paxil. It was making things worse.

Sometimes actions speak louder than words. By this point our adoption date was confirmed. We would be finalizing the adoption in June. As troubled as our marriage was, as paranoid as I was, as much as it seemed Jessica was at her breaking point, the adoption was going forward. In the foster training classes the most important piece of advice they gave was that the kids in the foster program have been through enough already. Don't get divorced. Divorce would ensure kids with horrible backgrounds would experience emotions ten times worse than where they came from. We both knew this. The fact that the adoption was going according to plan and moving forward told me that her goal was to move forward with us.

Over the next stretch of time everything went just the same as before. She would talk on the phone in the tree. I would watch television and take care of Manny. She told me that there was another CIA trip coming up. This one would be a week long, and she would be in Oregon.

After work one day the phone rang. I was silent. I watched her pull a marker out of the drawer and make some marks on the calendar on the wall. The dates for her first real assignment in the CIA were finalized. It would be in June, the week after the adoption was finalized.

I looked at the phone later and saw the caller ID of whoever called her. I searched for him on the Internet and learned about his position in the Air Force. I had always assumed covert trips would not be communicated over wireless telephones with easy access to caller ID. It seemed a bit odd to me that I suddenly knew who else she was working with in the CIA.

The timing worked out for us to visit her family in

Denver, which we had been planning for a while. The visit with her family would happen the weekend before she left for Oregon.

Still Vince's friend on Facebook, he made a comment about going to Oregon for a week. My paranoia was heightened again. What was he talking about? Were they working together?

"Did you see what Vince posted on Facebook?" Jessica asked me.

"Yes." I was hoping she knew what was going on.

"He did that just to fuck with you Matt. I told him to stop it and to remove it. He did." Huh, I was now becoming Vince's new target on the Internet. Excellent. And my wife, for whatever reason, remained friendly with this guy who clearly had it out for me.

The day for the adoption came and we arrived in the courtroom, planning to leave the courtroom as a complete family. Everything went swimmingly. Adopting a child whose parental rights had now been terminated was easy. Our lawyer presented us, and the judge asked us simple questions about our fitness, willingness, etc. to adopt Manny.

An hour later we were done, and Manny was officially our child. His birth certificate was changed to reflect the fact that he was born to both of us.

We got on the road to Denver, with Manny in the back seat. I have always joked that Wyoming has a population of three people. Every time I drove from Salt Lake City through Wyoming I was reminded of the sad realization that there was nothing in that state until you approached Cheyenne, unless you count *Little America*, a mini city set up in the middle of nowhere.

On the way to her brother's house, we stopped by a giant liquor store. Jessica needed to be properly lubricated before interacting with her family. She purchased a large number of mini-bottles of liquor, mainly because they are easy to hide, quick to consume, and for the novely since mini-bottles are not sold in Utah because of Utah's very conservative alcohol laws. The liquor store was humongous, and we called it the *Liquornacle,* a play on words for the huge structure built by Mormons in downtown Salt Lake CIty, the Tabernacle.

The weekend went very well, and Jessica would sneak a mini-bottle of vodka here and there to get through the day. Of course I consumed too. I wanted to be her equal, her partner. If she felt she needed to drink to interact with her family then she knew what she was talking about.

We drove home and had one more night with each other before she left. She didn't want to spend it arguing, which is what we did the entire car ride home. After Manny was asleep we jumped into the hot tub, which she had wanted and then rarely used. We started being intimate, and she turned around and gave me a show. Never once in our almost three year relationship had she ever done something like that before. It was sexy as hell, and something I could use to fuel me during our time apart over the upcoming week.

She left Monday morning to return the following Saturday. I missed her. Manny missed her. I hated that she had to do this job, but I couldn't stop her.

During that week a gay couple we knew was moving to Chicago so that one of them could attend graduate school. They had both participated in the feeling me up at the costume party months before. I hosted a small farewell party at our house. There were only a few of us in attendance. Sitting under the swamp cooler we all talked and drank. I stayed true to my refusal to drink too much as Manny was asleep in the next room. The gay couple, after a few drinks, told me that my wife had, on more than one occasion, approached them and tried to get them to have sex with me.

"Huh?" I was confused.

"Yeah Matt, she thinks you're gay," they responded.

"But I'm not gay."

"We both know that. You're as straight as they come."

Why was she trying to get me to have sex with men? I didn't get it. Was it some sort of "let's explore our sexuality" thing? Was it her way of trying to justify wanting to sleep with a girl? She had expressed that desire a number of times.

The farewell party died down and everyone left except for my friend Nadia. She helped clean up and we sat outside talking about our relationships. She was leaving her husband after years of a physically and sexually abusive relationship. I was trying to figure out what was going on with my relationship with Jessica so we more or less swapped stories and tried to figure out what the other person was thinking.

The next day I noticed that Jessica's cousin, Isabelle, and her two other cousins had removed me as "friends" on Myspace, the most popular social networking site at the time. I called Jessica and asked her why, hoping she would know. She told me she would find out and get back to me.

She called back later that evening and the first thing she asked was "What did you do?"

"What do you mean?" I replied.

"You know what you did. What did you do?"

I really had no answer, because I didn't know what she was referring to. I wasn't really great with confrontation, and she was clearly upset. She proceeded to tell me the horrible things I'd done to her cousins. She accused me of making passes at them by taking a shower in the house while her cousins babysat our son.

"I have been on the phone ALL DAY with our friends Matt. FOURTEEN PEOPLE have told me that things you do creep them out. They all told me things you have done, and EVERY SINGLE ONE of them warrants a divorce." She yelled; I couldn't get a word in. It didn't matter since I would have had no idea what to say to her.

I was spinning. I didn't know what to do. I wasn't much

of a drinker, but I felt I needed something to calm me down. I went into the cupboard and found a bottle of Everclear that someone had left from the farewell party the night before. There was about one shot left. I had never had Everclear before, but it turns out a shot of Everclear is just like a shot of rubbing alcohol. I started coughing and gagging.

"What's wrong?" she asked me angrily.

"I feel like I'm sick," I replied. The combination of her accusations and that shot of death was enough for me to want to just cry.

"Well, you should! You're a freaking child molester!"

Her cousins were all teenagers, with Isabelle, the oldest, being nineteen.

Jessica kept threatening divorce, taking Manny and getting as far away from me as possible. She repeatedly asked, "What did you do?" My responses of "nothing" were never enough. She wanted answers, and I didn't have the answers to give. She told me she had talked to Vince and he had told her a number of things I had said to him in the past about her cousins, and other women.

What Vince and I discussed over the years was strictly "guy talk," and nothing more. What did we talk about all those years back? We discussed women, previous girlfriends, ex-wives, which women were attractive, and other things normally reserved for the locker room. Jessica's cousin Isabelle, who by then had started modeling professionally, did come up on an occasion or two. Vince talked about having sex with a married woman, a former Mormon in an open marriage. It was the only time I had ever just talked about *guy stuff* with someone in years. I had followed his lead. In some ways Vince was teaching me how to just be one of the guys.

Apparently though, I was doing it wrong. The things I said to Vince was enough to make him concerned for Jessica, and to make him believe I was cheating on her with multiple women. I knew Jessica's accusations and Vince's corroborations were things that would never happen. I had this blind faith in her for so long. Why didn't she have the same in me?

Somehow Jessica had access to chat logs from before she and I were even married, and she recited them to me verbatim. It felt as though I was being held accountable for things I said or did before I found out about her cheating on me. I saw the double standard, but chose not to mention it. Clearly she was upset and pointing this out wouldn't fix anything. I wanted it fixed.

"You had better think about what you've done, and be prepared to tell me everything when I get home."

Of course the phone call was much longer than that, and truthfully I have blocked most of it out of my memory. It was around two in the morning, and I was so anxious that I was shaking. Back then, still smoking, I needed a cigarette badly to calm down. All I had were cloves, and since my son was asleep I couldn't just up and leave him alone in the house. I was stuck with cloves. I figured it was better than nothing.

I was sitting on the porch, shaking, smoking cloves, and frantic. Sure, some things I had done were probably not entirely appropriate. I had told one of Jessica's friends that she was "hot," I had referred to her cousin Isabelle as "Jessica's hot cousin," and there were certainly times when the idea of cheating had crossed my mind. I had never done it though. At that moment I was being accused of being not only a habitual cheater, but also a pedophile. my entire life was falling apart around me. Jessica was threatening to take our son and leave me. I didn't know what to do.

So I did what any mature adult would do in this situation. I called my mother. The phone rang and rang. There was no answer. I called back again, and again. She finally answered. For the next hour we talked. We discussed what had happened and what I was being accused of. She talked me down enough to consider going to sleep. I laid in bed for a few hours before being able to sleep.

I laid in bed, my mind racing. Where did all of this come from? How would I be able to fix it? I didn't *do* anything to warrant what was happening. I didn't even attempt to do what she accused me of. The life I had was being pulled away from me. Just one week after making our family complete, our family was being torn apart.

| NINTEEN |

My New Roommate
Summer 2007

I woke up anxious, unaware of what was going on. Every part of my body was on edge. I imagine what I was feeling was similar to someone stuck in a boat about to go off a waterfall. It is all going to be over, and there is nothing you can do about it. Except in my situation my new week-old family was going over the edge. Instead of accepting our fate I was frantic. Something had to be done.

I called the therapist we had been working with at Manny's preschool. I explained the phone call, the accusations, and the threats of divorce. The only reasonable explanation in my mind was that Jessica had some mental break or just went completely nuts. I was hoping I could describe the behavior and the therapist would recognize it, and readily diagnose Jessica's disorder over the phone. "Ah Yes, Matt, what you are describing sounds like a standard case of CIA-induced psychosis. We have the perfect treatment for that." Unfortunately nothing like that was ever said. Instead the therapist told us to come in soon and we could all discuss what was happening together.

One more day until she was to come home. No phone call. I wouldn't even know what to say to her if she called.

Her plane was scheduled to come home on Saturday

afternoon. She came barging through the door late Saturday morning. After she hugged Manny, gave him a stuffed animal, and talked with him for a bit, we sat down to talk.

"Are you going to tell me about your girlfriends in Utah?" She jumped right in.

"My *girlfriends*?"

"Yes, I know you have a number of girlfriends. And I know you have been seeing your ex-girlfriend in California."

"What? When could I have possibly done that?"

"You flew down to California a day before me a few months ago."

"Jessica, I was with my *MOM*. We were looking at cars."

"Whatever." She didn't believe me, even though a phone call could have easily confirmed my story.

She wouldn't let up. She claimed to know things that even I didn't know. She pulled the *you know what you did* card, followed up with the *you might as well just tell me* card. Why couldn't she just ask me specific questions? I starting grasping at straws to try to figure out what she was talking about.

"And what did you do to my cousins? Did you fuck them?"

"What!?" I was so confused by her accusations that a single word response was all I could muster.

"Teenage girls do not remove you from Myspace for no good reason. Are you having sex with them? You fucking child molester."

"No." It didn't seem like an adequate answer, but "no" was the truth.

"I think you're sleeping with Nadia." The accusations kept coming. Nadia, the friend who stayed to help me clean up the farewell party the night before, lived forty five minutes away.

"When would I sleep with Nadia? What are you even talking about?"

"You're both home all day. You would figure out a way to do it."

She clearly thought my sex life was something out of a romance novel, or a porn film.

Jumping from subject to subject, she started quoting things I had said to Vince, years prior, during our online chat "guy talk" sessions. How had she accessed that information? Did she hack into my computer? Does Vince hate me so much that he fed this information to her? Why was it even relevant to *us*? All of the conversations she quoted verbatim happened before we were married. They all occurred before our relationship was solid. They happened before we had a child together, a family.

I did not have the answers she wanted.

"Well Matt, you need to think about it then." As if thinking about it would produce the confirmation she so desperately sought.

"Okay," not knowing what I was supposed to think about. Not knowing how I could invent a transgression I had never committed.

"My entire family is creeped out by you. None of them want you around their kids."

I didn't understand what she was saying. I understood the words, but not the emotion or rationale behind them.

"I think that maybe you do things and think they are okay when they are not."

"Maybe you are right." I would have been willing to say anything at this point to make it my fault and put us in a place where we could work on the marriage again.

"That's a problem for me," she said quickly, "I cannot be married to someone so oblivious to what they are doing."

We had no resolution that day. Things only continued to get worse. I started seeing her accusations as ridiculous and as a result of this my willingness to participate in her accusatory conversations diminished greatly. I was secretly hoping there would be a therapeutic breakthrough that would explain her behavior. Perhaps she would wake up the next day and realize she was bi-polar. I was starting to place my bets on unlikely scenarios to save our marriage. The only thing that made sense to me was her being just completely crazy. I knew I didn't do what she accused me of, and I knew she loved me, so complete lunacy was the only viable explanation.

"I cannot sleep in the same bed as you Matt, I'm sleeping on the couch."

She slept on the couch that night. The timing for all of this was horrible. We had a family reunion planned that would be at our house two weeks later. We later decided her family could not know about the status of our relationship. After all, we were working through our problems, which implied to me an eventual resolution. If her family knew what was going on it would make everyone uncomfortable. She would pretend to be happily married to me while her entire family was in town.

While putting on the "happily married" act for her family Jessica told a story about her recent trip to Oregon.

"I just loved it there. We rented a car and did donuts on the beach. *I* could really see *myself* living there one day."

Her language said it all. She spoke in the singular and not the plural. She was no longer planning a future, or a life, with me. She was planning it for herself. When dealing with someone that would never communicate what she was really thinking or feeling, I had to read into everything she said in order to determine her intentions.

What I assumed from her speech was correct. As soon as her family left she retired into her bedroom in the basement. That room was going to be her room from then on. The basement needed to be set up as an apartment. Of course I was the one who paid for the entire conversion.

"For the time being Matt we need our own space to try to figure things out."

"What does that mean about us?" I wanted specifics.

"I think it means we will be allowed to go out and date other people, and sometimes we can even date each other. Maybe we'll fall back in love and it will work everything out."

We sat on the front porch smoking a cigarette together. I was confused. Fall *back* in love? When did we fall *out* of love?

She told me, "When we get *us* figured out, I still really want to have sex with a girl."

Talk about a mixed message. She just told me that she wanted to work on us, but also that she had every intention of having sex with a woman. I took it as a good sign. At least she was thinking ahead.

With Jessica moved into the basement, I closed the door and locked it. We decided that since I work at home I would be watching Manny during the week and that she would watch him during the weekend. Manny stood in the kitchen, trying to open the door into the basement, crying. He held his forehead, which was something he had always done since he was three years old. This behavior only occurred when he was upset. I had always assumed Manny was hit in the head as a baby and this was his default behavior when in pain. I had to pull him away from the door. He went back.

"I want to see Mom," he cried.

"I am sorry honey, let's go watch Spongebob." My heart broke, but the sooner he could get used to this situation the better. How could this have happened?

| TWENTY |
Don't Let Them Know
Summer 2007

One of our friends was visiting from out of state. She visited once a year or so and always stayed at our house.

Jessica and I were still trying to figure out our

relationship. She went to bed in her space in the basement. I went to sleep in the room upstairs. The only time we slept together was when her family was in town. We were putting on a show so they would not be burdened by our marital problems.

Our friend arrived and we all joked and laughed like normal. My beautiful wife, who I normally would be afraid to talk to about *anything,* was warm and friendly. She looked into my soul when she spoke to me, just like she used to do. I didn't feel defensive.

Perhaps her family visiting and our friend from out of town visiting was what we needed. Maybe she realized life with me was better than living in separate places and beating our heads against the wall trying to fix the marriage.

Fix. The. Marriage. That is all I thought about all of the time. No matter how hard I tried I could never find the right words or deeds to fix it. I became skilled at always making it worse.

And there was Jessica with her big brown eyes smiling at me.

"We should go to Wendover and party like rock stars!" Those words came out of her mouth. An impromptu road trip. Yes! Spontaneity just like we used to have.

"I think that's a great idea," I replied.

"I know you would Matt. I love you." Did she just say she loved me?

The plans for the road trip didn't make sense. There wasn't enough time and we didn't have a babysitter for Manny. We never went.

The three of us shared wine and laughed. Jessica sat next to me on the couch and grabbed my thigh.

We went to bed that night. Our visitor stayed in Jessica's room in the basement. I was fully prepared for Jessica to sleep on the couch away from me. She came into our room. Took off her pants. She looked amazing. She got into bed with me without a word.

"I love you," I told her.

"I love you too," she said. I pulled her closer. She was a little drunk from the wine. I was too.

I started kissing her and pulled off her underwear.

"Matt, don't have sex with me without a condom. I don't want to get fucking pregnant." I was okay with that. She was opening up to me. She was showing me she still wanted me. I was still desired by her. We had a chance.

The next morning Jessica and our friend got in her car.

"We're going to go look at houses, can you watch Manny?"

"Sure."

Jessica had been talking about buying an investment property for weeks. At first I was convinced she was looking for a place for herself until she reassured me that no, an investment property would be a great investment for *both* of us.

I sat at home with Manny waiting for them to come back. My thoughts fell to the night before hoping it wasn't just the wine talking.

That night our out-of-town guest and Jessica went out to a friend's house down the street. This was the same house where the gay pornography was viewed a year before. The occasion for this gathering was a "girl's night." Clearly, being a man, I wasn't invited. I had babysitting duty. The only thing I heard about from that event was a drunken Jessica proclaiming to the group of women, "I don't know why everyone thinks I slept with Vince! I have never slept with Vince!"

But I didn't know she had said that at the time. Jessica was convinced everyone was talking about her behind her back. She was certain they all suspected something about her. That was her way of setting the record straight.

She came home that night tipsy and crawled into bed with me again. It felt great to have my wife next to me.

"Wear a condom Matt," she had to remind me.

Our friend left for her home out of state and Jessica went straight back down to her basement hideaway. I didn't understand how she could have been so close, so longing, so *intimate* just the night before and then retreat back to her private apartment.

I tried talking to her about my confusion but remembered how talking never worked with her. She wanted action, not words. I had to prove I was capable of being the man she wanted me to be.

As if all of this was not enough, Vince was planning to visit Utah to pick up his daughters. This guy was oddly becoming a much bigger part of our lives, and I knew that Jessica was talking with him regularly about our relationship. I was reminded that Vince was was *her* friend and that I had no right to be upset with her sharing information about us. Before Vince came into town I extended an olive branch and told him he could stay upstairs with me if he wanted. He declined. He was going to stay with Jessica instead. Strictly as friends, I was told.

We met with Manny's therapist, who had turned into our own little private marriage counselor. Jessica started the conversation saying, "I felt like when we had three kids in the house that I really had four!" She didn't talk about me being a child molester. She didn't talk about my apparent numerous girlfriends.

She was upset because I was acting like a kid and might have been needy. This was extremely eye-opening to me. Jessica had nicknamed her previous boyfriend "The ManChild" because of his perceived neediness. I sat back and listened.

"I told you, Matt talking about this isn't going to fix anything, it's only going to make it worse."

This was the typical pattern for a while. Some weeks she would go to the therapist, other weeks she would not. I finally hit a breaking point at our next session. It had been weeks since our friend came from out of town when Jessica had shown genuine sexual interest. I had been living off of fumes of love since then.

"I think you want a divorce and are just afraid to say it," I started the session.

"Yes. Matt, you're right."

The therapist was relieved that a resolution was finally reached.

There wasn't much more to be said. We came home, and she apologized over and over again for waiting so long to just come out with it.

"It's just not what I want any more."

She then admitted that the *fourteen friends* she kept mentioning (the ones who apparently all had horrible things to say about my actions) was highly exaggerated. In other words, it was all made up.

After driving home, our first task was filling out the divorce paperwork online. We finished within an hour. We agreed that I would keep the house and that custody would be 50/50. Just like that, it was done. A relationship, a family, was thrown away based on false accusations. She put no effort into trying to fix it. I started wondering if this was her plan all along. I took off my wedding ring and sat in the empty first floor of the house while Jessica took Manny downstairs. He was oblivious that his family had only lasted a few months.

| TWENTY ONE |
A New Life
Summer 2007

We were meeting with Manny's therapist again, and I was still surprised Jessica kept showing up. Manny had been living with us for a grand total of eight months. During that time Jessica had played little to no role in Manny's emotional development. Now that she wanted out of the relationship, she suddenly cared about Manny. If anything good came from our separation, I thought, it would be her finally stepping up and being a part of all of Manny's emotional well-being.

"How are you two doing?" Susan asked us.

"We are doing great," Jessica responded. She was happy finality had been reached and that she was "free" from our marriage.

"And how about you?" Susan turned to me. She was no longer talking to a couple, but rather two individuals.

"Things are going great for me too." It was a simple, honest, and painful answer.

Despite our situation, Jessica had persisted in telling me that certainly, there was a *chance* we could end up together again. Maybe divorce was the best thing for this relationship? Our friend, the flamboyant gay man who married us, told me, "I have seen perfectly wonderful relationships ruined by marriage." Maybe that was the problem. Maybe we were better off just dating with all of the mystery and unknown surrounding us. I was still trying to make things work, trying to find a solution to a problem without an answer.

Friends of ours started calling me and told me that the only reason they stayed friends with Jessica for so long was because of me. My friend Archie recently told me, "Matt, you're a difficult person to get used to. They might have started being your friends for Jessica, but they stayed for you." It's true, I like to build long meaningful friendships. Jessica liked to collect people and then dispose of them once they have served their purpose. My friends told me they had wanted to drop Jessica as a friend years before. What our friends told me was extremely meaningful.

I had to know if any of Jessica's original accusations were about me true. She did say that *fourteen people* had told her horrible things about me. Were people telling her things about me? Finding out who my real friends were was extremely important No one believed anyone in our circle of friends would have talked to Jessica about me in the manner she claimed. None of them liked her that much. They all repeated that they have never had a problem with me. They always had had a problem with her.

I had to do something to move on and remove the pain that was inside of me. Still not knowing which way was up, being bombarded with information from my friends, and trying to fix the marriage, I embraced Jessica's idea that being apart might fix us. I accepted that maybe the only way back to each other was to be with other people. I created a profile on a popular dating website.

The same day I created the profile Jessica came home and started yelling.

"Can you imagine how embarrassing it is for me to answer to my co-workers about your dating profile?"

"You wanted the divorce Jessica. I'm trying to move on."

"It's only been a few days!"

"I'm sorry, it's what you wanted."

It wasn't what *I* wanted, but after suffering through months of rejection, I wanted to feel something, anything. Maybe the girl of my dreams would show up and make everything better. As far as I was concerned, however, the girl of my dreams lived in my basement, apparently *not* sleeping with Vince.

Her disgust with me trying to jump back into the dating was a double standard. As soon as she moved into the basement, she would spend a few evenings a week out until six in the morning. Normally her story was that someone had too much to drink and she had to drive them home. I had to assume she was already sleeping with people, but she was upset that I was looking for someone new. Her reaction to my dating was most likely caused by the embarrassment she experienced when her co-workers saw my dating profile.

Jessica's dating started to become something she would tell me about more and more frequently. I was unsure if Jessica did this out of spite or to just explore her options, but she started bragging to me about a girl she was dating. I remember thinking that maybe once she got her long desired female sexual experience out of her system, our relationship would become okay again. I thought maybe she would come back to me, sexually fulfilled, ready to be a family again.

"She's a co-worker. She has an expensive car, buys me stuff, and treats me right."

"Okay." How else was I supposed to respond?

"She's really wonderful."

A week later Jessica's short lived lesbian phase was over. She had had her same sex experiment, something which most people try out in their early twenties. The woman who was certain I was gay and tried to get gay men to have sex with me had become the very thing she was certain I was. The irony didn't escape me.

Our house was becoming *my* house. Jessica was only a tenant. If things were going to work out with us it was going to happen on its own. No amount of forcing was going to reunite us. I began redecorating, which is something I also did when I divorced my first wife. There is something therapeutic about making my space "mine" again. The first thing I did was add a dishwasher to the kitchen. Jessica had always insisted that we didn't need one. I hated washing dishes. *I* needed one. Our friend was over to help me with the install. He observed Jessica moving her belongings into the basement. "Wow Matt, she's really serious about this *living apart* thing, isn't she?" Yes, she was very serious.

It was July of 2007 and Vince was coming to visit. I had already suspected enough about the two of them, and after her unsolicited declaration of innocence during girls night I could not, in good conscious, stay in that house while Jessica and Vince were in the basement. I packed up Manny and left for California to visit my mother. I needed a break. I was beat down. I transported my dirty laundry eight hundred miles to wash it because Jessica had control over the washer and dryer in the basement. There was no way I was going to wash my clothes with *him* around me.

The trip away was worthwhile. I cleared my head and started thinking of starting a new life with Manny in Nevada where my brother lived. House prices were cheap there. We could start over without Jessica. She was psycho, and it took every ounce of strength to ignore it. I knew that all of the anger I felt had to have been fueled by the divorce, not something she had done. My feelings were not based on fact. We were just not right for each other. It was as simple as that. I kept telling myself this over and over again, needing to believe it. It was the only way we could both be on good terms for Manny's sake.

Upon returning home, Jessica needed to talk to me. It seemed important enough for her to come upstairs and ask me to sit down.

"My ex-husband charged up a bunch of debt on a joint account. I need to pay it off or else I'll lose my security clearance."

"What about your dad? He's rich." I remembered that he was filthy rich with high reaching connections.

"He won't help. I already asked. He told me that I got myself into this mess and I should get myself out. I wouldn't be coming to you if I had not asked everyone else."

Her father was right, and I did not want to enable her. I refused to allow her to know someone would always come to her rescue, as I had done many times before. I declined.

"I'm sorry Jessica, but you chose a life without me. I cannot help."

Through tears she plead, "I understand, but what about

helping your son's mother?"

She had me. I still loved her. I took out a second mortgage on the house and paid her her half of the equity in order to pay the collection agents. Her security clearance, and employment, would be secure once again.

She could continue on as a spy, a mother, and a short-lived lesbian because I came to her rescue, again.

| TWENTY TWO |

Moving on
Fall 2007

Soon after Vince left I was informed by Jessica that they were officially a couple, and she was in love. "I didn't see it coming, Matt. It just kind of happened when he was here this weekend." Good for them. I needed to move on. She clearly already had.

Since I had weekends free, I started going on real dates with people for the first time in my life. I had dated before Jessica, but it was dating in the same sense that running a marathon is a leisurely stroll. I had always dated in order to find my future wife and marry her. After the divorce, however, I was dating just to date, or sometimes just to have sex.

I learned a very important lesson from that experience. I learned that having sex with people, even attractive people, is not difficult. All that you need to do is recognize that women want sex too. The notion that men are sex hungry and women are prudes likely ends potentially great evenings every single day. Another key component was to not express a desire for a relationship. We always read that the "bad boy" gets the girl. From my experience this overused cliche was true. My emotional unavailability from the divorce was somehow working out in my favor.

Shifting from having the family I had always wanted to

divorced in such a short time ensured I wasn't even close to being emotionally available and wouldn't be for a very long time. At least this attitude provided what I perceived to be positive side effects.

Even though Jessica only had to care for Manny two days a week she still needed my help. She wanted to go out on the weekends and party. One weekend the popular band Muse came to Provo, Utah, approximately 45 minutes away. She and her cousin drove down and enjoyed the show late into the night. I always waited up for her to make sure she came home safely. She came home the next morning and resumed her parental role.

Recalling the concert, Jessica told me she stuck out like a sore thumb. Since Provo was the home of the Mormon Church's university the percentage of Mormons there was rather high. It was something like 110%. According to her, she was the only tattooed girl at the event, and all of the members of the band loved her. The members of the band invited her and her cousin backstage.

I was repeatedly reminded of how great she was, as she would almost daily tell me the lead singer of Muse kept calling her, inviting her down to Las Vegas for the weekend whenever Muse was in town.

"He wants to fuck me. Matt." She said it proudly and very matter of fact.

"So are you going to go to Las Vegas?"

"No way. I don't want to be just another slut to him and get a disease."

Even rockstars wanted Jessica. It was no wonder she wanted out of the marriage. She was way out of my league.

When our divorce became public knowledge in the ex-Mormon community, the majority of the community continued to rally behind me. I suddenly had friends to hang out with and a lot more time to do it. Most of the community more or less cut Jessica out of their lives, which she blamed me for constantly.

"I lost all of my friends because of you Matt! What you told people made them ditch me. You fucked up and cheated on ME, and I get punished for it."

Unfortunately she was only getting a taste of her own medicine. She had forced friendships to end many times over the years and often times just "cut people off" if they had too much drama in their lives. It seemed like Karma had a way of balancing everything out.

I was enjoying my newfound freedom as best as I possibly could. Repairing the marriage was still my ultimate goal, but with the announcement of her new love and rock stars fawning over her, but a renewed relationship didn't appear to be an option. I started to wonder if perhaps Jessica and Vince's relationship started long before we separated. Despite the curious timing of their relationship, I was told time and time again by Jessica that my fear was only a fear and nothing more.

"We never even considered this while you and I were together Matt." Not that it really mattered anymore anyway.

"Did you guys talk much back then?"

"Sure, sometimes we would email each other, but we would usually be talking about something silly, like cheese."

When Jessica visited South Carolina for her "work trip" back in May, she met with a number of our friends for lunch. One of them, a psychiatrist, told me later, "the sexual tension between those two was obviously very strong." I confronted Jessica with this information.

"Why would I have lunch with a psychiatrist, trained in human behavior, if I was sleeping with Vince? That would be the stupidest thing I could do."

Jessica was right. If she was trying to hide her hidden affair, why would she do something so obviously careless? She would either be the worst cheater ever or her story made perfect sense. Vince and Jessica's relationship was new, it had to be. It might have spawned *from* our divorce, but it had nothing to do with the cause of the divorce.

In October of 2007 Jessica took Manny to North Carolina for Halloween with Vince and his two daughters. It seemed like Manny really loved Vince's daughters and from what I could tell Vince was a positive male role model, despite his online harassment.

When they returned from North Carolina I picked up Jessica and Manny from the airport and told her that she might be surprised by something when she got home. While she was away for Halloween, I had purchased another car. I was still running a website dedicated to obtaining higher gas mileage and I found the holy grail of fuel efficient cars online: a Honda Civic VX. She saw my teal green civic parked in front of the house and said, "What? Did a girl move in?"

"No, I bought another car. I've been looking for this one for years."

"Uhm" she paused, "it's *green*. I don't know what kind of pussy you expect to get in that car, but you ain't gettin' any."

I now had four cars. I had my project car from the year before (1989 Honda Civic) which had sat untouched for quite some time. There was my new 1992 Honda Civic VX that was really a purchase to own the ultimate cheap/fuel efficient car. I still had my "family" car, the 2007 Honda Fit. In my driveway sat my prized possession, a 1971 Honda n600. The n600 had also not been touched in a long time, mainly because it wasn't safe enough to drive around in with a child. Hell, it wasn't safe enough to drive around parked in a driveway.

I clearly had a problem with how many cars I owned, and apparently none of them would get me any pussy. Classy.

My sex life was of little concern to Jessica, especially after what she told me upon returning from her trip visiting Vince. Jessica came home from that trip and told me that after months of being pressured by Vince to move to North Carolina, she had decided she wanted to do it. She needed to get on with her life, away from Mormon oppression. I could understand why. Mormonism had always been a dark shadow over former Mormons in Utah. She also was insistent on relocating Manny with her.

I was furious. No way this would happen. Her simple request turned into a yelling match.

"If you don't agree to this, Matt, I will take you to court for custody and move."

"Be prepared to answer for a lot of other things." I was trying to sound like I would have control in this situation, but the truth is I don't know what was going to happen.

"What *other things*?" She was getting more and more upset.

"Your *other job*."

"You cannot mention that in court. I will go to jail!" She looked panicked with her jaw clenched.

"Too bad," I responded. I had enough.

"Fine, I'll see you in court then." She stormed through the house, retreating to her underground lair.

Like all fights, emotions started to settle down and the next day we were able to talk again. I had considered her offer and I realized that what was best for me wasn't really what was best for my son. I agreed to let him go, knowing that the school systems in North Carolina had to be better than the school systems in Utah, which at the time ranked second to last in the country in test scores. It might have been the best for me too. I had a life to lead. Manny would be cared for by two loving parents, and I would be able to move out there eventually and be with my son. This also made financial sense, as my job had been affected by the economy and I was cut to half of my salary. I went from a dual income home to a half income home in less than six months. How could I support a child? I could barely support myself

Jessica taking Manny to North Carolina had two conditions: 1) She didn't deploy for the military. Considering Manny's background, him bouncing around the country to stay with me every time the military needed her overseas wasn't acceptable. He needed stability. 2) She didn't move in with someone. Her plan was to move in with Vince initially but to find her own place soon afterwards. She agreed on my terms for Manny to move and said my terms were reasonable.

Manny and I only had a few months together before he was to move to North Carolina. He was still only four years old and I was willing to sacrifice my own desire to raise him daily for what I felt was the best for him at the time. I could see that what I had to offer was not the best for him. The plan was for Jessica to move to North Carolina with Manny in March right after his birthday.

During this time period Vince and Jessica continued to incite more drama in our splintering community. After our separation and her accusations that I was having sex with Nadia, previously one of Jessica's best friends, people began accusing Vince of playing a role in our divorce. I still didn't know what was true, but I decided I needed to take the side of the mother of my child in order to make parenting easier for Manny. This choice was extremely easy to make. My son was much more important to me than people I saw once a month. This decision, however, made it appear to some people I was siding with Vince and Jessica. Since they were already viewed as pests in our group, this association caused further alienation from the people who were only coming to my aid.

In one particular online exchange Vince lashed out at James, who attended our wedding, calling him a "faggot." Yes, James was in fact gay, but it had nothing to do with what they were arguing about, which was my divorce and Vince's involvement. Because of this final straw Vince was banned from the community. He was an outcast after years of harassing and tormenting people in our community.

The person who ran the online community threatened Vince saying if he came back the police would be notified. Vince contacted me and tried to get me to ensure that the police would not be notified. He needed to ensure the threats against him were not serious. The law being involved would affect his employment and his custody of his children. Whatever his job was for the military, he was required to have a clean criminal record. Vince then told me, "contacting the police could affect my job and the custody of my children. I will do *whatever is necessary* to ensure this doesn't happen, and I think I know what you mean by that." Was he telling me he could kill someone for attempting to protect his friends from harassment? After a little prodding, yes, murder was exactly what he was insinuating.

Jessica came to the rescue with a solution to Vince's problem. Considering her renewed affiliation with the CIA, she was able to contact a number of people she knew from work. The people she reached out to were known for doing, shall we say, *morally questionable things*. I was told people in the CIA often times help each other in situations like this. Our friend who was threatening to contact the police lived just a few miles away from us. According to Jessica, four of her co-workers went to this man's apartment, slashed all four of his tires, and pissed on his windshield. "That should send a clear message," she boasted to me over shots of tequila. As she laughed I realized her formerly infectious laughter had become frightening laughter.

Who was this person? Who did I get myself involved with? A woman who had thugs destroy someone's car? A person with a boyfriend willing to fly out to Utah and kill someone for threatening to call the authorities due to harassment? I was honestly frightened. I started having second thoughts about sending Manny to live in North Carolina, but if Jessica and Vince were willing to go to such an extreme over an Internet argument, what extreme would they go to in order to ensure they had Manny? If my phones really were tapped I couldn't talk about it to anyone. I felt helpless and all I wanted was a way out.

Jessica was growing impatient with her move, wanting to be closer to her new found thug in shining armor. I couldn't wait for her to leave. Luckily she changed her plan to move from March to January. She was moving sooner than I expected. Thank God.

Even though it was Jessica's year to take our son for Christmas, she was kind enough to let me take Manny for his last Christmas with me before holiday visits would become all we had. Manny and I drove through the snow down to Southern California to spend the holiday with my family. Jessica had plans to visit with Vince in North Carolina. After driving for hours, watching the road and attempting to entertain a four-year-old who was clearly bored by out of his mind, my phone rang. It was Vince.

"Hello?" I answered. Even though I hate talking on the phone while driving I figured Vince wouldn't be calling unless it was important.

"Hey man, this is Vince. You need to get Jessica out of here man."

"I'm driving and over two thousand miles away." What was I really capable of doing? Besides, why was this my problem?

"You need to call a cab and get her out of here now." He was almost yelling at me, annoyed I would not help.

The phone went silent. He hung up. I called back. No answer. I looked at my phone and dialed her brother in Colorado.

"Hello?" He knew it was me something I could determine from the hesitant nature of his voice. I was surprised he answered at all.

"It's Matt. Something is going on with Jessica and Vince. Can you call him and figure it out? He said he needs her out of there now. It doesn't sound good."

"Okay, I'll call you back."

It wasn't until later that night, after arriving in Southern California, that I heard back from her brother. He managed to get ahold of Vince and the same conversation was repeated. "Just get her out of here. She's going crazy." Vince also hung up on him. Jessica's brother called the police, who came to Vince's house and gave Jessica the choice of going to jail or getting a hotel room.

Vince called me later and told me that she was extremely drunk and suicidal. She was trying to get Vince to enter into a suicide pact with him while his two daughters slept in the next room. He refused to join her ticket for two to eternal sleep. His refusal caused her to have a complete meltdown. Whenever he picked up a phone she would swat it away or hang it up. After we both acknowledged that she was in the CIA, he told me that something *work related* caused the meltdown.

I thought I was done with all of the drama. Why was *I* pulled back into it? What made me Grand Central Station for my ex-wife, her boyfriend, and her family? I was just trying to enjoy Christmas with my son and my mother.

The next day I received a call from Jessica around noon.

"I don't want you to be surprised when I come home, but I have a black eye."

"What?" I started to realize most of my initial replies to her were always one syllable words asking for clarification.

"Vince didn't hit me, but I cannot talk about what happened on the phone."

I drove back to Utah, and a day after I came home Jessica came home to her basement apartment. She immediately asked to talk. We each took a shot of tequila, which was a peace offering she purchased for me to soften the blow of what she was about to say. I stared at her very black eye, which you could clearly see despite a pound of makeup attempting to cover it up.

"I was freaking out at Vince's house, and I'm sorry you

were involved."

"It's okay," I replied. I'm always the supportive and understanding type.

"Here's what happened. Before I went to North Carolina I had to stop in New Jersey for my *other job.* I had to kill someone that had turned over." By this point she was in tears, bawling. Her emotions were real.

"What happened?" I was in a state of disbelief.

"He was a really good guy Matt. I knew him. We used to talk about our kids and families. He just got in with the wrong group and the Agency needed him gone. I went to his house while he was having a party and I took him up into the bedroom. With the lights out, I slit his throat and left."

I had nothing to say. How was I supposed to respond to that?

"I freaked out at Vince's because I couldn't deal with it. When the police sent me to the hotel my CIA contacts met me there. They knew all about what was going on at Vince's house, probably because they tap your phone."

"What did they say?" I imagined two muscular men confronting my 5'3" ex-wife in a small hotel room.

"They were trying to make me calm down. I couldn't calm down, so I punched one of them in the face and broke his nose. He then punched me right in the face and knocked me out."

Once again, I had no response. It was like she was living in an action movie.

"I was acting up. I deserved it."

I found out that years ago during her initial stint in the CIA, killing people is what Jessica used to do. She was a trained assassin, and I was so paranoid at the thought of the CIA tapping my phone I didn't know what to think or how to act with her around.

"We all have nicknames in the CIA," she continued, "Mine is 'trigger.' That should tell you how good I am."

| TWENTY THREE |
Saying Goodbye
Winter 2007

Jessica, whose *other job* I still had no way of confirming, still had not signed the divorce paperwork. She told me she would get around to signing the papers after she moved to North Carolina. One day she was in the basement complaining about how much noise I made, and then in what seemed like an instant she was out of the house. She was gone. She packed up her new truck, one I helped her purchase after she had totaled her smaller car, and drove across country with her dogs to her new home. The majority of her possessions stayed behind, packed in my garage. Her things would fill my garage for almost a year.

Hoping that her absence would stop the chaos, the threat of phones being tapped, the fear of CIA thugs coming to my house and slashing my tires, I relaxed with my son. My life was starting to get scary for me at this point, but this had nothing to do with her *secret life* or post-assassination meltdowns. It was the beginning of 2008 and the housing market had crashed. My job was working with construction companies in Southern California (where the market crash hurt the industry the most). The company I was working for went from twenty employees down to five. I was laid off. Just six months after forming a family I was accused of being a child molester, I lost my wife, I lost my job, and soon my son would be living two thousand miles away from me. If I didn't find a job quickly, I would also lose my house.

The only positive things going on at the time was when my website promoting fuel efficiency started becoming popular. It's popularity amplified after it was mentioned on 60 Minutes and MSN Money. The rising cost of gasoline helped too. The years I poured into the website were finally paying off. I knew it couldn't last forever. I had been following gasoline prices for years now, and I had started to notice a trend. The prices couldn't stay this high forever, not with it being an election year. I took action and sold my website. I was able to live off of that money for a few months while the dust settled. I also started collecting unemployment for the first time in my life. Since my previous job was in such a niche market, it was nearly impossible for me to find a new job, although I tried relentlessly.

I took this time to give myself a much needed vacation from the turmoil that had become my life. I still visited with Manny's therapist and I still got him to and from school, but when I wasn't applying for jobs I started religiously watching television shows. I channeled the emotional turmoil of my life into ten seasons of Stargate: SG1, which only took me a few weeks to finish. I spent more time trying to get the basement ready to rent out, considering my financial situation made paying the entire mortgage by myself a difficult task.

If it wasn't for that time I had to myself, I would have cracked. Everything was different, and I had to ask myself if I was the type of person who would adapt and make the situation work, or if I was the type of person who would let my bad situation get the best of me. I was the former, not the latter. It was time for a change.

The first change I made was becoming extremely frugal. I needed to simplify my life. My goal to live cheaply would require me to change my spending habits. I would buy used and be as thrifty as possible. I would barter for items. I would try to grow my own food if possible.

But how was I going to live off of little money when my mortgages would exhaust my monthly income? Finishing the renovation on the basement was my only option. I needed to get the remodeling done myself so I could rent it out. Had I put more time into it I am certain I could have done it, but living cheaply took a lot of time and planning. I didn't have the time or energy to hang drywall when I was busy bartering with people to get free food.

Since I was unemployed I had the time to be more frugal, but I was never the best at planning. I did stick with the simplifying though, and I still buy some items at thrift stores. Spending hours a day coordinating how to barter the guy down the street out of some pears from his tree, or trying to get my neighbors to give me some eggs from their chickens was something I couldn't do. I wasn't motivated enough, probably because I still had a small nest-egg of money from selling my website.

Living on unemployment and not being too careful of my purchases (despite every intention to do so) started to have some casualties. I sold my prized Honda n600. The only memory I have of this car now is the tattoo I received of it burned on my forearm. Months of getting new parts, installing new upholstery, etc. were all wasted. I also had to sell my Honda Fit. Finally, I reluctantly sold the 1989 Honda Civic. If saving money and being frugal was my goal I opted to stay with the car with the best fuel economy and the lowest insurance. My quest for the perfect car was now reduced to a quest of affordability. Dreaming about what *could be* would have to wait until I got past being broke.

I kept selling things, which was part of my desire to simplify and also get some cash. I was removing the clutter and removing the stress. I had the time and energy to focus on Manny's emotions with the divorce, which was no easy task.

A local radio station was having a contest to be a fill-in host for a week on their popular morning show. I was still out of work, and since I had always wanted to work in radio I gave it a shot. I sent in my audition to their producer. I also sent them a copy of a radio interview I did for a popular Los Angeles based radio show. The interview was titled *Ask a Mormon*, and I hoped the combination of this clip and my audition would make me a shoe-in for this position. I waited to hear back. Nothing. Nada. I listened to their show every day and heard they were looking for unpaid interns. My heart was so set on the idea of being on radio that I applied.

Since I could no longer find work in my profession, I decided it was time for a career change. Radio had always been something that fascinated me and I was certain I had natural talent. Getting in the building by being an intern would be my first step. Working in radio wasn't something I could do with my son around as my hours would start at five in the morning. Fully pursuing that dream would have to wait, or my schedule would need to be more flexible.

After talking with the producer of the morning show, Richie T. Steadman, for a few minutes he told me I had the job. He wasn't picky. My experience editing audio was more or less all he needed from me. This was my shot at the big time and I had every intention of making it work. Fantasies of having my own show flashed through my mind. Local celebrity status would be granted. I was certain it would help me get women too. I initially worked from nine until eleven in the morning. This would be my regular routine until Manny left. After Manny left for his new home my plan was to amaze and wow everyone with my long hours of unpaid dedication.

As Manny's birthday approached I prepared for his party. I also packed his bags and was getting him ready to move away from me. Jessica was flying in to attend Manny's party and then would fly out the next day with Manny back to North Carolina. The night before the birthday party the phone rang.

"MATT!" A drunken Jessica yelled into the phone.

"Yes?"

"These motherfuckers won't let me on the plane! They said I had too much to drink! I only had ONE BEER! Motherfuckers, I only had ONE BEER! I have a receipt."

"What can I do to help?"

"You can help me sue these assholes." Her speech was slurred. "My dad's lawyer is Robert Shapiro!"

"The same guy who defended OJ Simpson from murder charges?"

"Yes, I'm going to sue this fucking airline."

My classy wife, the divorce paperwork still was unsigned, was stuck in Chicago's O'Hare airport for the night because she couldn't control her drinking enough to make it through a layover. If she was punched in the face by the CIA for acting up in North Carolina I wondered what her punishment would be for public intoxication.

"I just want out of here Matt. I just want to come home."

Did I hear her right? *Home*? Was Utah, and my house, *home* to her? Was there a chance she would be coming *home* and not going back to Vince? I was willing to forgive the past if she wanted our life together again. I didn't know what she meant by *home*, but I did know one thing: she was drunk. She was so drunk that airline employees noticed it, which said a lot. I envisioned her telling random people, "I don't know why everyone thinks I slept with Vince!"

| TWENTY FOUR |
Living the Dream
Spring 2008

"Today I got mail from Jessica. I miss her so much.
Right now though, I honestly think that we'll make it through this."
  -private missionary journal, Matt Timion, July 6, 1998

I haven't changed a single bit. Looking back on my journals from when I spent two years as a Mormon missionary to the Philippines, I'm the same person. The above quote is from my journal, just six days into my missionary experience. I had a girlfriend who I left behind. She was named Jessica, of course, and she was going to wait for me. She was seventeen, I was nineteen, and she was going to wait two years for me to come home and then we would be married. We were going to have kids, attend church, and be happy. She used to send me letters signed "Jessica Timion."

She couldn't do it. She waited *three whole months* into my Mormon mission. I wish I still had the "Dear John" letter she sent me while I was in the Philippines. Being broken up with while on your mission is common for Mormon missionaries. These break-up letters are called "Dear John" letters, and are viewed as a rite of passage. I no longer have that letter because I had a little therapeutic exercise in Caloocan City, Philippines when I was twenty. I burned all of her letters and let her go. Our relationship was over, in smoke. I always hope, and *want* someone to see me for someone amazing, someone worth fighting for. With everything I had experienced with Jessica over the years, I had seen nothing but the opposite. Something must have been wrong with *me*.

It was Manny's birthday, and Jessica flew into Salt Lake City despite the fact that her drunken layover made her late. She was, however, able to show up for Manny's 5th birthday party without missing much. He loved his party, which combined friends from his preschool and kids from our neighborhood. The sad reality was despite the cake, piñata, and presents, it was a goodbye party. We all knew it.

We three spent time together as a family, which was something Manny longed for. Then, like the quick whirlwind that tore my family apart, it was time for Manny and Jessica to go. Out of desperation or compassion, Jessica invited me to her brother's house for dinner. I had not seen her family since the family reunion at our house. They were just as surprised to see me as I was them, but I loved that I was able to see them again and also spend a few more hours with my son.

An unexpected consequence of her invitation was a

possibility for a relationship between her siblings and me. Her invitation sent the message that I was okay to have around and that Manny and I were okay to involve in family functions. I have always felt that her family were good people despite their connection to the CIA. I wondered how much of my behavior was noticed and how much of what I did would be reported back to the people I was certain were watching my house and tapping my phone.

The next morning Manny was gone. Drunk Jessica never wanted to come home. She didn't want me. She had found someone better. There was no noise in the house. The spaces normally filled with children's laughter were silent. My cats looked up at me and then went back to sleep. Opening Manny's bedroom I saw his empty bed, still dressed with sheets from the night before. I laid down on his bed, wrapped myself in the quilt I made for him, and cried.

My family was gone. I had uprooted my life for a life with her, for us. They left me, even if I had allowed her to take Manny. I was the only one left. The only noise I could hear were cars driving by on the street outside. I was all that remained of the dream Jessica and I had together. The only conclusion that I could draw from the emptiness around me was I was not good enough.

Alone in my house, originally purchased for a family, I couldn't help but realize just how quickly everything had happened. I had been in Salt Lake City for just a little over three years. It was March and we adopted Manny the previous June. Just like that, in an instant, it was all gone. It was gone before it even had had a chance to live.

After Manny and Jessica landed safely in North Carolina, I received a phone call from Jessica's number. I had assumed that it would be Manny. It wasn't Manny. It was Jessica telling me everything I did wrong as a parent. She must have had a list of grievances to throw at me, but it included how I hadn't made sure he brushed his teeth (not true), how his clothes were dirty (not true), how I didn't pack the right things for him (subjective). She just ranted and yelled about how horrible of a parent I was.

Jessica, who was recently denied access to an airplane because of her inability to control her drinking called *me* a bad parent. At least I had never killed anyone.

With Manny being out of state I was now able to finally start working in radio full-time. I would go in at five in the morning and leave at eleven in the morning. The rest of my days were filled with television shows and silence. My new unpaid job, taking up six hours in the morning was truly me doing something I loved. I was an intern for *Radio From Hell,* easily the most popular radio show in the entire state of Utah.

Radio From Hell was the *alternative* morning show for the unbelievers. The show, right down to its name, was a part of the counter culture of Salt Lake City. The show was so shocking that some people wouldn't listen based on the name alone. While the show was not as controversial as Howard Stern, the show played up the shock factor. This show was the radio version of tattoos on a former Mormon. I fit in perfectly.

My duties as an intern varied, and my computer skills definitely helped the producer do his job more effectively. I was thrust from a life of being a rejected nobody to being someone who was associated with some of the most famous local celebrities in Salt Lake City. Their appeal to me wasn't what it was to everyone else because I wasn't raised in Utah. I understood the importance of their role as a dissenting voice in a state that had nothing else like them to offer. Mostly I just recognized them as regular people. Perhaps my perception of them was because that was all they were: regular people who were lucky enough to talk on the radio.

Ironically enough the radio station that aired *Radio From Hell* was owned by a number of devout Mormons. Money speaks louder than words, especially in Utah.

My involvement with this show suddenly made me feel special. I was important. I was allowed to talk on the radio. Sometimes people would even recognize me on the street. I was allowed to be a part of the show, even in a limited intern capacity. It was my dream job. I knew that as long as I stayed there and waited long enough, I would be able to be a part of something bigger. Perhaps I could get my own radio show one day too. Perhaps the popularity and validation I needed would come from radio.

Being part of a popular radio show, regardless of my being an unpaid intern, gave me opportunities I had never had before. Flirting with women was easier. They all liked me. My self-confidence increased. They all wanted to be around me. Some of them even wanted to go home with me. Perhaps Jessica had done me a favor by leaving.

There I was, a twenty-nine-year-old who worked in radio and owned my own house. I was clearly a success. Women loved that. Most men they were used to meeting still lived with their parents or had roommates. They also loved that I didn't care about them. I couldn't commit. I was aloof. This was partially due to the emotional baggage caused by my divorce, and partially due to my new identity as a "rock star." My apparent disregard made women want me more. I secretly wondered if Jessica would have left this version of me. Tattooed and on the radio I was easily more popular than her new boyfriend. In some circles that made me the dominant male, despite another's muscles, money, great tastes, and good looks.

I would call Manny every other day, and we would connect. Talking to a five year old on the phone is as easy as having a conversation while underwater in a pool. A five year old's attention span is limited enough when you are right in front of them. A voice on the phone? He couldn't care less. He wanted to watch television, run in the park, or eat Cheetos. He didn't want to talk to me. Our conversations were short and sweet.

My days were simple. Radio was good to me. Television was good to me. Dating was good to me. Being in the place where I didn't want to date anyone in a serious way somehow just made my entire life about me. For the first time in my life I focused on me.

I was loosely seeing a two women at the time. They both knew about it and neither of them cared. We were all in the same boat of not wanting to have anything too serious. During all of the fun and games both of them mentioned how much they would love to try a threesome. I saw an opportunity to cross something off of my bucket list. I contacted both of them, and we planned a tentative date. I couldn't believe the ultimate male fantasy could actually happen.

They both showed up at my house, nervous to meet the woman they might be having sex with that night. They greeted and seemed to enjoy each other's company. I was cooking dinner for all of us, trying not to screw anything up. I realized that situation might be a once in a lifetime opportunity. We dined, we wined, and then my phone rang. It was Jessica. Always afraid something might be wrong with Manny I answered the phone.

"Hey," she started, "I fucking hate Vince." That escalated quickly.

"Okay." I just wanted to know what was wrong.

"We're in Washington D.C. with the kids.... I just don't know any more. Vince is such a dick."

"Is Manny okay?"

"Yeah, he's asleep. Sometimes I just wonder what I'm doing. Like maybe Manny's life would be better if I were not around."

This wasn't the first time we had that conversation. Jessica always seemed to believe that suicide was *normal* to think about. It was *normal* to consider as a viable option. I told her that night that Manny would NOT be better off without her.

Manny would need a mom. She didn't buy it. She was clearly drunk, upset, and angry at Vince. They got in a fight and he left her alone with the kids in the hotel room. Her mood made me upset.

"I don't know Matt. I just don't know if I am cut out for this world."

"Jessica, go to sleep, and call me tomorrow."

I got off of the phone. My dates were patiently waiting for me. One of them took my phone and told me, "You don't need to worry about this tonight." She put the phone on my dining room table and we went out to a club, the same club Jessica and I used to go to, and we danced. Men looked at me longingly knowing I had two women with me. I was enjoying my evening without Jessica and without stressing about her life.

The evening ended at my house just as I wanted it to. Waking up the next morning with a woman on each side of me confirmed that the evening before was not a dream.

| TWENTY FIVE |

The Voice of Reason
Late Spring 2008

Still living on unemployment meant that money was becoming scarce. Despite my lack of money I was still determined to make my way in radio. Radio was, after all, my dream job. Getting my shot in the big leagues was a waiting game and I was willing to wait. Five months after I started my internship, I volunteered to be Tom Barberi's co-host for his early morning show. The hours were from five in the morning to seven in the morning. It was also unpaid, but I wanted to pay my dues.

Tom Barberi (long nicknamed "The Voice of Reason") was a Utah radio legend. During a time with people needed a voice, he was there. He helped rally citizens to march on the state capitol. For over a decade, he had helped change public opinion in Utah. Unfortunately radio politics got in the way. He was soon left with no following and no pulpit from which to preach. Some say he lost his edge, but from what I saw that wasn't true. The truth was that people changed, and what was once important no longer mattered.

People in Utah had become more complacent and as a result, visionaries like Tom Barberi had started to become irrelevant. The radio industry also was becoming more and more corporate. They found it was cheaper and easier to syndicate a national talk show for a fraction of the cost of having an employee. All of these factors, including the rising trend of portable mp3 players and satellite radio made the veterans of radio start to look like technological dinosaurs.

Tom was, just like me, working for free. He did it all for the love of radio. And so it began. I was Tom Barberi's co-host. *This could be my shot*, I thought. I felt it was a move up in the radio world, even though the people who listened to terrestrial radio were diminishing every day. I had a speaking role, and I was part of the show. To make things even more exciting, I was sitting next to and talking with one of Utah's legendary voices. All it would take would be one more break and perhaps I would be able to have some sort of midnight deejay shift. Perhaps I would be able to take over for Richie when he quit due to being so terribly underpaid.

Time went by and I started planning for Manny to visit me for the summer. During one of my regular phone calls with Manny, Jessica got on the phone.

"Why haven't you made plans yet to get Manny?" Jessica was yelling in a way so that no one else could hear her.

"I haven't purchased the tickets yet."

"I think you don't care about him. I think you're just disregarding him. I think you are not going to pick him up."

I sent her my flight information the same day. I could

barely afford the plane ticket. I still co-hosted with Tom Barberi for free, but I needed to actually make money. I decided to take a day job working in the radio station's web department, which only paid slightly more than unemployment. My job kept me in the building, awaiting my big shot.

My experience with Tom Barberi lasted six weeks. Tom Barberi finally had had enough. He was sick of not being paid. He was sick of getting a horrible time slot and being marginalized. In one of the most amazing two hours of radio I have ever heard, Tom quit while on the air. He was able to say goodbye to his listeners. He was able to say his piece. Since it was so early in the morning he was able to do it without being stopped. I was there the entire time. I was part of what I consider to be Utah radio history.

The timing was perfect. Tom Barberi quit his show just before I was going to have to quit. Having a child at home full time wasn't conducive with coming in to work at five in the morning. I was going to have to stop the radio dream, or at least the version of it where I arrived at five in the morning.

I flew out to North Carolina. My connecting flight was in New York. I arrived at the airport, rented a car, and did the best I could to find the sandwich shop where Jessica was waiting. Her directions were horrible, and the people at the gas station were not much help either. Eventually I found them. I picked up Manny and gave him a big hug. Jessica looked like an anorexic version of herself. I started referring to her as "Bobble Head Jessica."

At her heaviest during our marriage Jessica was a size sixteen. As a man I don't know what a size sixteen really is, but I'm told it's big. She had become a size zero, which she loved to brag about. Her curves were gone. He once large breasts were now tiny. The only thing that remained was her giant head. It was like looking at a stick with an apple on top, and it was NOT a good look for her.

"Cool tattoo dad!" Manny was referring to my newest tattoo: a vintage microphone. Since tattoos to me have always been a way to tell my life story, I had inked the microphone on my arm as a sign that my longtime dream of working in radio coming true. The skin around my tattoo was peeling and flaking, but Manny thought it looked cool.

Manny and I got in the rental car. I couldn't believe that she expected me to get a rental car and drive an hour to pick up Manny when she could have just driven him to the airport herself. While we were driving back to the airport Jessica called me and yelled at me for being late.

"And why did you fly to New York as a connecting flight?"

"It was the cheapest." I didn't understand the issue.

"Why would you fly one thousand miles out of your way to pick up your son? You're a horrible father. You clearly don't care about Manny."

If there was a world where her screams made any sense, I clearly had never been there. I hung up to make our connecting flight. We landed safely in Utah.

Manny visiting for the summer was filled with playing, water fights, gardening, and his making friends with kids his age. Manny was excited and optimistic. He knew his visit with me was only for a few weeks, but we made the best of it. I felt like a dad again. Nothing could have made that summer bad. In fact, some things made it even better.

Towards the end of the summer I received a phone call from Jessica. The details of her private life were something I didn't know much about. Honestly, I didn't care. Whenever she wanted to talk to me I just assumed she was drunk.

She started the conversation with an abrupt statement. "I'm being sent overseas to Qatar," she said. Being sent overseas was an unfortunate reality of military service, one she could not avoid no matter how hard she tried.

"For how long?"

"At least three months. I want to have Manny come back for a few weeks and then I will send him back before I deploy. He can attend school there until I get back." She was the defacto custodial parent so I felt I could not argue. I agreed that he would go back to North Carolina for a few weeks only to return to start Kindergarten here.

She had just broken rule number one of our verbal custody agreement. She was deploying and bouncing my son all over the country. His stability was extremely important to me. She had already broken rule number two. She was still living with Vince. Manny's "bedroom" for the last five months had been an office with a bean bag. He didn't have a bed. He had a bean bag.

It was as if Jessica paid zero attention in our classes while we were being trained to be foster parents. It seemed as though she was actually trying to make Manny's life more difficult and disjointed with every single action.

The divorce still wasn't finalized. The divorce papers still had not been signed. I was starting to think letting Manny live with Jessica in the first place was a mistake. Fortunately I had time on my side to figure that out.

| TWENTY SIX |

Daddy Time
Summer-Autumn 2008

The door was opening. I was there all alone fiddling with my fingers. I wanted to leave. Waiting was killing me. People started coming out of the door and all I wanted to see was my son. I looked and looked. He was nowhere. Suddenly a flight attendant came out with a little five year old in a denim jacket. His backpack was almost as large as he was. "Dad!" he yelled right before he ran up to me.

"We need to see your identification sir," the flight attendant told me, "and you'll need to sign him out of our care." It was the first time we had experimented with Manny flying by himself on an airplane. His flying unaccompanied was a little more expensive than a normal flight, but ultimately much cheaper than the cost of flying out with him and then flying back.

Just five weeks before Vince picked up Manny to go back to North Carolina. With Jessica going to Qatar for a few months Manny was required, by law, to live with me while she was gone.

"How have you been?" I was carrying him through the airport. People turned and looked at the man carrying the little boy, smiling.

"Good," he answered. "I'm hungry." He was back, and even if was only going to be for a few months, he was back. Even though I suggested to Jessica she just leave Manny with me so he could start school in Utah only, she was adamant Manny be returned to her for five weeks. While in North Carolina he started kindergarten, something I was upset I did not get to witness myself. Luckily, at least for the next three months,his school was close to our house.

The next morning, before I could get Manny fully registered for school, I brought him in to work. He toured the radio station and met some of the people I saw every day. He was also able to meet Krystal, the woman I had started seeing while Manny was away for that long five weeks. She worked at the radio station with me.

"Oh my gosh! You're so cute!" Krystal said upon meeting Manny.

"Thanks?" Manny's face turned bright red and he placed half of his body behind my leg.

"Give me a hug!" Krystal put her arms out. Manny reluctantly walked into her arms and hugged her back. He held on tight.

What Krystal and I had was different. It wasn't love. It wasn't even a defined relationship. I wasn't ready for anything close to a relationship yet. We were seeing where things were going, what could happen. Before Manny came for the summer I was seeing someone else and told her to stop coming over so it would not confuse Manny. I never asked this of Krystal, so she was either *better* than the previous girl, or I had changed in that time period.

Manny's enrollment in kindergarten was easy and we were back on our way to a normal routine. While taking Manny to school one morning we walked up to the door of his classroom and he stood like a thousand pound statue in the doorway. He did not want to go into class. I pushed and he held onto the door frame, pulling himself out. I removed his hand and a leg would appear out of nowhere also preventing his admittance. Slowly all of the children in the class started looking at Manny, one at a time. He was reduced to a pile of *crying child* on the floor.

"Don't worry about it," his teacher said. "This happens all of the time." The look on my face must have been an indicator to her I was worried. I had never raised a kid before. Was this normal? According to Manny's blonde twenty-something teacher, it was normal. Considering within six months Manny had moved from Utah to North Carolina to Utah to North Carolina and back to Utah, not wanting to let go of me made perfect sense. All of his detachment issues were amplified by his foster background.

Nothing was working out the way it was supposed to. I was supposed to have a family and a child we could raise and help *together*. Instead Manny was bouncing all over the country with no real idea of where his home was. He had no concept of stability. If anything we took him out of an unstable foster system and introduced him into an even more unstable world.

I had no preparation for being a single parent of a

school-aged child. I had completely forgotten about "non-student days," which I loved when I was a kid. Any day without school was a good day as a child. As an adult, days without school meant finding a babysitter or leaving work. It meant that my normal twelve dollar per hour job would be put on hold for a day while I sat in the house while Manny played with the neighborhood kids. Luckily Krystal was there. Her work schedule allowed for her to watch Manny most of the time.

I came home from work on one such occasion. Halloween was approaching, and I saw two pumpkins on my dining room table. In the kitchen were Manny and Krystal making cupcakes. They had spent all day together. They ate, picked out pumpkins, played. It was like a real woman was around. It was great for Manny. My emotional walls were still too tall for anyone to scale them, even if Krystal had so quickly stolen Manny's heart.

It was Halloween of 2008. "Dad, where are we going?" It was easily the fifth time Manny asked me that question within the last hour.

"We're going to your aunt and uncle's house." When Jessica invited me over to her family's house months before she had sent an unspoken message to them I was okay to be around. Knowing Manny was in town they gladly asked us to go trick-or-treating with them.

"Dad, is my aunt and uncle's house far away? I'm bored." He had only been in the car for five minutes with another forty minutes to go.

"No, it's not too far, just be patient." A little lie wouldn't hurt, would it?

With Manny's face painted white and fake blood dripping from his mouth we toured the neighborhood. With us were Manny's three cousins, one of whom was also adopted. His adopted cousin stood out with her dark native Mexican skin while the rest of us were pale in comparison. The adults stood back and watched the children run from house to house, always excited for their next possible sugary jackpot. We finished the night and ended up again at Jessica's brother's house.

"I want to go home," Manny told me. His normal smile was gone, and he looked at the ground. It was a little difficult to take a three foot tall dracula seriously when he was pouting.

"What's wrong?" I was enjoying the time with Jessica's family.

"I want to go home." Manny had enough interaction that evening and no amount of coaxing him to stay was going to change his mind.

"We need to leave," I told Robert, Jessica's brother.

"Oh, that's too bad." He stood up and we shook hands, like men do. Manny didn't want to shake hands or give them hugs goodbye. He just wanted to leave. "Why don't you plan on coming over for Thanksgiving?"

"We would really like that." Not having any family in Salt Lake City meant most holidays were spent alone unless we were willing to drive hours to see my family. Thanksgiving at Robert's house sounded perfect.

"Good, my sister will be here, and my brother too from Denver."

Jessica and I talked regularly, and she was glad Manny enjoyed himself at her brother's house. Since Manny's communication skills were still lacking at best, I usually told Jessica what Manny did on any given day.

One night the phone rang and I saw it was her. She normally called much earlier than ten o'clock at night. Usually she would try to call and talk to Manny before bed. She could have only been calling to talk to me. Her voice did not have it's normal pep behind it, as if someone had put her candle under a bushel.

"I don't want you to freak out, but I was raped last night."

"What?" My mono-syllable retorts to her returned. Despite everything she had told me in the past, being a CIA agent, being an assassin, and receiving a black eye from her CIA handler, nothing could have prepared me for being told she was raped.

"A bunch of us at work were celebrating for the upcoming deployment to Qatar. Someone put something in my drink and took me into another room and raped me."

I felt the blood gather in my face. My jaw clenched. I saw only red. Despite our differences and our failed marriage, *no one rapes the mother of my child.* I wanted to fly out to North Carolina and be Trigger's sidekick, taking out the monster who could do this to her, the woman I still loved.

"Oh, I know who did it. I called my dad and he said it is going to be *taken care of."* Her father did have connections, after all.

"What do you mean *taken care of?"* It was an ambiguous statement. I hoped she was saying what I hoped she meant.

"You know what I mean." Her voice had a slight hint of laughter as she said it. Her dad was going to kill the guy, or at least arrange for someone else to do it. Good. *He'll get what he deserves,* I thought.

A few days later Jessica left the country. Once she landed we chatted online.

"What is the progress with *the guy* from the party?" I didn't want to say "the guy who raped you." Jessica had spent a few months being a rape crisis counselor while we were still married. Because of her training, and my own failed experience at graduate school to become a therapist, I knew never to ask the wrong question. I didn't want to invoke some sort of flashback or horrific spectacle for her in front of hundreds of military strangers.

"They took my blood when I landed here. I am told I tested positive for Ruffies."

"So what is next?"

"That motherfucker is already in jail for what he did. My dad is going to ensure he ends up in prison. Military prison. It's worse than any other kind of prison you can imagine." I knew what happened to rapists in prison. Karma had a way of coming back at them over and over again, delivered by multiple messengers. I was okay with the possible world where that man would get what he had coming to him.

After all, he raped the woman I loved, even if she no longer loved me.

| TWENTY SEVEN |

And I am Thankful
Thanksgiving 2008

Jessica had recently begun telling me about all of the *hot guys* on the military base in Qatar. "It's like being a fat kid in a candy store," she said. I am unsure why I was the appropriate person to tell about her romantic endeavors, but I was. She sent me pictures of someone she only described as, "the guy" a few times. She said her rape sent Vince over the edge, and he wanted nothing to do with her. She was moving on.

I read her most recent description of how she could have any man she wanted on the military base, and I closed my laptop.

Manny and I drove to Robert's house for Thanksgiving dinner. It was nice to be invited to spend the holiday with Jessica's brother. I refused to impose myself on anyone that holiday weekend, so an actual invitation, by family nonetheless, was perfect. I knew the special significance this holiday represented. Despite our failed marriage I was still a part of Jessica's family. I was still welcomed. To say I was grateful for being taken in would have been an understatement.

"Hi Jessica," her brother said while I held the video camera. "We miss you and hope everything is going well."

"Hi Jessica!" her sister said next. "Be safe."

Videotaping her family and sending it to her was the least I could do. After all, regardless of our living apart, our families were combined.

My family never had a big Thanksgiving tradition. We never sat around a giant oak table telling everyone for what we were thankful. At the very most we ate food and watched television. Even that tradition had not happened in years. I was glad to be a part of a real family gathering for once in what seemed like forever. Had we gone around the table and proclaimed what we were thankful for I would have said, "I am just thankful to be here." I was.

Manny and his cousins were in rare form that night. Having just watched *Madagascar* for the one hundredth time, Manny taught his cousins one of the songs. He taught them one verse of the song, which they sang over and over again. "Oh, I need to record this," I told Jessica's family. "She'll love this." They all smiled at me, not saying a word. I liked to send videos of Manny to Jessica, partially for moral support and partially because I wanted her to know I was a great father. I was someone she could rely on.

The kids kept singing and singing. Their little voices became background noise as the adults went into the dining room to sit down and prepare for dessert. We sat around the table, making small talk. I am sure my presence was awkward for them, but they did invite me after all.

All of her family was Mormon. I was an outsider, so that meant we couldn't talk about church or service. We couldn't talk about the most recent speech the Mormon Prophet gave and how it was *so inspiring.* We had to find something to talk about. Talking about Jessica became the only common ground we had.

Jessica was an elusive member of their family. Just like she had done with our ex-Mormon friends, she would occasionally cut her family out of her life for months at a time.

All it took was one misstated remark, or a misinterpreted gesture, and Jessica would be gone. Because of this her family only spoke kindly to her. They had to walk on eggshells in order to keep her around. She was just as much of an enigma to them as they were to me. Maybe they thought my presence would shed some light on their sister, who they barely knew.

We discussed Jessica's apparent inability to communicate properly and how her reactions could be caused by something else. Her brothers and sister verbally threw their hands in the air, expressing, "I don't get it!" I, however, understood why she acted that way. She had to learn English at the age of ten. The rest of her siblings were already fluent in English when they moved to America. Perhaps how Jessica communicated was different than how the rest of us did. I held on to this notion for so long, if only to comfort myself. I felt the need to defend Jessica to her family.

"It's understandable she has communication issues, considering she moved to America and learned English when she was ten." From my own personal experience in the Philippines, despite speaking the language very well, properly expressing something emotional was terribly difficult.

"What do you mean Matt?" Robert spoke up. I scanned the table to see every adult looking at me like I had just told them the best use of toothpaste was as hair gel, or that peanut butter was a great underarm deodorant.

"She didn't learn English until she was ten. She probably has a difficult time still conveying her feelings properly." I thought perhaps I misspoke the first time, or maybe the sound of the children in the background somehow muffled my previous statement.

"Jessica was four when she moved to America. *I* was ten, not her," Jessica's sister told me. She looked annoyed, like I had taken her science project and tried to pass it off as my own in the fair. We stared at each other. I was waiting for them to say, "Gotcha!" I waited. There was no surprise joke in her statement. Her siblings all looked at me waiting for my response.

"But," I paused, unsure of what to say next. "But, she speaks Spanish, right?" Her family laughed like I had just told a dirty joke during church. It was subdued laughter, implying something secret or dirty. Jessica's sister-in-law sat at the table unmoved, breastfeeding her newborn baby.

"What?" Her brother Stewart, from Denver, spoke up. "She can barely speak Spanish. We all make fun of her for how horrible her Spanish is. That's why we never speak it around her." It was true. I never saw them speaking Spanish to each other. Jessica even refused to speak it when we were at Latino markets by our house.

None of what they just told me made any sense. Someone wouldn't lie about that, would they? Why? It seemed like such a silly thing to lie about. Besides, I *knew* she spoke Spanish. She used it for her *other job,* which I knew at least one of the people at the table knew about.

"She told me she was a professional mixed martial arts fighter for a while." Their laughter persisted, but this time it was if I had said something actually funny.

"Her first husband was really into mixed martial arts, and even trained for a while. Jessica never fought." I told them the story about her professional fights and how her father refused to support her in her hobby after she had received a broken nose. I recalled Jessica telling me about a time a woman in a bar was being upfront with her, so Jessica broke her arm. Her family didn't know how to respond.

"She trained in martial arts, right? She said she had her third degree black belt in Brazilian Ju-Jitsu."

"No." The game was no longer funny to them. Their faces had turned serious.

Either Jessica had lied to me, or her three siblings were lying to me. It was difficult to decide which was true. Reading people had always been something I was good at, and they appeared to all be telling the truth. Then again, I always believed everything Jessica said too. My people reading skills could not be correct in both situations.

I had to find something, anything, that was the truth. I started grasping for straws. "At least tell me your mother died of breast cancer," I blurted out.

"Oh yes, that happened," Stewart said. Robert had stood up to take their newborn to bed, reminding the children to be quiet while the baby slept. Jessica's sister sat back and didn't contribute much to the conversation at that point. She was just as interested in the outcome as I was. What else could be a lie? I needed to know more.

I took a chance and asked about the CIA. "Jessica says that all of you are in the CIA and your father has money and influence in Washington, D.C."

Stewart laughed. "Our dad is completely broke. He has no money."

Robert chimed in from the other room. "I was approached once to be in the CIA." Finally, there was some truth to the stories. Robert quickly told the story of his interview for the CIA, which he ultimately decided he could not pursue. The reason he did not want to be in the CIA was simple: sometimes they are required to do *whatever is needed* to get information. Robert, a faithful married Mormon man, refused to even entertain the idea of using sex as a weapon. He had standards.

His story mirrored Jessica's story almost exactly. Jessica had used her own brother's story as her own. I realized that nothing was sacred any more. I had to ask a very personal question.

"Okay, this sounds ridiculous," I pushed on, "and I've been told to never discuss this with anyone, but Jessica told me she had two stillborn babies in her first marriage."

Robert was back at the table by that point. He and his

wife looked at each other for only a second. They seemed to have had an entire conversation with each other with that look. He slowly turned his head toward me amidst the silence of the room. Robert's wife spoke up. "She had a miscarriage when she was five weeks along. She told us later she was happy the pregnancy ended because she didn't want a baby."

"Wait," I paused. The story of her miscarriages had been something I had known for years. It was one of our first *bonding moments* when we first started dating, sharing each other's pain. "She told me she had a stillborn at nine months and another at six months." Maybe if I stated it another way they would suddenly remember.

"That was *us*, Matt," Robert's wife responded. She was clearly agitated by what I was saying. "I'm not surprised I'm hearing this, honestly, Jessica has never been trustworthy." No one stood up for her. In a room filled with her closest blood relatives not a single one of them said, "Hey, that's my sister you're talking about!"

"What about the story where a woman in church came up to her and asked when she was going to have a kid, right after the stillbirth?"

"That was us *too,* Matt. That never happened to Jessica."

| TWENTY EIGHT |

Seeing the Forest for the Trees
Winter 2008

I drove home from Jessica's brother's house in a weird state of amazement and bewilderment. What just happened? Who was this person I married? Every single thing I learned was a revelation. Every single thing we talked about made me question every story she had ever told me. I laughed.

"What's so funny dad?" Manny was still awake and curious.

"Life is funny Manny." The profound nature of what just happened, along with it's implications, had yet to sink in. I finally knew that Jessica was either completely nuts or a pathological liar. Being a pathological liar would also make her nuts. During the drive home I couldn't help but wonder how much of my divorce experience was also fabricated. I had spent months trying to repair a marriage beyond repair. I had accepted the divorce was my mistake, somehow believing *I* did something wrong and someday, *maybe*, we could be together again. Finding out who she really was not only removed the possibility of that ever happening again, but it also removed a year of self-induced guilt for a failed marriage.

Jessica wasn't able to call much due to her deployment to the middle east. She was able to contact my son on Skype, which she did on a weekly basis. I still felt badly for her rape, but was that true too? I hated being the guy who had to doubt someone's claim of being raped. I thought to myself, "She wouldn't lie about *that*, would she?" I didn't know. I needed to collect more information. I needed to figure out where I drew the line in the sand. Jessica called. I wasn't about to bring up what I learned. I was still trying to process the new information.

"Uhm," she started, "I *met* someone."

"Really?"

"Don't laugh, but his name is Ricky Bobby. He lives in Kansas. He's a Christian." She mentioned that Ricky Bobby was Christian because we were both atheists. She knew I wouldn't want Manny raised in a religious home. Ricky Bobby, it turned out, was *the guy* she was sending pictures of to me.

"Kansas?" Kansas was such a random place. Just a month before Jessica went on and on about how North Carolina was her definition of perfection.

"I think I want to move there when I get back. He has a kid and I think he and Manny can be great together. He wants me to be a housewife, and we can have more kids."

I couldn't believe my ears. She was going to keep moving Manny around the country. I had initially agreed for Manny to live with her for his stability, which I thought I couldn't offer him. Now she wanted to move herself again, with Manny, to Kansas?

"Well, if you want to take some time when you get back to figure it out, I can keep Manny for a bit longer." It was a legitimate proposal. She laughed.

"Nice try!" She laughed again.

Jessica proceeded to email me pictures of her new beau. I had no idea on what planet it was okay to send pictures of your new boyfriend to your ex-husband, but I played along. She was definitely twitterpated with him, like a child is with a puppy. Whatever happened to her setting up base in North Carolina? Was her bouncing from one guy to the next normal for her? How would this affect Manny?

I cannot remember who initiated the friendship, but somehow I became friends with Jessica's former co-worker on Facebook. She worked with Jessica in the intelligence squadron in the Air Force years before. I had met her a number of times. I had to know what the truth was.

"Did you guys really work together?"

"Yes, why?" She replied to me in an online chat.

"I learned some very concerning things about Jessica recently. I'm just trying to get the facts straight. Did you really deploy ten months a year?"

"Yes, we did. But Jessica never did."

"I thought she was a member of your unit."

"She was, but she was in charge of the warehouse. She possibly deployed one month a year."

All of the stories of boarding her dogs for months at a time were a lie. All of the adventures she went on were a lie. It seemed that all I had to do was ask simple questions and the truth would be obvious. Why hadn't I asked these questions before? Why was love such a blinder to my skeptical side?

Still anxious and unsure of which version of the world was real, I put it all out there.

"She told me she works for the CIA." I waited for a response. Did I hit a nerve? Perhaps she was calling her supervisors and a black SUV was going to roll up in my driveway at any moment. A few minutes went by.

"Hahahaha". She was laughing. "There is no way she ever worked for the CIA. She couldn't even get into our unit because no one trusted her. We all knew she was full of shit."

The worst part of this experience, for me, was realizing that I had spent the last three and a half years in a lie. I felt like I had just realized that Mormonism was not what it claimed to be all over again. The difference, however, is that I did not buy a house with Mormonism. I did not share a bed with Mormonism. What was I doing? None of this made sense.

I started calling friends of mine to find out if she ever told similar stories to them. A part of me was convinced that I had a serious mental problem. There was no way someone would lie about being in the CIA, having stillborn babies, how old they were when they moved to America, being an MMA fighter, or working in an intelligence unit. All of this information couldn't be real. People like that don't really exist. I began to question my own sanity.

Luckily everyone I talked to repeated the same stories to me. One person remembered Jessica telling her that Jessica had killed someone and was in the CIA. A number of people remembered hearing about Jessica's time in military intelligence while she was on the ground during *Shock and Awe*. Everyone, including my mother, recalled the story of the two stillborn babies. This was the mother of my child. We adopted Manny together. I didn't know what to do. And she wanted to move to Kansas to follow some guy named Ricky Bobby? I had had enough.

My friends, and Krystal, the woman I was seeing, were very supportive. Most of my friends had refused to believe Jessica for years. They could see her for what she was. Why couldn't I? They all responded to that question in the same way, that I was "blinded by love." I have heard that expression before, but it never meant anything until that moment. I finally understood it. To say I was devastated is an understatement. My friend Nadia then said to me, "Jessica is a very believable person. I believed her stories about stillborn babies too. It's not your fault."

I have already compared finding out the truth about Jessica to finding out the truth about Mormonism. There is a distinct difference, however. Mormons legitimately believe in their religion. Despite scientific evidence, historical evidence, or just obviously *non-Christian* behavior performed by their church leadership, they believe it. To say that my Mormon friends had been lying to me during my years in their church would be untrue. Saying I was misled would be untrue. These people really believed what they were saying. I just got swept away in it years ago.

Jessica, on the other hand, knew what she was doing. She had known that she was lying, or at least I hoped she had. She told other people's stories as her own over and over again. She consciously did it. She made the choice, and she let me live my life in a happy stupor never knowing any better.

Finding out she lied was worse than finding out that Mormonism was hollow; it was like comparing an apple to an atomic bomb. There is no comparison. I had to confront her. I refused to let Jessica take my son to Kansas. I refused to let my son be raised by someone who thought that lying was normal. Manny was too important for that.

| TWENTY NINE |
Confrontation
Winter 2008

During this time, my friend Nadia needed a place to stay. She had left her husband a year prior and couldn't afford to stay in her apartment any more. Nadia had been there for me during some of my worst times. She was a constant in my life. Opening my home to her and her kids was never even a question. She only needed a place to stay for a month while she was getting back on her feet. I had a basement that was empty.

I offered my basement to her for a month with the understanding that she would be moving out quickly. She and her three kids moved in. My house went from being empty to having myself, Manny, Nadia, and her three kids. I still also had my two cats. We tried to keep separate living spaces for a while, but it didn't last too long. It was one big household filled with kids and animals. On top of this Krystal came by every night. She stayed over most of the time.

I spent a while digesting everything I learned. I was trying to decide if I should spring my new knowledge on Jessica or if I should confront her in an email. Her family all told me they supported me because staying with me was what was best for Manny. Some of them told me that they felt Jessica had only wanted to be a mother when it was convenient for her.

With my new roommates in the basement my cash flow was getting even tighter. I was starting to run out of the money I had made selling everything I had. I asked Jessica if she could send me some of the money she promised to send for watching Manny while she was deployed. She had originally promised to pay me three hundred dollars per month for watching Manny.

Instead of paying money she sent twenty dollars worth of food every month. While the gesture was appreciated I would have preferred to receive help paying the heating bill. Instead I had twenty organic yogurts delivered to my house each week. After my request she sent a few hundred dollars, but then told me I shouldn't expect any more.

Life went on for a little bit and I was able to pay the bills, at least for that month. Manny had no idea just how broke we were and I planned on keeping it that way.

One evening Jessica called Manny on Skype. They talked for a bit and then I wanted to talk to her. I was agitated, upset. She could tell. My plans to construct a massive email outlining all of the lies she had told over the years was melting away. I couldn't hold it in any longer. My living room cleared as Nadia and Krystal knew what was about to happen.

"Why are you being such a dick, Matt?" I'm sure Jessica's confusion was genuine. After all, I had been a pushover with her for so long. I was suddenly talking back to her. I went for the throat.

"Jessica, how old were you when you moved to America?" I went for the easiest lie first.

"Ten, you know that."

"Then why did you siblings tell me you were four?"

"Why were you talking about me?" She was yelling. She had always hated people talking about her when she wasn't there. I finally understood why.

"Answer the question," I insisted.

"I was ten, Matt. Jesus Christ. You already know this."

"So if you were ten, are you saying your brother moved here when he was eighteen?"

"I guess."

"So he never went to high school in America?"

"He did."

"You've told me stories about him in junior high and

high school. You told me stories about him playing for the high school football team. Do you see how your math doesn't add up?"

"You're right, Matt, it doesn't add up. But that's just how I remember it. I don't know."

It was the same answer she had given me years prior. "I don't know." I wasn't falling for it this time. I started talking.

"Why does your family have no memory of your stillborn babies?"

"You were talking about me to them?" She was livid.

"Jessica, none of them know about your two stillborn babies. You would think that your family would know about this."

"What!?! Listen, there was a year and a half where I didn't see them. I never told them about it." I didn't buy this one either. I knew that she talked about her family trying to console her after the lost babies.

"Bullshit." I called it like I saw it.

"It's true Matt. There is a lot about me they don't know. Where is all of this coming from?"

I continued pointing out more and more examples of her lies. Her defenses were no better than her previous attempts to answer questions. I saw right through them.

"There is no way you will take Manny. I will not let him be raised by someone capable of this level of deception."

Silence.

I continued, "The divorce isn't even finalized yet. You haven't even signed the paperwork. Expect new paperwork."

All that I remembered was her yelling back, "You cannot take my son away from me! He is all I have! What would people think of me if a mother cannot even raise her own child!?" I was so furious, so enraged that I cannot remember all of the conversation. I do know that true to form her concern wasn't about Manny, but rather about how others would perceive her.

After this conversation, she didn't call for a while. I didn't know when she was supposed to come home. I didn't know what to expect. I had to prepare for a legal battle, and after a few phone calls I had some backup. The caseworker from the foster agency and Manny's former therapist were both willing to report their observations about us. The observations were highly in my favor. I also had a number of friends willing to back me up and corroborate the stories, but the ex-Mormon group was dwindling in size. The caseworker and therapist had to be good enough.

From that night on and over the next few months, I kept having a recurring dream where my father was still alive. In this dream my parents had faked my father's death. There was a good reason for hiding my father's continued existence, but I cannot remember what it was. In this dream I remember visiting my father in a rundown duplex. It looked like it should have been condemned. He was there like always, drinking, but still very alive. He didn't look healthy. The confusion and pain I felt every time I had that dream caused me to wake up. I always had to take a moment to decide if what I dreamed was real or not.

Unfortunately my father was not still alive. At that point he had been dead for over twelve years. I had never been a fan of interpreting dreams. The only thing that made sense to me was that my brain was comparing the deceit I had experienced with something greater. Being lied to for all of those years was as hurtful to me as if I had just found out my father were still alive, and it had all been a big lie. I was coming to grips with the fact that our entire marriage was fabricated. I never really knew her.

I refused to let my son be raised by someone capable of that level of deception. I needed a lawyer.

| THIRTY |
Anticipation
January 2009

A month had gone by and I still had no idea where
Jessica was. Was she so embarrassed that she just ran and hid?
Was she so humiliated by me finding out about her years of
deception that she would never show her face again? I hoped so.
I hoped she would no longer be a part of our lives any longer.

My houseguests needed to go. Nadia and her children
were only supposed to live with me for a month and they had
already stayed longer than that. It was taking them longer than
anticipated to get their own place. If Jessica dropped by
unannounced, which was something I was prepared for, Nadia
and her kids living in the basement would be used against me. I
knew that Jessica already thought that Nadia was a horrible
person. I was certain she could argue that a household of kids
and people would not be a suitable place for Manny to be raised.
I couldn't give Jessica any ammunition to use against me if this
custody situation started to get any uglier.

In the month that went by so quickly, I contacted a
lawyer to rewrite the terms of the custody arrangement. It cost
me $1,000, which I really didn't have. Money was becoming
more and more tight and my $12 per hour job wasn't cutting it
anymore. Winter was upon us and there were so many things up
in the air that I didn't know what to do or how to fix.

My friend Alan moved in, taking the place of Nadia and
her kids. One extra person in my house was a lot better than four.

Alan had moved from Salt Lake City to Chicago over a year ago and decided it was time to come home. Perhaps he would finish school. He was still looking for something in his life and he felt Salt Lake City had the answers. He moved into the basement and paid rent, which helped release some of the financial burden. He helped me by offsetting the cost of the house, and I helped him by giving him an affordable place to stay.

Krystal was around more and Manny was really taking to her. Krystal was raised Mormon and still considered herself to be a member of the Mormon Church despite the drinking and sex. She fit into the Mormon version of "cafeteria religion," where she could pick and choose what she wanted to believe. Mormonism for her was her cultural identity more than her religious identity.

When Manny found out that Krystal was Mormon he was confused. "You can't be Mormon," he proclaimed. "You're not brown." All of the Mormons that Manny had been exposed to were either Latino or Polynesian. As far as he knew it was another way of describing brown people.

I am still surprised Krystal put up with my situation as long as she did. She really wanted a relationship with me. I can look back now and see a pattern of women who knew I was not emotionally healthy enough to be in a relationship. They still saw something in me so great that they were willing to wait it out.

Krystal being around made everything a little bit easier. I never told her I loved her. I don't know if I was capable of love back then. She stayed though, thinking long term. I sometimes wonder how different life would have been had I been emotionally available to return the feelings Krystal wanted me to feel.

Still without hearing from Jessica, I was always paranoid that she would suddenly show up. One evening while Manny, Krystal, and I were watching television the phone rang, and it was Jessica. She was back in the country and was LIVID that I had contacted her family. She was LIVID that I had talked about her to them. I told her that I had the support of the caseworker and the therapist. She reminded me that her dad had a lot of money and that family would support her. I was going to have a long road ahead of me.

I was then forwarded an email from one of her brothers. She sent an email to her brothers asking the following:

Stewart and Robert,
Matt told me that the two of you agreed to testify
against me in a custody hearing which determines if
he or I will have primary custody of Manny. Is this
true? That's all I would like to know.
Jessica

She had lied again. She didn't have the support of her family. She was only then attempting to obtain their support after our phone call. Her brother Stewart from Denver replied to her saying:

Jessica,

For the record, I supported Matt's desire to seek
primary custody. However, since you felt the need to
corner me like this, I'm thinking I just might
testify if it ever came to that.

I'm not going to go over every reason for my stand,
but I will say that Vince managed to single-handedly
get the ball rolling. My contact with Vince during
that crisis highlighted his lack of concern for you.
He refused to tell me what was happening to you, and
hung up on me while I was frantically trying to
assess the situation. Thoughts of you being
victimized by a stranger out of our reach crossed my
mind. I was scared for you and your safety. I later
felt dissatisfied with your poor explanation of
events. The whole thing got me questioning

everything, from your alcohol abuse to the environment Manny is exposed to in NC.

I don't, for one minute, question your love for Manny. But I also don't see a problem with Matt seeking primary custody, based on what I've seen.

Stewart

Jessica knew she couldn't do anything. She was bluffing. Her other brother, with whom we spent Thanksgiving, told me about his response to Jessica. He said he would not take sides, but that he would also not lie. A judge hearing the truth was something that Jessica couldn't have. I imagine she was panicking at that point.

I emailed Stewart shortly after to find out what his thoughts were on the emails and the threats of legal battles. He replied.

It wasn't easy, but I'm done with diplomacy. I think she'll be quite surprised by my response, because it's not in my nature to be confrontational. But it's the right thing to do, and she's terrorized people long enough. If her plan was to disprove our support, I think it just backfired.

I don't care what she says about Vince. [My wife] and I don't ever want to meet him.

I'm glad, you deserve some rest. I remember how exhausting it can be to chase after a little one :)

Take care,

Stewart

I shot off another email a day later asking if Stewart had heard anything. Asking if Jessica had perhaps replied.

Yeah, she replied the next morning saying it's unfortunate that we chose to side with you, and that any further communication from Robert and me is unwelcome and will be ignored.

We kind of figured that would happen so it doesn't come as too great a shock. I spoke with Robert later and her e-mail hasn't changed his mind. Needless to say, neither one of us have replied to her message.

No point in doing so. We can't force her to be a part of our life. If at some point she changes her mind, we will welcome her back, as always. Life goes on!

Let me know if she says anything. Take care...

Stewart

Upon reading his email,I sighed in long overdue relief. Her family knew she was crazy and they still supported me. Jessica apparently had no issue cutting off her family just like she had cut off so many friends over the years. It oddly felt great to know that the family of my ex-wife supported *me* instead of their own flesh and blood.

During all of this I lost my job. This was the second time in less than a year. The company I had worked for would routinely lay off half of their employees every year right before Christmas. I was a victim of this mass layoff. My experience running my fuel economy website and working on the radio station's websites allowed me to find a new job within two weeks. It was closer to my home than my previous job. I would be working as a computer programmer for a website selling skin care products. It wasn't glamorous, but it paid a little more than my fantasy job in radio, which unfortunately was now something I had to abandon. Working in radio would have been easier if I didn't have parental duties. Now that I was a full time parent, some dreams needed to be put on hold or disregarded completely. Raising Manny and being a father were more important.

Over the course of a few weeks Jessica kept calling me to give me strict rulesthat she wanted me to follow so she could allow me to keep Manny. She accused me of being an alcoholic and a drug addict. I took the afternoon off of work and took a drug test. I had the lab send her the results. "I never want to be accused of this again from you." I proceeded with my lawyer ensuring that he was always in the loop. The irony is that had she signed the divorce paperwork in the first place it would have been next to impossible for me to change the custody agreement. Her inaction gave me the opportunity.

Soon she requested that I mail her the new copy of the divorce I had filed. My lawyer sent it to her. She still had not agreed to my having custody, but from what I could see the case was a simple one. There was no way she could win. There was also no way that I could afford it.

Jessica wanted to come for Manny's birthday party again. It had been almost a year since she had moved to North Carolina, and it was now almost seven months since she had last seen Manny. I wasn't sure how the visit would work out. After all, we both *still* had legal and physical custody of Manny. Nothing was finalized. Could she just take him and leave? I called my lawyer and he assured me there was no way Jessica could take Manny out of state with her. "Let her come," my lawyer said, "there is nothing she can do."

| THIRTY ONE |
Is There a Doctor in the House?

It was March of 2009 and Manny's birthday was worth celebrating. He was turning six years old, meaning he had been with us (Jessica and I) for over two and a half years. I was the primary caregiver for all but six months of that time. His home was with me in Salt Lake City.

Jessica emailed me her flight plans. She told me her father was driving from Arizona in order for Jessica, her father, and Manny to have breakfast. Their breakfast together would provide me some time to buy decorations, pick up Manny's birthday cake, and get the house ready for the birthday party. Alan, my new roommate, and Krystal helped set up. Manny was ready and waiting to be picked up at seven thirty in the morning. He waited. Eight o'clock came, and he still waited. He sat patiently by the door until Jessica finally showed up around ten o'clock. She didn't get out of the car. Manny ran outside and Jessica opened the car door to give him a hug. "You've gotten so big!"

After a few hours Jessica's father knocked at the door. He was dropping Manny off. Jessica was nowhere to be found. "Jessica lost her purse. She'll be here later." I offered to let Manny's grandfather to stay for the party. He declined. The party started at one in the afternoon.

Two hours later Jessica showed up. She sat by herself on the couch watching Manny and his friends run around, play instruments, and destroy a piñata.

We chit chatted a bit, but it appeared my fears of her kidnapping Manny were overblown. After all the lies she had told me over the past few months, I had assumed the worst of her. I was glad that my worry was unfounded.

The party died down and the guests left.

"I'm so sorry I was late." I didn't know if she meant for the breakfast or the party.

"My alarm didn't go off in the hotel room, and my dad just waited for me in the lobby. He never called. He never tried to see if I was okay."

"Manny waited for you for a long time."

Jessica looked past me not making eye contact. "That's too bad," she said.

"And what about the party?"

"While at lunch someone stole my purse. It had my drivers license in it. I had to get a new picture ID before my flight tomorrow."

She was either the most unlucky woman in the world, or all of the bad things that kept happening to her were intentional.

She took Manny out to buy some presents for his birthday. They came back a half hour later, and Manny was beaming. He loved being with his mom. He missed her so much and seeing all three of us in the same house together was probably the best birthday gift he received that year.

Jessica and Manny went back to his bedroom to play with his new toys. They got to spend some time together for the first time in over seven months. I heard Jessica go into the bathroom a few times. It must have been weird for her to be in my house for the first time since she moved out. She had picked that house out herself. She had painted some of those walls. Every morning she had showered in that bathroom. I have always wondered if it was as weird for her to be in my house as it was for me to have her there.

Alan, Krystal, and I were in the living room talking. Jessica came out of the bathroom and into the living room.

"Do you have a doctor you go to locally?" It was an odd request, especially so late at night.

"Is everything okay?" I thought that maybe something was wrong with Manny.

"Manny's fine. I have been throwing up blood."

"Krystal is a nurse." I only stated it. I wasn't trying to volunteer Krystal, and luckily Krystal didn't jump out of her chair and take Jessica's pulse.

"Oh, I'll be okay," Jessica replied.

Manny's birthday turned out great despite his mom being late twice and her vomiting blood in the bathroom. Manny was just happy to see his mom. I was happy to see her go.

A few days after the birthday party Jessica called me.

"Hey, I know you don't believe anything I say," she started. I was so glad that she finally understood the issue I had with her lying. "But I saw a doctor today, and I have cancer."

"Cancer?" I had graduated to two-syllable retorts.

"Yeah, it's ovarian cancer. Vince and his girls are pretty upset about it."

Once again I had no idea what to say. I let her keep talking.

"The doctor thinks that's why I threw up blood at your house. Matt, if you want the name and number of the doctor here it is." She proceeded to give me her doctor's name and number, who I called the next day. I was never permitted to get her medical information. I could neither confirm nor deny her story.

"And..." she paused, "I think it was all for the best that Manny stayed with you because I don't want him to see me get sick like this. I don't want him to worry. I'm certain I'll be starting chemotherapy, and I won't have the energy to help take care of him."

I talked with my mother about this new development. We both concluded I had to play along whether I believed her or not. I really didn't know what the truth was. I did know, however, that if someone was willing to lie about cancer they had to be one of the craziest people in the world. Jessica seemed off balance to me, but not *I-will-lie-about-having-cancer* crazy. I had to push forward, and at her request, I didn't tell Manny that his mom might only have six months to live.

It finally felt like closure was happening. She was going to sign the divorce paperwork, and I would have custody. Manny would be away from her craziness. But then the cancer added a new weird element to the equation. Jessica's mother had died of cancer so I knew her family probably had a higher predisposition. Considering she only had six months to live if untreated, her only option was a partial hysterectomy, which she had planned for the following week. I started to really think that

Manny would enjoy being around his mom more. If her time was limited I might regret not giving him the opportunity.

I spent some time looking on the Internet for houses in North Carolina. I wanted Manny to have both parents available, and honestly I wanted it too. I wanted to be able to take a weekend off. I wanted the freedom once in a while to do something that I wanted to do. Maybe I could even watch a movie that wasn't made for five-year-olds.

For the next few weeks, I kept looking at houses while Jessica started calling more frequently to talk to me and Manny. A few times I asked her how the chemotherapy was going or how her hysterectomy went. I was always answered with one word answers such as "fine," or "okay." I figured she didn't want to talk about it. I figured the cancer treatment was taken care of. As much as I hated her for lying about her past and the CIA nonsense I didn't want to see her die. Manny didn't deserve that.

I was on the hunt for options. My job didn't pay well so I had no real attachment to it. I just wanted what was best for my son.

While searching for options, I received a wedding invitation. It was one of our friends from the ex-Mormon group, who I had seen less and less of after becoming Manny's full-time parent. I just didn't have the time. I decided to bring Manny. Weddings are, after all, a family affair.

Half of the group no longer liked me. Since I more or less had to publicly side with Jessica and Vince for the sake of raising Manny a number of them were highly offended. It hadn't helped when Vince had called one of them a "faggot." I was hoping to see Lester, our flamboyant yarn-loving minister, at the wedding. He was one of the people who was turned off by my presence. He couldn't even stand to be in the same room as me.

I found Lester, introduced him to Manny, and said to him while gesturing towards Manny, "This is what all of the fuss has been about. This is what I have been fighting to protect."

"I know." Lester was calm.

"I need to find a way to obtain forgiveness from you and James." James, who also had attended our wedding, was the one whom Vince called a faggot.

"I forgave you a long time ago, Matt. James, on the other hand, is his own person."

"Can you have him call me?"

"I will tell him to answer when you call." I had every intention of calling James. I wanted to apologize and make things right. I never did though.

That evening I saw a number of people I had not seen in a long time. It was good to reconnect with these people who had been a major factor in my decision to move to Utah. I had a drink with a friend named Evelyn, who was oddly enough Vince's former girlfriend. I told her I would love it if she came over sometime to catch up. Evelyn was the woman who had hosted the costume party about two years prior.

Spring break was fast approaching, and it was Jessica's turn to take Manny. She had made no mention of the divorce paperwork or her cancer. If I had been in her shoes I would have been so overwhelmed with just trying to survive that divorce paperwork would not have mattered to me either.

On a play date with Robert's kids, the topic of Jessica came up. I told him about Jessica's cancer. "I'm sorry Matt, and I know this sounds harsh, but I'll believe it when she's dead." These people had known Jessica her entire life and knew what she was capable of. I started wondering if perhaps the cancer was real or just another shot at getting sympathy.

Soon afterwards I put Manny on a plane to visit his mom for the week. Even if I didn't want him to go I didn't have much of a choice in the matter.

| THIRTY TWO |
Time Together, Time Apart

Spring 2009

Manny arrived in North Carolina safely, and from what I could tell Jessica was okay with Manny living in Salt Lake City. There was no talk of his living with her again. She talked about her time with him as a temporary thing. It seemed like my worries were going to be over.

Due to Manny needing to fly out to North Carolina as an unaccompanied minor, connecting flights were out of the question. Airlines do not allow unaccompanied minors to have connecting flights. Since Jessica lived in North Carolina, the closest direct flight was at an airport five hours away in Baltimore.

Until just a few weeks before his Spring Break, Manny's trip to North Carolina was in question. Jessica called me one night crying.

"I was in a car accident. I got a ticket. I totaled my car."

"Oh my God. What happened?"

"I was taking someone home late one night after a party," she said. The story sounded all too familiar. "It was raining and I hydroplaned. I ran off the road and my car is totaled."

"At least you're okay."

Sobbing, "I don't have enough money to bring Manny here for Spring Break." I didn't know if she was trying to get me to pay for it or not.

"Let me know what you can figure out Jessica." This was *her* time with Manny and I refused to fund it.

Soon afterwards, the tickets were purchased. Jessica bought another SUV, this time a Nissan Xterra. This was the second car she had totaled since we had separated. Her excuses were always valid ones, usually ones having to do with the weather. I wondered though how so many bad things could keep happening to her. Rape, cancer, two totaled cars, and all of her furniture that I had sent to her was ruined.

The weeks without Manny were always stressful. I wondered if she was going to try to pull something. I was still unsure what she was capable of. In the back of my mind I kept thinking of her cancer and how she didn't have much time to live. I researched ovarian cancer relentlessly on the Internet. If someone has ovarian cancer, even with treatment, there is a good chance that it will spread to the stomach. Stomach cancer rarely results in a cure; treatments maybe delay the inevitable.

Manny needed to be near his mom even just for a few years before she died. It would be a disservice to him to refuse my son time with Jessica before she died. I realized nothing was really holding me in Utah besides ensuring Manny's stability. I told her of my plans to possibly move to North Carolina. She was excited at the idea.

During the week Manny was away, Krystal and I stopped seeing each other. She knew she was not the only person I was dating, but I guess the reality of it finally got to her. One day she left and didn't come back. It seemed like the strings holding me to Salt Lake City were getting cut left and right.

It was time for Manny to come back from visiting Jessica and our future was unknown, but I was willing to do whatever I needed to do to ensure Manny grew up to be a well functioning adult. The phone rang. I saw the all too familiar number from "Jessica Timion" on my phone.

"I want you to know I didn't do this on purpose, but we were late and missed the flight back."

In a state of disbelief, I responded. "Okay. What are your options?"

"We cannot get another flight until next week. I am so sorry. Vince is pissed at me too for this, saying that I'm totally irresponsible."

"Well, then I guess we don't have much of an option, do we?"

"I was thinking, since you were thinking of moving here anyway, why not just let him stay until the summer and then you can move out here? After all, Kindergarten isn't that important."

"No." What she was suggesting was so absurd I didn't think it warranted much else of a response.

"Okay, I'll get him back next week and send you the ticket information."

Her irresponsibility and disregard for Manny's education was too much for me to handle. Every so often she would appear to care about Manny, and I'm sure she did in her own way, but it wasn't in the way that he needed. I decided at that moment that there was no way we would be moving to North Carolina. If she could not get him on a plane with a week of notice, what else was she incapable of doing?

Manny arrived a week later. In his suitcase was the divorce paperwork. The papers were signed. Finally.

I submitted the paperwork to the courthouse knowing it would take ninety days to finalize. Almost two years after we had split, things were finally ending.

Another phone call. Jessica had something important to tell me.

"I'm not living with Vince any more."

Unbelievable. She was trying to get me to let Manny stay for the rest of the school year and then suddenly she was out living on her own.

"Well, we've been planning this for a while. We waited until Manny left before I moved out. We both decided that we needed our own space in order to be a better couple. We needed to date and be separate in order to stay in love." The story eerily reminded me of what she told me when she wanted a divorce.

"So is Vince okay with this?"

"Yeah, it was his idea. He even bought me furniture to help get my new place in order."

After everything we had been through, Jessica's

unpredictability affected me less than it did before. At least I knew that I had custody of Manny. Jessica could keep messing up her own life as long as Manny was not a part of it. I could live with that. I sighed in relief and had the best night of sleep in years. It was really going to be over. I no longer had to worry about if she lived with Ricky Bobby in Kansas, or Vince in North Carolina, or by herself in North Carolina, how how her deployments would affect Manny's stability.

Evelyn, who I had reconnected with at the wedding, came over. Evelyn was still talking with Vince. Vince had told her that he and Jessica had in fact broken up. This didn't match with Jessica's version of why she had moved out. We laid in bed talking. Despite a bad breakup years before, Evelyn wasn't over Vince. A part of her still wanted to be with him. "Vince thinks Jessica is totally crazy. Like completely nuts." This really didn't surprise me. I was indifferent at this point, but still elated by that the divorce paperwork was signed.

Evelyn and I dated for a while, which usually consisted of her coming over. I didn't have the money or the motivation to try to have a formal dating relationship. I wasn't ready at the time. She stopped coming over; she said that my version of dating was not the same as her version of dating. I think it had more to do with our six year age difference, her having three teenage children, but ultimately it was because I wasn't ready for a relationship. I started to see a pattern in myself. I clearly wasn't relationship material. I had to change that.

The school year ended, and Manny had his kindergarten graduation. I was the proud dad with the video camera. The kids sang songs for the parents and every time the lyrics "I love you" were part of the song Manny would look straight at me and gesture that he was saying those words to me. I started crying.

Kids from a foster background often times have a difficult time forming emotional attachments with their caregivers and their adoptive parents. This is known as an attachment disorder. There are a number of theories as to the cause, and a number of controversial treatments, but attachment disorders are fairly common for children with Manny's background. This disorder has been seen even in kids adopted as infants. Manny's love and affection towards me (and his mother) had always been legitimate. His emotional bonds had formed and they were real. Part of me hated that the bond he developed with Jessica was also real.

My little guy was getting bigger. He had graduated kindergarten, his first rite of passage. Now I just had to worry about him getting a driver's license and getting accepted into college.

The summer of 2009 was fast approaching. I was waiting to receive the finalized divorce documents so that I could frame them. It was going to be one of my proudest accomplishments. I had wanted to do the same thing when I resigned my membership from the Mormon Church years back. When I received the letter confirming that I was no longer a Mormon *on record* I had gone so far as to buy a frame. Suddenly though my disassociation with the organization seemed like gratification enough. I didn't need to brag about it. Perhaps I would feel the same way about the divorce.

Despite being required by state law to give thirty days' notice of making any travel arrangements, Jessica still had not given any notice to take Manny for the summer. Two weeks before the departure date, she sent me flight plans. I could have fought it, but the last thing I needed to do was disrupt the divorce process. It was all in my favor now. I welcomed the six week vacation from parenting. According to Jessica, Manny would be spending an equal amount of time with Jessica at her new apartment and Vince's house. She said that they were still dating.

In our familiar routine, I took Manny to the airport, and watched him get on the plane. He was going to fly unaccompanied again. Hopefully this time he would return on time.

| THIRTY THREE |

Back into the swing of things
Summer 2009

"I think that I've decided that if I don't end up with Jessica, I'll move
to Utah and go to BYU or something. I have too many friends there.
Man, one thing is for sure, the friends you make on your mission are
real, genuine friends. I love everyone here, all servants of God, with a
holy calling. Wow."
        -private missionary journal, Matt Timion, April 1, 1999

I had started talking with an old high school friend from
Illinois. I started talking with Courtney online. My obvious
desperation is something I am embarrassed of to this day, but
during one of our first interactions I said, "If *this* moves forward,
how quickly would you be able to move to Utah?" Was I really
asking someone I had not seen in almost fifteen years to move in
with me? How desperate could I be? Luckily, Courtney did not
run the other way when my emotional desperation reared its ugly
head. I talked with Courtney almost every night, and we started
really getting to know each other. We began really liking each
other. She seemed to be someone I could be happy with. She
made me laugh every night.

Manny came back without a problem from Jessica's, and
his summer in North Carolina went well. Manny's homecoming
was happy, and Jessica kept in contact with me over the entire
summer. She even sent pictures every few weeks to let me know

how Manny was doing. I partially felt like she was being *overly* nice, but I dismissed the idea as paranoia.

Manny was enrolled in the first grade; he started attending school just one week after coming home. His teacher was kind and a veteran educator. His after school program was understanding and patient. Just a few weeks after school began, however, Manny's behavioral problems began to resurface. Manny's inability to focus and stay on task required him to be relocated to a different class. In the after school program he would often times get in trouble or be sent home early because he had acted out. He bit, he kicked, and one time he stabbed another child with a pencil. When I talked to him about his behavior, he would shut down. One time, however, in tears he told me, "I don't know where I'm going to live." He didn't know if home was with me in Utah or in North Carolina with Jessica. My goal to provide stability for his life was a complete failure.

Manny needed someone to talk with so I worked with the school to take advantage of their resources. Talking with a school counselor on a regular basis seemed to help quite a bit. While he lied and stole sometimes, I wasn't as concerned about those behaviors. I was more concerned about how he behaved when he was upset. Manny would normally go into a violent rage. It was no different than how he acted when he was three years old, but now he had the ability to use his words instead of using his body to bang his head against the wall. However, he still would, bang his head against the floor or punch himself in the head.

I decided I needed to take Manny back to his therapeutic preschool to see if they had something for school aged children. Certainly our situation was not unique. Anything, even a monthly support group could help. We met with Susan, Manny's former therapist, again. I noticed that the last name on her office had changed.

"What happened to your name?"

Laughing, she said, "I thought you'd notice that."

"Divorce?"

"Yeah, and when I was going through it, all I could think about was what you and Jessica went through. Matt, I suddenly knew exactly how you must have felt during the whole thing." I had wondered what she *really* thought when Jessica and I were sitting in her office the year before, but I could never ask.

The options available for Manny at the preschool were rather limited because of his age. We tried to make a number of therapy appointments, but scheduling became such an issue that we opted to just stick with the therapist at the school. Manny was not a bad kid, but he needed a lot of extra support and attention. I knew to expect this from former foster kids, but actually having to deal with it was another matter completely.

Dealing with his issues was what I had signed up for though, and Manny's behaviors were really not uncommon. Resolving his behavioral problems was going to take time. I noticed that the longer he was back home with me, the better his behavior became. He was calmer and he made some progress in school despite the fact that his reading and math were a year behind. The excellent teachers and school administrators knew what to do, and we benefited from their experience.

Time went on and Manny got back into the swing of things. I had purchased a vintage Atari 2600 while Manny was gone for the summer for him to play. He played it and its sixty or so games for a few months before growing bored with it. He liked his Nintendo Wii better. I had this weird belief that my son should experience all of the things I did as a child because I turned out okay. As a result we had an Atari, we listened to vinyl records, and he knew all too well what a VCR and a tape deck were. This also extended to movies we watched. He knew more about children's movies from my childhood than he did about modern children's movies. We mixed vintage items with their modern counterparts like the rotary phone in our living room, but

I feared that Manny would one day feel unfamiliar with modern technology. Luckily he recognized those relics were old. He always referred to those items as "things from the old days."

There was close to no contact from Jessica. She would call once a month and talk with Manny for awhile and call a month later. I interpreted this as her letting go and moving on. She still had not paid any child support, which was beginning to really hurt me financially. I was still paying for my house, Manny's day care, food, clothes, bills, etc., all on about fourteen dollars per hour. What had become my life was a stark difference from years before when I had so much money that I could afford to buy cars and still have money saved away. Life had definitely changed.

Being a single parent affected my ability to interact with my ex-Mormon friends. I didn't have the time or the money to socialize with them like I used to. On top of that, I was not entirely welcome around some of them. Lester, the de facto leader of the group, had a problem with me. Even though he had said he had forgiven me for my association with Jessica and Vince, what he said in private was completely different. He talked about the "dark energy" around me and how he could not be in the same room as me. The way I saw it, everyone loved Lester. I had zero desire to make other people feel uncomfortable in my presence so I opted to absent myself from the ex-Mormon social gatherings. The group of people with whom I was so close at one point had become a group of people I would see on the Internet.

The only ex-Mormons I still associated with were my roommate Alan, my friend Nadia, and my friend Mary Ann. Nadia and Mary Ann were great because they had kids as well. As the ex-Mormon group splintered further, those of us with similar lives tended to band together. From our old group of friends, a new one emerged. Those in my new smaller group were all parents. At the very least it was an easy way to organize a play date or find a babysitter in case of emergencies.

Just like I had assumed that my fellow Mormon missionaries and I would be great friends for the rest of our lives, I assumed that these amazing relationships I had formed with my fellow ex-Mormons would be life-long friendships. Only a few of my co-missionaries would talk to me anymore, and it seems that only a few of my fellow ex-Mormons considered me worth the effort.

It dawned on me that once again, ex-Mormons were no different than their former selves. The ingrained belief to avoid evil or the appearance of it at all costs. The only difference was that ex-Mormons didn't view evil as disbelief in a church, but rather disbelief in their new religion whether it be partying, open sexual relationships, liberalism, conservatism, atheism, or diet fads) Obviously, they had rejected the religion, but they couldn't remove the cultural influences they had been raised with.

I was no different. I myself did the exact same thing when I bought into the religion of Jessica. I never questioned a single thing she said. Her words were gospel, and her actions were infallible. I should have recognized her lies, but my unquestioning devotion to her made me no better than a person who would enthusiastically put his or her faith in a new diet fad or some other ridiculous belief.

Alan, Nadia, and Mary Ann were the only family I had in Utah. My biological family was out of state, and I had been given strict instructions to never talk to Jessica's family again. Jessica didn't want me talking with her brothers or sister. I honestly never knew if this edict was given to her siblings as well. They never reached out to me either. I always assumed that her declaration to keep us from associating with each other was an attempt to control the flow of information. I was okay with not talking with her family. I finally saw Jessica for who she was. Unfortunately the person who suffered the most for the lack of family interaction was Manny. He had cousins nearby that he could never see.

Courtney was going to visit soon. My feelings for her were becoming more profound. With all of the women I had dated since Jessica, none of them held a candle to this woman that I still had not seen in person. Unfortunately, in an act that I can only justify with a bad metaphor, I continued to see other people for a short while. Like an atheist who still celebrates Christian holidays, I would occasionally have women over from my past.

There were only two of them, and it only happened when they were in town from out of state, but it somehow made sense at the moment. I just wanted to feel wanted again if only for an evening at a time. That behavior had to stop, and it did. I couldn't be that guy any more. I felt like I was no better than Jessica while she was cheating on Vince with Ricky Bobby.

| THIRTY FOUR |

Courtney
September 2009

Courtney's flight was booked, and she was scheduled to spend a week with us. We had been talking on the phone for quite some time and she had vacation time she needed to use. It was one of those "make it or break it" trips. When she arrived, I found out that Courtney was a lot more aware of cleanliness than I was.

I liked to blame my messiness on me being a man and her being a woman, but her observations about my house were spot on. I had neglected my house. The overwhelming nature of being a single parent with negative cash flow affected me in more ways than I previously had realized. Who had time to clean when I was busy trying to raise my son? Raising Manny was a full time job by itself.

Truthfully though, I didn't even know how to clean the

place. When Jessica had lived with me she had been in control of the whole cleaning process. She told me to do something and I did it. She told me to vacuum a room or dust the table and I did it. We would get the entire house cleaned in under two hours. Since she had left my motivation to clean and organize was not there. No one was there to lead. No one was there to tell me I did something right or to try again. I cleaned when I could and in a way I felt acceptable. The absence of Jessica in my life meant the person I assumed was my guide into normal adulthood was no longer there. I was left to make up my own rules and figure it out myself.

The first night of Courtney's first visit was amazing. After she acclimated to a "guy" house we pressed forward.

The next morning the sun woke us up. Well, that's not true. What woke us up were the morning sounds from my neighbor's chickens. There must have been ten of them.

Courtney shot up. "Matt," she said, trying to wake me up. "Matt! What in the hell is going on?" She was referencing the chickens. She had gone from living in an apartment building in Chicago to staying with me in my house in Utah. She went from traffic and trains to neighbors with chickens clucking at six in the morning. I imagine she felt she was in the country, a total hick town.

We laughed about the chickens and just how out of place she felt. I wished I could have related but truthfully the idea of chickens sounded wonderful to me. Free eggs. I was used to my neighborhood and my neighbors with their six kids and cars parked on their lawn.

Courtney, Manny, and l went to Snowbird, a ski resort in Utah, for the annual Oktoberfest celebration. Oktoberfest, which in most places is an excuse to drink and dance, was oddly tame in Utah. Since I had never attended an Oktoberfest in any other state, it was completely normal to me. Courtney, however, was the first to comment that "this is the most low key Oktoberfest I have ever seen." In other states people dance and drink, eating bratwurst while celebrating. In Utah it was more of a chance for people with German heritage to dress up in formal Oktoberfest garb and dance to music reminiscent of polka. There was beer too, but it was by far not the focus of the event. Their German ancestors would have been ashamed of them.

I told Courtney about people I knew in Utah. I told her about the polyamorous couples, the swingers, the pot smokers, and the guy who drank a shot glass of his own urine every day to boost his immune system.

"You *do* realized you know some of the weirdest people I have ever heard of."

"What do you mean?" All I had ever known were those people. As far as I knew it was normal. Tyson had been the only person to tell me otherwise.

"This kind of thing isn't normal, Matt. Those people are weird." This might have been the first wake up call I had ever had in regard to Mormon culture. Mormons and ex-Mormons were all that I knew. Perhaps they were not normal, like Courtney said. In Salt Lake City though, especially among the ex-Mormons, they *were* normal. They were often praised for their ability to fight the system or to go against the grain.

That very night Courtney and I retired to bed. We held each other and it felt like a missing piece in me was right next to me. She was someone I could see myself with. She was a woman unlike any of the other girls I had known.

"Marshmallllooooooow!" We heard our neighbor's housemate yelling at around midnight.

"Marshmallllooooooow!" He yelled again. He was looking for his dog Marshmallow.

Courtney and I both burst into laughter. "Seriously, Matt, Utah is weird!" I had to agree.

Despite my lack of cleanliness, my apparent weird friends, and the mellow Oktoberfest, the visit with Courtney was a success. We continued talking and started becoming a lot more serious. Despite our limited interaction, I could really see a future with her. She was very attractive, smart, and one of the funniest people I knew.

Over time we started to fall in love. It felt like *real* love like love that they write about in romance novels and make teenage sitcoms about. In October of 2009 she sent me the following email.

I was thinking today: what did I do to deserve Matt in my life? It's inconvenient, it's slightly frustrating, and so much seems unknown. But just seeing your name on my caller id makes me smile, talking to u on the phone is the favorite part of my day, and hoping(knowing) that one day we won't be so far away from each other makes it worth it.

My emotional connection to you has been quick, unexpected, and unlike anything I've experienced in a long time.

So to answer my own question: I really don't care what I've done to deserve you; I'm just really happy that I did it.

I felt the same way.

| THIRTY FIVE |
Finality
October 2009

I received a letter in the mail. It was my completed and finalized divorce decree. Jessica and I were finally divorced. It was official, and I had custody.

I don't know what I was expecting to feel. Perhaps an official court document would have given me closure. I was officially single again. No new feelings emerged. It had been almost a year and a half since I received *the phone call* from Jessica and we were divorced. Finally. Everything felt the same though. It just felt normal.

Five years of marriage, lies, fatherhood, CIA Assassins, and people throwing up blood had become a part of my identity. The effects of those experiences don't just get wiped away with a judge's signature.

This is the same way Mormonism still affected me even though I had removed my name from their membership records. Mormonism had defined me for so long that to completely erase it would be impossible. To discount its influence on me, even to this day, would be a disservice to the Mormon Church and myself.

I called Courtney and gave her the good news.

"I'm officially divorced!" I was expecting excitement.

"Awwww," she said. She sounded disappointed. "But I liked knowing I was sleeping with a married man." I imagined her putting on a pouty face as she said it.

It was a running joke we had. She was dating a married guy. Now that joke would have to be put to rest. We started planning another visit for her to come out and spend some time with her new non-married boyfriend.

Still an atheist, something had happened that made me wonder if Courtney and I were meant to be. Fifteen months prior, while still working for the radio station, I had had a psychic reading. It was the first time I had ever done such a thing. Margaret Ruth, the radio show's resident psychic who had a weekly hour-long segment giving love advice, read my tarot cards.

I wanted to know when I would find *the one.* Her answer was simple. She blurted out, "fifteen months." I was disappointed it would not be sooner. "I see you with a family and a dog and kids. You won't meet her for fifteen months." The exactness of her prediction has always stuck with me. I was aware of the coincidence, and I always wondered if perhaps Margaret Ruth really had had some hotline to the spiritual world. The timing seemed too perfect since I was falling for Courtney. I even told her that I loved her. It was the first time I had told someone that since Jessica.

Courtney visited over the months when she could. One night I locked my bedroom door so that we could have privacy. Manny knocked. It was after midnight. I told him to back to sleep. He yelled, "You're just like my mom!" The next day I asked him about his outburst. He said that over the summer when he had been staying at his mom's house, the air conditioning stopped working. Manny and Jessica then went to stay at a male friend's house. Manny assured me this friend wasn't Vince. "Dad, my mom locked herself in the bedroom with this guy I didn't know. I was having a nightmare, and she wouldn't let me in. I was scared." That poor kid. I always left my door open after that. He needed to know that he was safe.

Money was becoming more and more of an issue. I had none. If I had had more items to sell I would have, but by this point all of my big items had been sold already to the highest bidder. In order to make up for this I had spent a lot of time that year growing my own garden. I had tomatoes, peas, onions, and everything else I could think of. The goal was to preserve them and save them for the rest of the year. At least I knew that they had been grown locally, and, most importantly, they were essentially free. Besides, it gave Manny and me a reason to go outside and work in the dirt. I would also take pears from a neighbor's tree while walking back from Manny's school. Free fruit. I took what I could get.

One day I came home from work at lunch to eat. I was riding my bicycle to and from work in order to save money on gas. I tried to do everything I could to save money. I opened the door to find that my house had been ransacked. Drawers were opened and items were tossed all around the house. Someone had been in my house. Who? Part of me thought Jessica or one of her goons had done it, even though I knew thinking like this was irrational.

I called the police and they sent out a Crime Scene Investigator. They took pictures, took my fingerprints, and took my statement. They did the same thing for Alan as to avoid accidentally thinking we were the thieves when they found fingerprints.

I couldn't live like that. I didn't feel safe in my own house. I needed a solution. I needed a dog. Yes, a dog! People never could have broken into my house if I had had a dog in there. I needed a big, strong, loud dog. To make it even easier, Jessica had recently told Manny who desperately wanted a dog "There is no way your dad will ever buy a dog. He just says stuff and doesn't mean it." I wanted to prove to Manny that his mom was wrong.

It was one of the least mature decisions I had made as a parent. I agreed to take in a dog just to prove to Manny that Jessica was wrong.

We found Jojo, an emaciated red nosed pit bull at a local pet store. The cost? Free. She had been rescued from the street not too long before. She was ten months old and extremely timid. Manny was in love and was so happy to have that dog in our lives. My cats were not as happy, but I don't think I've ever seen a happy cat before. Before Jojo, Manny had had nightmares around three times a week about "bad guys" coming to get him. He would run into my bed and sleep with me. After Jojo, his midnight trips to my bedroom turned into once a month. Soon afterwards the behavior stopped altogether. Our new dog had a real purpose.

It was getting colder out, and I was unable to ride my bike to work any more. I didn't have much money or food. I had received a letter from the Utah Foster Agency saying that they were having their yearly free day at an amusement park for current and former foster families. I saw this as an opportunity to get free food and free entertainment for Manny for the day. I started looking for events like this because I could not afford to do much else for Manny's development besides rent movies or take the dog for a walk.

We walked in the amusement park, in the bitter cold, and took our place in line. The warm chili filled me up. Manny was less interested in the food and more interested in the rides outside. We were walking around and saw bumper boats, which Manny was too young to ride on, at least by himself. Just then I heard someone yell my name. "Matt! Manny!" We looked over and there was Ariel. I had secretly hoped to run into either Peter or Ariel there. I was glad one of them showed up.

Ariel was now living with a family and was working towards being adopted. According to Ariel's foster father, Ariel and Peter lived together for a short while, but the two of them were too much to handle. They were both sent away. At least I wasn't alone in being overwhelmed with those kids. By this point Peter was fifteen years old and had decided for himself that he could do better on his own. He kept running away from his foster homes and always ended up at his grandmother's house. The three siblings had been removed from their grandmother's care originally by the state. Eventually, because of his tendency to run, the state found Peter a home so far away he wasn't able to run away again.

Ariel's foster father and I talked and exchanged information. We planned on visiting and keeping Manny and Ariel in touch. We both agreed that Peter might not be the best influence on the kids, at least not initially.

A short while after reconnecting with Ariel, my water was shut off due to non-payment. I had started to juggle bills in order to get them paid, but this usually meant I was always behind on a bill or two. Alan had stopped paying rent because of his own financial situation, and I was left to pay all of the bills myself. With no water I needed to figure something out. Luckily I was able to pull together the thirty dollars needed to ensure my son would be able to bathe that night.

Jessica had still sent no child support. She called no more frequently than once a month. Manny was happy, and he had no idea his dad was broke. He didn't even know what being broke meant.

I started looking for new jobs, a process that could take a while. Making so little money was unacceptable. I needed to stop hemorrhaging money every month.

It was Thanksgiving of 2009. My friend Nadia was putting on a big Thanksgiving for her friends and family. Manny and I were invited. It was free food,my favorite part, and all of my good friends would be there. Courtney sent me a text message that day. "I am thankful for you," it said. Surrounded by friends, I only wished Courtney lived closer. I hated the feeling of loving someone so far away and going to bed at night with no one by my side.

| THIRTY SIX |
Trying to Find a Way Out
Winter 2009

I started applying for jobs every day. I had to change my situation. I had to make more money. I could see a trend and knew the longer I stayed at my job, the faster I would be completely broke and possibly lose my house. I couldn't be homeless with a child. I had stayed so long at that job because of how flexible they were with Manny's schedule. Counting down to my impending financial demise, I would have taken *any* job that paid more. *Anything* would have been better regardless of the schedule.

For Christmas I had managed to save enough money to

get Manny a number of presents. Christmas that year was just he and me at the house. I would have preferred to travel down to Las Vegas, where my mother had recently relocated, to spend Christmas with my family. Unfortunately it was Jessica's year for Christmas, and she would be coming to town to pick up Manny and spend Christmas with her family in Utah. I made the mistake of telling Manny that his mother would be coming. She never came. He started to learn that anxiously waiting for her would not make her magically appear.

I knew exactly how he felt. When my parents divorced, I was thirteen years old. My father stayed at a friend's house for a while, but before he left he told me that he was going to take me to a concert coming into town. It was going to be my first real rock concert. ZZ Top was coming to the Moline, Illinois, and I was thrilled. Mostly I was finally going to be doing something with my dad. I put on my best Grateful Dead t-shirt and waited. We had not heard from my dad for a week, but there was no way he would forget about me. I sat. I waited. I waited for hours before my mom told me that there was a good chance my dad wasn't coming. We didn't even know how to get ahold of him.

I found out later that my father had taken his new girlfriend to the concert. My father's priorities were obvious. My father never apologized for forgetting about me. He never mentioned it. I never mentioned it either. Like my father, Jessica never acknowledged that she was supposed to come into town. She never apologized to Manny. She never apologized to me.

Dmy video camera was one of the items stolen from my house. I had a long tradition of filming my son on Christmas when he opened presents. I did this mostly because there is almost zero film of my childhood. I didn't want Manny to grow up without a record of his past, with no funny videos to show his own children. My video camera was gone. I rummaged through the basement and found an old VHS camcorder that I had been bringing with me from house to house for years. It was missing a power adapter, but I figured out a way to to jerry-rig one out of two other power adapters I had had. Although it would be on VHS, I could film Manny's Christmas. At least it wasn't reel-to-reel.

Faced with the fact that I had to use a fifteen-year-old video camera to record my son's Christmas, I was motivated yet again to get a better job. Anything that paid more would do. I saw a job online to be a recruiter. Recruiters are those annoying people that call you and ask you if you're looking for a new job. They then get you the interview and if you get hired their company makes twenty percent of your first year's salary. It's a terribly lucrative business. With my knowledge in technology and my bachelor's degree in psychology, I thought I had the right combination of skills required to do the job. I applied.

New Years came and went. I kept the house at sixty-five degrees in order to save money on heating. Warm air escaped through the sixty year old windows in the basement. We made up for the loss of heat with small space heaters in our rooms, which were still ridiculously cold.

Jojo, our dog, slept in my bed. Sometimes she would sleep on the couches themselves, which had been mended with needle and thread over a dozen times to repair the tears she had created while "digging" for crumbs of food left behind by Manny. I couldn't afford to buy new couches. I couldn't even afford to pay my gas bill some months. Our dog was a money pit. My son loved her though. He adored his dog, even when he would sometimes wrestle with her and get hurt.

After being tired of constantly having to mend my furniture and clean up after a dog too stubborn to house train, I decided to try to kennel train her. This process of kennel training involves leaving the dog in a small kennel all day so they won't go to the bathroom. They are supposed to hold in their natural urges until they are let out of the cage. Apparently dogs don't like to lay where they waste. Jojo was the exception. Not only did she go to the bathroom in her kennel, but she would then lay in it and when I let her out of the kennel she would spread it all over the house. Eventually our dog figured out how to break out of her kennel. Since the kennel could not keep her in, I tried to give her a room in the basement. It was an abandoned bedroom that used to be Jessica's room. I figured Jojo could do whatever she wanted in there and at least the mess would be localized. Still not content being locked up, Jojo tore a hole in the door and escaped. If it wasn't for the love my son had for that dog I would have gotten rid of her right then and there.

My house was chaotic and owning a dog cost more than I had anticipated. I kept applying for jobs.

My roommate Alan still wasn't paying rent. It had been four or five months by this point, which had really taken its toll on my ability to do much of anything. Although we never talked about it, I know he had had his reasons for his lack of payment. He would avoid me like the plague and come in and out of the basement without saying a word to me. There was a door to the basement in my kitchen that always stayed closed. I only heard him coming and going as he never opened the door any longer. I only opened the door when I had to do laundry since the washer and dryer were in the basement. If I went down to the basement his room would be closed. It was like a stranger was living downstairs. This behavior went on for a few months.

I was on the phone with Courtney one night. We talked almost every night. While talking with her and cooking dinner I heard a blood curdling yell. "Nooooo!" I heard Alan screaming and then something was thrown against the wall.

"I need to let you go," I told Courtney.

I opened the door that divided the upstairs from the downstairs and saw Alan slumped on the landing of the stairs crying.

"Alan, what's wrong? What happened?" His cell phone was on the floor next to him.

185

"It's my mom, she's dead."

"Oh my God." In times like these, there are no real words to help people. All you can do is be there for them and listen.

"She was in a car accident with my brother. He's in the emergency room."

I quickly realized that Alan's mother and brother were in the hospital where my ex Krystal was a nurse. Expecting to be ignored, I called her. She did answer. I asked her to keep an eye out and let me know of anything she could. She agreed.

"Do you need a ride to the hospital?" If I were in his situation I wouldn't want to drive.

"No, I can get there. I just need to get out of here."

I knew the feeling.

Over the next few days the hospital saved Alan's brother's life. As a result of the accident Alan and his siblings each received a settlement from the driver's insurance company that killed their mother. Alan had enough money now to pay me back and get his own place. Moving out wouldn't happen overnight, but it meant I was going to be alone in the house again (minus the child, the two cats, and the door-eating dog).

Salt Lake City wasn't working for me, or perhaps I just didn't know how to make it work. I needed to get out of there badly. I had no idea where to go, or even how to do it. I felt so helpless. I needed a real change.

| THIRTY SEVEN |
A Way Out
January 2010

After months of job searching, on January 15th I received a job offer as a recruiter. I started on February 1st. The job proved to be worse than I had imagined. Not only were the expectations ridiculous, but the management was unethical. I was used to bad managers, but never before had I been so verbally abused and honestly sexually harassed. The owner blamed his brash style on being from New York (he was really from New Jersey, which I imagine he was ashamed of) but the truth is he was just an ass. I started looking for an escape from my new job too. I began applying for jobs again elsewhere. It would take me a few months of searching before I could get out of there. Until that time I would have to keep my head down and do my best, which wasn't really that great at all.

As February rolled around I sent Courtney some roses for Valentines Day. It was the least I could do for the person I was seeing half a country away. I wished I could have done more. She regularly flew out to see me and Manny to visit for a weekend and all I could afford to do was send flowers. I felt like a complete loser.

I started to get the impression that no matter what I did in my life, I was wrong. I couldn't be there for my girlfriend. I couldn't afford my bills. I couldn't even afford to get Manny new clothes as I bought them all used. It was just one thing after another, and I was still the only one carrying all of the weight. I had no one to hold my hand some days.

Manny's birthday came again. We had a house filled with his friends from school and the neighborhood. Once again Jessica wasn't there. At least this time she hadn't promised she would be there. Jessica's family was also nowhere to be found. I am sure they received the "no contact order" from Jessica. She did not want me near her family because she couldn't control the flow of information. The year prior Jessica's father and stepmother had sent a card for Manny's birthday. This time around they sent nothing.

Manny always had nothing but great things to say about his mom, and her absence didn't seem to phase him. When we were training to be foster parents, the teacher warned had us that foster children will often overly idealize their biological parents.

They will tell stories about how wonderful their biological parents are, and sometimes they will even talk about their parents as rock stars or superheroes. Sadly after adopting and abandoning Manny, Jessica had taken the role of the absent biological parent.

Manny would talk about how great Jessica was. He would have her pictures on his wall when I was the parent doing all of the work. I was also the parent who received the talking back, the punches, the kicks, and the insults: Manny told me that I was the worst parent in the world. It became difficult *not* to tell Manny that his mom wasn't the person he thought she was, but I bit my tongue. I justified this by telling myself that I would only tell the truth if he asked. This was smart because I could almost guarantee that my son would never ask, "Dad, is my mom a pathological liar?"

On March 20th the phone rang. I looked down at the small screen on my phone to see if the caller warranted being talked with. It was Vince.

"Sorry to bother you, but I just wanted to talk to you. Jessica is totally fucking nuts."

"Yeah, I know." He could have told me the sky was blue, and I would have responded the same way.

"The cops came here last night. We got in a fight, and I punched her. Her dad and brother flew out to get her out of here."

"What?"

"She has been pushing me and pushing me for so long. She kept hitting me, and I couldn't take it any more. I snapped and hit her back. Matt, I've put the last three years of my life into this relationship."

"Three years?"

"Yeah, we started dating in May of 2007."

"You realize we were still married right?"

"She told me that you filed for divorce. She called me in

April telling me how much she wanted to fuck me, but I wasn't cool with that because you were my friend and I didn't want to screw a married woman." Suddenly I remembered Jessica vanishing during Evelyn's costume party and talking on the phone in the gazebo.

"Was it during a party?"

"Yeah, she said she was at a party and it was the anniversary of her mom's death or something. She said she always drinks on the anniversary of her mom's death."

"Yeah, we didn't even talk about divorce until after her work trip to Oregon."

"That wasn't a work trip Matt. It was a vacation with me."

"Wait, what?"

"And her trip to South Carolina, which she told you was a deployment for work, was to see me too. I swear Matt, I thought you guys were already divorced."

"She had me convinced she was CIA."

"Yeah, I fell for that one too for a while. I think it was just her way of going out and fucking other dudes. I know she's been sleeping around on me too."

I wasn't shocked. I was upset, however, that it took three years for me to get validation of the feelings I felt so long ago. I knew something was off with our marriage. I *knew* Jessica was cheating, but I had dismissed my suspicion as something being wrong with *me*. I thought *I* was chemically imbalanced. It turned out I had been right all along. Vince continued.

"Dude, just keep her away from your son. She latches on to men and uses them up. As soon as her looks fade she'll latch on to Manny and do the same thing to him."

"I agree." I pictured an adult Manny happily being controlled and emotionally abused by his mother. He would give her money, a place to live, cars, anything just to receive the validation from her that he was loved. The thought frightened me.

"I lost my girls because of her. Her bullshit cancer story made my girls cry for days. Then she never talked about it again." I was just glad that she had told the story to someone else too. He continued, "I think my kids were so freaked out by her all of the time that they chose to live with their mom over me. They couldn't handle her anymore, and I don't blame them."

Vince told me that after Jessica had come back from overseas her behavior continued like it had before. He had had enough and was ready to kick her out and end their relationship. He was about to break up with her. Then she was suddenly diagnosed with cancer. In his mind, she had made up the story in order to get sympathy and to avoid being sent packing. It apparently worked.

The phone conversation continued on for a while, and we started putting pieces together. We discussed Ricky Bobby, Jessica's short lived ex. I told Vince how Jessica had told me that she and Vince had broken up after her rape.

"What?!?! We never broke up. Well, maybe for a week or so, but we got back together soon after she was in Qatar."

"She was messaging me about guys as late as December," I told him. I scanned my email and found messages from her about guys she was trying to date. I knew she had slept with at least one of them because she had asked me to deactivate her Facebook account. Before doing so I had read her private messages. She had told me she and Vince were "only friends."

This was why Jessica never wanted people talking to each other. When people talked to each other about her they found out the truth about her. I now had confirmation Jessica had been cheating on me while we were married. She had been sleeping with Vince and planning her escape all along. She had waited for the adoption to be finalized before she ended the marriage.

What kind of person would do that? Who in the world

would act that way? Worse yet, who in her right mind would allow me, her husband, to take the blame for the divorce when she was the guilty one? How dare she accuse me of being unfaithful when she was the one who was unfaithful all along?

Vince wrote Jessica a letter that he posted on Craigslist's *Rants and Raves* section. He knew Jessica would read his message because it was posted in her favorite section of the popular website. Vince sent me an email with the contents of the message.

From: Vince
Subject: Re: Thought you might like this.
To: "Matthew Timion"
Date: Sunday, March 21, 2010, 11:32 AM

This is the email I want to send her, but I've been sitting on it. I'm not sure there's a point at this point. I posted it in the CL rants and raves section because I have to do something with all this shit that's inside of me.

Dear Jes,

I am the biggest dipshit in the world. Three years of your lies, distortions, manipulations, and cheating. When you love someone so much you're willing to abandon common sense & intuition and give the trust that isn't deserved over and over again.

As much as I'm hurt right now by your lies, manipulations, and cheating (yes, you did, multiple times) I still love you, and because I know you read this site you need to do the following or you will repeat this behavior, and you will continue to be miserable and ruin another man's life:

Stop drinking at all costs. You cannot drink. Not even a beer.
Keep going to therapy at all costs.
Get meds to manage your brain chemistry.

Do you want to know why I was going to leave the country? I'm sure you do. I have to get away from you. And in all fairness, I can't provide you with whatever it is you think you need from a partner to balance out. The only way I'll be normal again is to ensure you and I aren't together. You make others as miserable as you are. You say the most outrageous things that only a dupe like me would believe, and then when things don't pan out... I have a drink. I'll tell you why I started to drink. It was to deal with you; your behavior, your lies, your manipulations. They say women are ruled by their emotions, but I think men are ruled by their heart, too. It's been my heart, a good heart, that has kept me in this horror of a relationship.

Now you'll destroy the man you cheated with. It's inevitable.
You'll destroy the man that you're currently interested in.
You'll destroy the next one, too.

You'll make them crazy with insecurity claiming that they're being controlling when in reality they're right; your incessant need for male attention translates to feeling "confused" and making a "mistake" that "doesn't mean anything". Well, woman. It means something. It means something to the man on the other side of your actions. If this is the life you want then by all means keep doing the thing that makes you and everyone else miserable. If you want to be happier than you are now, then you have to make sacrifices (booze and male attention), and find healthy outlets for your energy. I hope you do. I really do. You're a very beautiful woman, so you'll continue to have opportunities to meet a variety of men. Pick wisely next time, and act wisely next time.

As for me? I'm good looking enough, motivated enough, and focused enough to have a good life again and I will find someone that will be everything you weren't: Honest, Loyal to a Fault, and Healthy.

I'm glad I put the pieces together. I'm glad I saw incontrovertible proof of your lies. I'm glad I talked to enough people to sort out the lies from the truth, and wow, there was a lot of deceit. Now I have the opportunity to find something and someone that I deserve. I wish I could have had that with you, but looking back it was always an impossibility. You're completely incapable of normalcy, but I hope that changes. I really do.

Love,

Vince

His email was followed up with a note to me.

Matt,

Count your blessing, dude. I know you might think you were wrong, but all she did was move onto another vulnerable male once she was done fucking you up. I think she clued into my personality type, and is somehow attracted to men that she subconsciously knows she can control. I'm not sure. It's either that or she's a fucking bull in a china shop that destroys everything she touches, and can't understand the consequences of her behavior. Someone always bails her out. She'll find another man. It's inevitable, and the she'll hide her craziness for a while, but it will come out little by little until it consumes everything, and then she'll start over.

You. My friend. Caught a break. Because I can fucking testify that the last three years has been mostly Hell. She really fucks a dude up.

- Vince

It had been a little over a year since I found out about the *real* Jessica. Jessica the liar. Jessica the cheater. Because of what

I knew about her ,everything Vince told me was not surprising. Putting pieces together about the secret life she had while we were married was not shocking.

Jessica had simply used me and Vince to get what she wanted. While Vince told me about the DUI charge she had against her, describing her vehicle as a "mini-bottle grave yard," I could not help but remember the mysterious bottle of vodka Krystal found a few months back above my refrigerator. Jessica the drunk.

I sent Vince an email with a link to an old episode of NPR's *This American Life,* titled, "Liars." It was about this very subject. People who lived with pathological liars and later had to pick up the pieces. One of the people interviewed said and I'm paraphrasing, "You try to regain some control. You try to put all of the stories into two piles: truth and lies. Then you start realizing that there is a third pile: I don't know. By the time you're done you start to realize that almost everything that person ever said to you goes into the *I don't know* pile."

After talking with Vince that day I symbolically took some items out of the *I don't know* pile and put them into the *Lies* pile. I went to bed that night with a smile on my face. I knew that I had done nothing wrong. The divorce had nothing to do with me. It had everything to do with Jessica being a crazy person. Before we got off of the phone, Vince told me that he would sign a statement attesting to Jessica's detachment from reality and why she was dangerous. "Anything I can do Matt to keep her away from your kid I will do to help."

| THIRTY EIGHT |

An Exclusive Club
March 2010

I was like a newly born-again Christian. I had to share the new knowledge I had just learned with everyone I knew. I had to tell every one of my friends who had been there and listened to my woes over the last few years, every family member, everyone. I had to say, "You see? Do you see? I was right all along! I did nothing wrong." However, my audience already knew I was right and Jessica was a nut. The only person who hadn't known the sad reality was me. Finally I knew. I'm certain my mother and Courtney were sick of hearing about my ex-wife, the liar. Always supportive, they kept listening anyway.

Vince and I talked a lot over the following weeks. We chatted online. We emailed. I kept learning new things about my marriage. For example, while we were married and she had been locked in the bedroom she was talking with Vince. They talked every night. She wasn't talking with her friend like she said. I knew it. The feeling of justification and some sort of holy righteousness overcame me. Because of the incident where Vince punched Jessica, they were scheduled to talk with the police. Vince called me after the meeting with the authorities.

"Dude, we went to the courthouse and the prosecutor dropped the charges."

"Why?" I was hoping something would stick. A paper trail would be nice.

"I just don't need this, man. Because of her and all of this shit I'm moving out of state. The Army told me I can resign or get transferred. I'm moving to Alabama. I'm done."

"How was she when you saw her?"

"She looked defeated. The detectives figured out almost everything she reported to them the other night was a lie. The charges were dropped on the condition she wrote a letter to the arresting officer and apologized for lying."

"Defeated?"

"She only said a few words to me. She told me that none of this matters and it's all pointless. I think she's suicidal again."

I had never wished death on anyone in my entire life. I remembered back to years before when Jessica was suicidal and questioned if Manny would be better without her. I started to wonder if maybe Manny's life *would* be better without her influence. I knew *my* life would be better if she was not involved. But back then what I knew about her was so limited. Sure, I had my doubts of her faithfulness, but after Vince called and filled in the pieces, I had confirmation. I had a real life person talking to me on the phone. Vince continued.

"I called her dad to tell him she's suicidal. He basically told me that I was scum and that if he was here he would kick my ass. He told me I'm a disgrace to the uniform. I don't know man. I'm washing my hands of this. I'm done."

We continued talking and putting more pieces together. We talked about Jessica's rape, which he always doubted. He was certain that she had cheated, and it was just an excuse.

"Dude, I'm such a fucking idiot. After she got her DUI and crashed her car, I gave her five thousand dollars to buy a new one. I could have spent that money on my kids." The new car Vince had purchased for her was her fourth car in three years. Since our separation, she had totaled all of her cars. I wondered if all of her car accidents had been alcohol related.

Like a battered wife running back to her abuser, Vince, after talking to the police, tried to give Jessica another chance. Despite there being a restraining order against them being near each other, the two of them drove two hours from their home to spend the weekend together. They were at a bar with plans to go to a hotel that night.

"She kept texting all night saying it was work related. I didn't believe her. I knew something was up. We got in the car and all she could do was tell me about how she was going to fuck me better than I have ever had before. We eventually got to the hotel, and she just passed out because she was so drunk. So I went through her cell phone."

"Did you find anything?" I liked that Vince was being a detective too. It was the only way to find out the truth when

Jessica was in your life.

"She was smart, but not that smart. Matt, Jessica acts like she's so smart but she's really stupid. She deleted all of her text messages, but her emails were still there. I read her emails."

"What did they say?"

"She was talking to some guy about how much she loved fucking him and how she cannot wait to fuck him again."

"So did you talk to her?"

"Fuck no. I drove home and left her there. She had to take a fucking cab back home, over two hours. That bitch. She deserves it."

Motivated by his revelations Vince sent me a timeline of his relationship with Jessica.

```
From: Vince
Subject: Re: Thought you might like this.
To: "Matthew Timion"
Date: Sunday, March 21, 2010, 11:05 AM

Sociopath: Antisocial-type personality,
pleasure-seeking, remorseless, and not bound by law,
code, trust, or friendship.

Oh my god, Matt. Three years of my life wasted on
sleepless nights, bullshit, and her endless prattle.

I suppose it doesn't matter at this point, since
she'll just continue to lie about her lies and
infidelities. I wish there were a way for me to find
out about how many guys she's hooked up with. I don't
know why I care. I guess I just don't want to feel so
foolish for having that sense that something was
wrong.
```

Vince went on to detail their entire relationship. Some of the things he described to me were new, but most of it was old news for me.

One of the most fulfilling things Vince mentioned was

her insistence that she was in the CIA. She told him the same lie. He even believed it for a while. A man in the US Army fell for the same gag hook, line, and sinker. I had always assumed my naivety towards this topic was because of my unfamiliarity with military culture. Nope. Jessica was either a skilled liar or knew how to find men who would easily believe her.

What I didn't know, however, was just how crazy Jessica had become since we were married. Vince described meltdown after meltdown. He talked about suicide attempts. That night when Jessica called me from Washington D.C. talking about suicide she had apparently tried to do it: sleeping pills, booze, and Manny in the next room.

Their relationship was rocky, and he could not seem to shake her. They would break up and get back together. They were addicted to each other.

I felt like I was reading the secret history of what my life could have been had I stayed married with Jessica. Vince told me multiple counselors and therapists had said that Jessica was either bipolar borderline, or both. I had suspected as much all along.

I felt like I was part of some sort of exclusive club. This guy knew exactly what I had gone through, but on some level his experience was worse than mine. We had been both dealing with the same woman for years. We both dealt with her lying, her manipulations, and we both finally saw through them.

We talked about the meltdown during Christmas the year before when Vince called me to get a cab for Jessica. I told Vince how Jessica's family perceived Vince as the bad guy during the meltdown and subsequent rescue. They viewed Jessica as the victim, or at least a crazy participant in the insanity. He wrote me:

```
Matt,

That sucks he thinks I started this, and was
```

victimizing her. I didn't hang up on him. I freaking
called the guy because I was so freaked out by Jes.
She, in fact, gouged my eye, took the phone, and hung
it up because she didn't want them to know what she
was doing/going through. Remember, she was
threatening suicide and was hysterical. I didn't know
what to do. I had never, in my life, been exposed to
that level of insanity, and I thought if I called her
family they would have an idea of what was going on,
be able to calm her down, and get her help. That was
the first time she attacked me... Scratching and
gouging me in order to get to the phone.

I'm sure her family thinks I'm a big piece of shit,
but they have no clue what I've experienced and how
much I've tried to be there for her. The reasons why
I ended up kicking her out was because I didn't want
my kids around her behavior, and like an idiot I kept
getting sucked back into her life. I accept my part
for keeping Jes in my life, but I'm not the monster
they think I am. I don't blame them for not really
knowing who Jes is because they don't live with her
the way you and I lived with her. How can you tell a
family that their sister/daughter is the way Jes is
without looking like a complete and utter asshole?

I'm glad you have bonded with them, because that will
help you find the best way to care for Manny. But,
remember, blood is thicker than water and Jes is very
good at being Jes.

Brother, I hope she gets it together. I hope she gets
to a place where you feel good about her being
involved with Manny. Maybe supervised visits are a
good start? I don't know. I had that happen to me
with my ex-wife, and it was hurtful. But the bottom
line is you have to do what is in that child's best
interest.

- Vince

Vince was trying to start over, and he tried to mend old

friendships in order to help repair his life. He logged back on to Facebook and added all of the old friends he had had, most of whom were a part of the old ex-Mormon group that had been long gone. To be honest, that group mainly imploded due to Jessica and Vince. Every single person in our dissolved community would have freely acknowledged Jessica's role in destroying the community. Lester, the de facto leader of the group, put out a message on Facebook telling everyone, "If you add Vince as your friend, you are no longer my friend. I can not be friends with anyone that is friends with him." The remains of a once strong social group was shattered once more. I saw Vince as awakening from the spell Jessica could cast on a person.

About a week later I felt empowered by righteous indignation. Jessica called to talk to Manny and I told her off. I knew exactly what she had done and who she was. I stood in the back yard so Manny couldn't hear and I yelled in the phone, "You lying fucking bitch." She hung up the phone. I called Vince to brag about what I had done.

"I don't know Matt, you need to get a grip on yourself." Those words sounded oddly familiar.

"What?" His words took the wind out of my sails.

"You need to calm down, and maybe talk to a therapist or something."

I was confused. He had told me he was coming to visit in a week or so to see his girls for Easter. He wanted to stop by and visit Manny. His daughters loved Manny. "Sure," I said. I was still confused. I wanted to see the only other member in my exclusive *screwed over by Jessica* club. I had fantasized about finding Jessica's first husband to hear his stories. I was willing to bet that they were just as screwed up as mine. Perhaps her first husband could be the guest speaker at our annual meetings.

PART 4

| THIRTY NINE |

Enemy of the State
April 2010

I liked this guy. He was shorter than me, but not by much. He was probably 20 years my senior. He was friendly. He had slightly blotchy skin, just enough to show you that he probably never wore sunscreen. He showed me his badge. "State of Utah," it said. Underneath it said, "Department of Child and Family Services (DCFS)." It was the second time I had seen a state badge. The first time was when an investigator came knocking at my door asking if I had any information about my neighbor, who was apparently taking state money for disability and not really disabled. I let the state employee into my house.

"I'm not here to judge you or anything. We just received a report and have to check out it. Since you are an adoptive parent I was called. I'm an internal investigator."

I knew who he was and what he was saying. Normal investigators are called for normal people. Internal investigators are called for people who have adopted or fostered children. It was a checks and balances thing.

"I just need to take a look around the house and see if anything is alarming."

"Go right ahead," I told him. We toured the house. I showed him Manny's room, my room, and the rest of the house. He was fixated on the kitchen.

"We received reports specifically about the kitchen. Do you mind if I take some pictures?"

I moved the inch tall tomato plants I had in a small greenhouse off of the sink. The rest of the kitchen was bare. He took a few pictures of the kitchen.

"Normally I only do this when things are really bad, but I feel the need to take pictures to show how unwarranted this is. May I continue?"

He took pictures of the living room, the dining room.

"Do you want to take pictures of the basement too?" I asked.

"No, this will be okay. I would like to talk to your son."

Manny was playing two blocks away at a friend's house. I walked the investigator there. While we walked we talked. I started to figure out what was going on.

"Can you think of anyone who might report you?"

"My ex-wife, but she hasn't been in my house in over a year."

"The report was that there was thick mold all over the house, and animal feces everywhere."

Just one day before the investigator appeared, Vince had come to my house with his daughter early in the morning. I had no warning as to when he would come. He knocked on the door after Manny and I had only been awake for thirty minutes. We were still in our pajamas.

He was greeted by Jojo and Annie, Mary Ann's dog who I was watching. The night before we had had spaghetti and the dirty dishes were still in the sink covered with night-old spaghetti sauce.

Manny was in the living room watching *The Goonies* on our oversized television. A bowl of cereal was on the coffee table as Manny focused more on the movie than on the drips of milk escaping his spoon. When Vince and his daughter arrived, Manny ran with Vince's daughter into Manny's bedroom to play.

Vince and I talked about everything going on with Jessica. I was happy to see him. I would never have welcomed him in my home had it not been for the two weeks of phone conversations we had shared. Had we not hashed things out and put pieces together I would have never have known that we were part of the same exclusive club. He was unresponsive whenever I would bring something up about Jessica. I still wanted to talk about her and how much we were screwed over by her. I still wanted to put even more pieces together. Vince had already moved on. I was only a little jealous.

At one point Annie jumped on the coffee table and ran towards me. I hated that dog. She was so hyper. Before dogsitting Annie, I had considered Jojo to be hyper, but Annie's energy level made Jojo look like a dead horse. Annie ran everywhere and she licked everything. She ran all over the coffee table and jumped over all of us. I pushed Annie off of the table. Vince and his daughter didn't stay long, but Vince left a gift for Manny for Easter. "It's from Jessica," he said. Vince and his daughter left.

Did Vince call the state? I have no idea. The stories kind of matched up, but only a little. The investigator met with Manny. I was asked to walk away so that they could meet privately. A few hundred feet away, I saw them talking. A few minutes later the interview with Manny was done. Manny yelled, "Dad, can I go back to my friend's house?" I said yes.

The social worker and I walked back to my house. "I can tell you right now that this case is unfounded. Due to confidentiality I cannot tell you who reported it, but I can tell you how it will be filed."

Months later when I requested the case report, the complaint was as follows:

Referrer had not seen this family for a while before this. Referrer indicated that the home was filthy and dusty. There was dog feces and waste on the floor. In fact, the pit bull urinated in front of him. Referrer states that the whole place reeks of the dog waste. The pitt bull tore up the couch. Purported Victim had dirty clothes on and unkempt hair. There were moldy plates in the kitchen. The dog walked across the table. Dad drinks almost every night. He has passed out before, and the purported victim has had to find his own dinner. The frequency is unknown.

The conclusion stated:

This CPS case is being closed at this time as unsupported regarding the single allegation of "Environmental Neglect." The home was not in the condition as reported to DCFS, and there is insufficient evidence to make a finding that abuse and/or neglect occurred.

I toured the home, both upstairs and downstairs. I saw no dog feces on the flooring of the home. There was no dirty dishes or spoiled/moldy food. The condition of the home was not a safety/or health concern to the family members residing in the home. The floors were somewhat dirty, and there were a number of small particles, but given the age of the Purported Victim (7) this is not a health or safety concern.

The Purported Victim looked to be cared for in that he was groomed, and dressed appropriately. Interviewed the Purported Victim without the alleged perp present, and the Purported Victim did not disclose any concerns to me.

I asked the Purported Victim if he had anything he wanted to talk to me about, or any questions for me... and he asked, "Why do bats have wings?" I told him that I didn't know.

No ongoing DCFS services at this time.

After the visit I phoned the investigator. I still couldn't believe that this was my life. His advice was solid. It was sound. "I would just make certain to keep your place clean if someone like that is in your life." That was it.

At the time I didn't have the DCFS report. I didn't know what to think. I knew someone had called the state on me, and my suspicion was directed towards Jessica. I couldn't trust Vince any more. It felt like something sinister was going on; I was a fool for trusting him in the first place. The ex-Mormon leader Lester might have been right to try to keep Vince at an arm's length.

The rest of the night was a mixture of elation and confusion. What was happening? Why was the state being called to investigate *me*? I was the guy who had rescued my son from an environment like the one someone claimed. Elation came over me because whoever reported me to DCFS clearly had an agenda, and they were proven wrong. I felt like I wanted to call whoever reported me and say, "nice try, sucker."

I called Jessica. I already knew that she was aware of the allegations. The investigator told me that he had already contacted her. How would the DCFS investigator have her phone number? It was clear to me whoever made the report to DCFS knew Jessica. Her new North Carolina phone number was something that only I and her family had.

"DCFS came today." I told her.

"WHAT?!?! DCFS WAS CALLED ON YOU!?!?! WHAT THE FUCK!"

I don't know why she acted so surprised. I already knew that she knew about the investigation. When the investigator had come over he had told me Jessica had already been informed.

She went on and on about how I was an unfit father. She then told me that everything I said to Vince was well known to her. According to her she had been sitting right next to him every time Vince and I spoke, laughing with him. "You're pathetic, Matt."

Maybe she was right. Maybe I was pathetic. I still had to know who called DCFS. I felt the same as I assume my son will feel one day when he wants to know who his biological family is. Sure, it didn't *really* matter, but I needed to know.

"It wasn't me, Matt, if that's what you're asking."

"Then who?"

"I heard about your place and called someone to check it out. MY FAMILY came out there and checked it out. It was MY FAMILY Matt."

While I found it hard to swallow, I supposed anything was possible. Perhaps her family came and looked in my window and saw something they felt worth reporting. I really didn't think it was true though. Everything pointed to Vince. Vince, the only other member of the *screwed over by Jessica* club, reported me. I didn't understand why. He had told me he was done with Jessica. He was gone to move to Alabama to be away from her. He was going to be free, something that I could never have because of my connection to Jessica through Manny. Why would he throw that beautiful freedom away?

I didn't contact Vince again. I didn't know what the truth might be. I was no longer his "friend" on Facebook, but his profile was public so I could still see everything he posted.

Alabama is a Lynyrd Skynyrd dream come true.

Great, he was in Alabama. Hopefully he was away from Jessica.

The same day he had one more update.

Eloped.

I sat at my computer snickering. As if my life couldn't get any more strange, the guy who had called me to tell me that Jessica was a cheating crazy bipolar alcoholic whore had turned around and married her. She hadn't even invited her son to her wedding. Vince's behavior over the last weeks was either an elaborate ruse or he was just as crazy as Jessica was.

Vince then posted pictures of their makeshift wedding. She wore a black dress. It looked like it was a civil ceremony with only the two of them. The first person to respond to Vince's wedding pictures said, "dumbass."

I couldn't have agreed more.

| FORTY |

Foraging
Spring 2010

I remembered the feeling of the old nail cutting my hand. I started dripping blood on the ground but kept moving forward with my project. Sweat dripped from my forehead into the wounds. It stung. Finishing my project was all that I cared about at that moment. I found the perfect piece of wood. It was exactly what I needed.

Once a year, Salt Lake City had a program where people would put all of their junk outside on the curb. The city would hire men to come around in dump trucks and take it all away. It was the perfect way to declutter, but it was also the perfect way to get free stuff. My neighborhood was filled with dozens of cars driving around looking for something to keep. Mostly people looked for anything metallic so that it could be recycled for a profit. I always looked for wood though. For years I had been collecting wood for firewood or for building things. I always have had this idea that I could build something myself, with my own two hands. This time I was rummaging through a stranger's discarded garbage looking for wood to build Manny a club house.

Looking back it is slightly humiliating to admit that yes, I was rummaging through someone's garbage. I couldn't afford the raw materials needed to build a clubhouse so instead I found the materials another way. I had never been so poor in my entire life. The cuts I received from this activity went untreated. Even though I finally had health insurance for the first time in two years there was no way I could afford the co-pay.

I remember how life was with Jessica. We were finishing the basement. When we bought our house - my house - the basement was only half finished. We bought wood, paint, and materials together. Money was not an issue. I did the work and the supplies to do so were abundant. It was a stark contrast to how meager my life had become.

My life had turned from opulence to poverty. I was using those salvaged materials to build my son a clubhouse. It would be a testament to myself that I could build something out of nothing. I could build something out someone else's trash.

I had enough materials together quickly to finish the clubhouse using salvaged wood and doors from Jessica's former wardrobe. It was a hodgepodge clubhouse literally built with blood, sweat, and tears.

When the clubhouse was finished, Courtney commented that one day Manny would see his first pair of breasts in that clubhouse. I flashed forward to the image of a teenaged Manny sneaking off into the backyard to make out with his girlfriend. I felt accomplishment in what I had built. I was literally building a legacy and a memory for Manny out of scrap wood. It leaked when it rained. It was his clubhouse and he loved it.

Since Jessica and Vince's secret marriage I had had no contact with them. Jessica seemed to have dropped off of the face of the earth again. The unknown of the entire situation, especially after the interaction I had with Vince for a few weeks, was extremely concerning to me. My stress level peaked, and I didn't know what to do about it. I fully expected Jessica and Vince to show up at my doorstep out of the blue and take Manny. I let Manny's school know that under no uncertain terms was Manny allowed to leave school without my consent.

Amidst my paranoia and constant stress over Jessica and Vince's possible kidnapping of my son, it was time for another one of Courtney's visits. Her visits always came at the right time because I was so lonely doing this parenting thing myself. I had friends to help, but it's not the same as having a living breathing person next to you cheering you on. I didn't need Courtney to raise or parent Manny, but rather remind me that I was doing the right thing and doing a good job. She was great at that. Whenever she was around she motivated me to be a much better person than I already was.

I wish I could remember what we did during that visit, but it was probably nothing more than talk about how crazy Jessica was. I think that's all I did for two years: talk about Jessica. Courtney must have loved me more than I knew because I am unsure if I could put up with someone constantly talking about their ex ad nauseum.

Courtney, a high powered director of a retail beauty chain, loved visiting. She loved the predictability and the monotony. She loved that we had dinner time and stories before bed. She loved just how *normal* our lives were. I loved that she loved it. Where most people go on vacation and travel or see beautiful cities, Courtney's version of a vacation was visiting me where nothing exciting happened. She traveled and saw amazing cities for work. She wanted a taste of normal life.

It was May 2 and Courtney was scheduled to leave that day. Her flight was in the afternoon. I was still asleep on my bed when she came in the room fully dressed.

"Get up," she said. She looked pissed.

"Uhh." I moaned the kind of moan you make when just waking up.

"Do you think I'm an idiot? Let me answer that for you. Yes, you do. God damn it Matt. I'm such a fucking idiot." She paused, seemingly expecting an answer. I remained silent. "You need to take me to the airport."

Courtney wanted to go to the airport because she opened my computer to check her email while I was sound asleep. I left my chat program open. She read the messages I wrote trying to woo other women. She refused to be disrespected like that. She was done with me.

***

With everything going on in my life, I had never been so lonely. The social interaction was gone except for work, and I hated most of those people. I rarely saw my friends. The most real life adult conversation I had in any given day was with the caregivers in Manny's after school program.

I talked with Courtney almost every night, but it was still not enough because she was so far away. I considered moving to Chicago to be closer to her but getting out of my financial situation seemed impossible.

I was upside down on my house loan and I had a second mortgage that was almost entirely maxed out. I couldn't even afford to buy lumber at a hardware store, let alone move. I was stuck in Salt Lake City.

I kept telling myself I stayed there to ensure Manny had stability and consistency, but that was only partially true. The truth is I was *too poor* to dig myself out. I had tried for so long to get out of the hole that I was exhausted from trying.

I needed more people near me. I wanted to feel special again. Feeling *my-girlfriend-sees-me-once-every-six-weeks* special was not good enough. I wanted to feel wanted and desired. I didn't want to feel invisible. I did the only thing I knew how to do previously: I created an online dating profile.

Perhaps I would find someone who would sweep me off of my feet. Perhaps this person would see me, my profile, and recognize me for this amazing person that I was. Perhaps they would live down the street. In hindsight it was a stupid idea and really just one of fantasy because I didn't have time to date, and I didn't have the energy or money to do it. Besides, I was already taken.

***

We drove up to the terminal at the airport. Manny was confused as to why we were taking her there early. No one said a word the entire trip, which was about a five minute drive from my house. I grabbed her bag. "I'm sorry this couldn't work out with us." I was sorry too, but I was still so numb from everything going on in my life. It was sad to see her go for good.

She dumped me, just like every other girl had dumped me my entire life. This time was different though: I definitely deserved it. I was seeking attention elsewhere while in a relationship. I still wonder if I felt the need to emulate Jessica in order to understand her. Even though it had been years, living with Jessica and having it all vanish was still affecting me.

Even if it was just for a moment, I needed to feel something from someone.

Courtney called me to tell me she had landed safely. She wanted to understand *why* I could do that to her. I really didn't have any answers other than telling her that I was incapable of a long distance relationship. I couldn't explain it. As much as I try to now, I still cannot explain it other than blaming it on the mental state I was in at the time.

I was alone again. I somehow felt okay with being alone, as though solitude was my ultimate life goal. The only person I could count on was myself so eliminating other people from my life seemed to make sense. Perhaps I was sabotaging everything good around me because I didn't know how to live a normal life. Chaos and destruction were all I knew. As much as I tried to understand *why* I did certain things in my life, understanding *why* would never change the simple fact that they happened. It was pointless to figure out my motivations so I stopped psychoanalyzing myself. Self reflection had been replaced by the need to simply exist.

In a moment of desperation and clarity, I recognized that I needed to get out of the house more. I needed to interact with people. I couldn't keep letting myself drift and drift until I was completely gone. I was putting on more and more weight again. Manny's social interactions were also gone because no one wanted to play outside during the winter.

We signed up to take martial arts. Affording the classes was difficult, but I figured that I would find a way, somehow, to pay for it. Perhaps these people would be my new community? Maybe the trick was to surround myself with health-conscious people and to participate with my son in a fun activity together. Maybe if Manny knew how to punch and kick he wouldn't be so afraid of bad guys all of the time. Maybe I could meet a girl there and fall madly in love. Maybe this girl would understand my life and the bad choices I had made, and she would tell me how I amazed her and how lucky she was to be my girlfriend.

Courtney still didn't call, and I still missed her. I wondered if she missed me.

| FORTY ONE |
Something to Prove
May 2010

Jessica called and informed me she wanted to take Manny for the summer. I spoke with a number of lawyers trying to see if her craziness could warrant eliminating her parental rights. They all said no. Even though she had been a non-factor in Manny's life for almost the last three years, being his mother *on paper* made it extremely difficult to remove her parental rights. The only way her rights could ever be terminated would be if she abused Manny or cut off all contact. I had no choice but to send Manny to her house over the summer. She told me she would be in town on June 8th and would take Manny back with her. She also wanted to bring Jojo with her. I declined that suggestion. Like always, our conversations turned into a yelling match. I just wanted her to *admit* that she lied our entire marriage. I wanted her to acknowledge that she cheated. I wanted her to admit she was married and was in Alabama with Vince. She wouldn't budge. I hung up the phone.

From: Jessica Timion
Subject: RE: Manny
To: "matt"
Date: Tuesday, May 18, 2010, 5:49 PM

I have no problem talking to you on the phone, you're the one that freaked out the last time we talked. I'm fine with it.

If you don't want to send the dog, fine. I was just thinking of Manny and didn't want him to miss his dog. I have dogs and I know what I'm getting myself into. The cost would be mine. No worries.

Also, I'll be in Utah on the 8th of June, and plan on taking Manny back with me on the 12th. I have family traveling to meet us, so please don't change this on me at the last minute.

I'm in North Carolina. If I move I'll give you a forwarding address within 24 hrs like our decree spells out.

I sent her the parenting agreement that we had signed. She was to give me sixty days notice if she moved, not twenty-four hours. She then admitted that she was, in fact, in

Alabama. She planned on taking Manny for the summer and if I had not figured out she had moved I would have thought Manny was in North Carolina instead of Alabama.

I started receiving phone calls from multiple members of her family expressing concern for Manny's safety while in Jessica's care. A call from her sister was the most shocking. Her sister was so concerned for Manny's well-being that she called DCFS and tried to express her concerns. DCFS said that all her sister could really do to help was to call me. Members of Jessica's family knew she wasn't stable. Her marriage to Vince, the man who punched her, also made her family afraid for Jessica and Manny's safety.

During Jessica's visit to pick up Manny, there was a scheduled family gathering with her family. Her brother was supposed to drive in from Denver. Her dad was supposed to drive up from Arizona. It would have been the first time all of them were together since the family reunion at our home. As soon as her father and brother found out that Vince would be in town everyone canceled their trips. No one wanted to see that guy. Who could have blamed them, really? After all, her dad and brother had flown to rescue her from Vince just a few months prior. Another one of her siblings was on the phone during Jessica's drunken meltdown years before.

As soon as her family backed out of seeing Jessica and Vince, I received an email from her.

Matt,
there has been some scheduling conflict and i want to pick up Manny at your house on june 9th. can you have him packed and ready to go that afternoon?

Vince and Jessica showed up alone in Jessica's new car. It was the car he purchased for her after she had totaled her last car while drunk driving. Vince stood by the car and didn't approach me. Part of my initial motivation for taking martial arts was to be able to handle myself if Vince ever tried to punch me. With his military training I wouldn't have stood a chance, but the thought kept motivating me. I'm glad that I didn't have to demonstrate my white belt techniques that day. I really dislike pain.

It was June 9th, and Manny was outside waiting with Jojo for Jessica and Vince to come. Manny had been playing outside all day and was dirty. I didn't see the need for him to shower before Jessica showed up. What kid wants to shower at 2 PM? I handed off his luggage and I remembered that Manny had made a paper flower for Jessica. I ran back inside to get it for her. "Thank you Matt, that is really sweet."

I had the house to myself. It was so quiet. A chirping sound came from my phone. It was a text message. Was it Jessica? Was Manny okay? I worried too much. It read, "Manny shit his pants while he was at your house and he stinks. All of his clothes stink. We had to take his clothes to the laundromat and wash them. I had to shower him. What the fuck is wrong with you?" I didn't respond. Manny may have been dirty, but he didn't stink. All of his clothes were washed. If Manny had an accident it wouldn't be the first time. Manny would sometimes just decide that playing was more important than coming inside to use the bathroom. This had been a problem for years, and his therapist had just told me to wait it out. It's not uncommon.

The next morning I found a soiled pair of children's underwear in my front yard. At least they hadn't slashed my tires and pissed on my windshield.

Jessica was supposed to buy a return plane ticket for Manny to come back home. Normally both parents split the cost of the children traveling, but since she was so behind on her child support she was supposed to pay the entire amount. I kept waiting for the ticket to be sent to me. I knew that she always did everything last minute so I really didn't expect to get the travel information until a week before Manny's travel date.

Time went on. My days consisted of going to work, attending martial arts classes six times a week, and coming home to tend to my garden. I think I had over twenty tomato plants that summer. I would easily have enough tomato sauce for the year.

Still no word from Courtney. Still no luck on the dating websites. Men were a dime a dozen, and women didn't want a single dad. They wanted a guy who could devote all of their time to them. I remembered that Courtney was different. She loved that I put my son first. Why did I mess things up so badly with her? Although I no longer had to tend to Manny's every need, I really didn't go out much. The problem wasn't being a parent, it was me. I think I just preferred a life of solitude and drinking wine while I watched television.

For the first few weeks Jessica was nice and cordial with me. During one phone call she said, "Oh My God," while holding back laughter, "don't be mad, but Manny called a crow a *nigglet*. It was so funny that Vince and I just started bursting into laughter." His mother's laughter told Manny that what he said was okay so he kept repeating it. They kept laughing. I took personal offense to this because my niece and nephew are half black. Was she inadvertently teaching my son racism was okay? I was not amused.

Seemingly overnight Jessica's tone changed. Jessica sent me an email spelling out all of her concerns with my taking care of Manny. Was she serious? The woman who lied about her entire childhood, cheated, almost moved to Kansas on a whim, and let my son sleep for five months on a bean bag was talking to ME about parenting? Her claims were outrageous, but I had come to expect nothing less. I was finally done talking about her constantly to everyone I knew, and then this happened. She threatened a court battle if I did not voluntarily give up primary custody of Manny to her.

From: Jessica Jacobs
To: Matthew Timion
Cc: Vince Jacobs
Sent: Thursday, July 8, 2010 10:22 PM
Subject: RE: Status for Manny Timion

Matt,

I propose you let Manny stay here with Vince and me.
You and I both know he is neglected under your
custody. However, when he is with me he has the care,
structure, and nurturing this child requires in order
to overcome some of the challenges he faced when he
was younger.

First I want to provide you with my observations as
to why I want to modify the divorce decree returning
primary custody to myself:

*when I pick Manny up, every time he is filthy; his
body is reeking of urine or feces
*his teeth were not brushed in days & in some cases
were rotten (I had to take him to the Dentist twice-
you did not help offset the costs)
*had not had a haircut since, I imagine, the last
time I took him for one
*torn/tattered/ill fitting clothing & shoes; I have
to buy him a new wardrobe every time I pick him up
*improperly packed (not having adequate clothing,
toiletries, etc); junk food wrapped in saran wrap,
dirty clothes, suitcase stinking of cat urine
*you are a very serious alcoholic, drinking yourself
to the point of passing out daily, with Manny in the
home; Manny talks about it quite often, and it's a
sad thing for this kid to be in a home with an
alcoholic father
*you're underemployed and you can't meet his basic
needs
*you've admitted you weren't giving the child proper
care, and feeling guilty about your alcohol abuse
*your home has a pungent odor of urine and feces
*you have an unruly dog inside the home that is
hyperactive, jumps, and bites

*you were dog-sitting when a dog squatted and
urinated directly in front of Vince, his daughter,
and yourself and you did absolutely nothing about it,
no clean up
*you have torn up & soiled (animal urine & food
stains) furniture and pieces of furniture lying about
*your floor is literally covered in animal dander
*you have food and dirty dishes all over the kitchen,
and some dishes are covered in thick mold
*you yourself are typically unbathed, and wearing
obviously dirty clothing on a regular basis which
sends the wrong message to Manny

Additionally, when Vince and I picked up Manny at
your home on June 9th Manny had defecated himself
hours prior to us picking him up. When we got Manny
in the car, we immediately smelled it. When we
arrived to our hotel we changed his underwear. It was
full of feces, and had already started to dry. It was
obvious that he had been in that state for a long
time. You were either completely unaware of Manny's
state, or unconcerned. This is extremely unacceptable
behavior. Also, you were very drunk when we arrived
at your home (slurring words, unable to stand up
straight, alcohol on your breath and coming out of
your pores).

Apparently wetting/defecating himself is something
that has been happening frequently. Manny told us
that he does it sometimes, and sometimes you care,
and sometimes you don't. Since he has been in my care
this has no longer been a problem.

A few more problems:

*you have told Manny that I am a "bad person that
hurts people"
*you have told Manny that I am an "unsafe driver and
need to go to school to learn to drive"
*you call me from time to time while drunk. You yell
at me and call me vulgar names while Manny is in your
home
*you are required to maintain health and dental

insurance for Manny. You do not. Manny's only coverage is Medicaid, provided by the state of Utah and only effective in Utah. Anytime this child travels out of state, he has no health coverage whatsoever.

I *knew* something like this was going to happen. A feeling of panic came over me as I continued reading.

Manny also tells me that he prefers living with me and his step-dad. I am a stay-at-home mom, and here he has:

*structure, age appropriate chores and responsibilities, bedtime, etc…
*he eats nutritious home cooked meals every meal
*we buy him clothes, shoes, and toys
*he is groomed, provided with proper toiletries, and gets haircuts
*constant interaction, love, and attention.
*stimulation- we go swimming on a regular basis, take him to museums, outdoor activities, (nature walks, river, etc), play games, reading time
*extracurricular activities (Soccer- Vince will be coaching his team)

Matt, we've retained Counsel in Utah and are filing to modify the decree based on the sheer level of neglect we've observed. There is no doubt Manny is better off in Alabama with two parents who have the time, means, and energy to devote to him in every possible way. We can try to work things out between you and I so it saves us the time, heartache, and money that a custody challenge will cost. I will tell you that we are willing to see this through to the end no matter the cost; whether we hire a Guardian ad Litem (which you will most likely have to pay for half), travel back and forth from Utah, or anything in between I can assure you Manny's well-being is my primary concern and I will do what it takes to ensure he is no longer neglected. Any court will not look at the issues you have with Vince and I, but will focus on Manny's welfare. I'm confident that an unbiased Judge will compare our two situations and adjudicate favorably for Manny, which is here in my care.

As a reminder, you have stated on multiple occasions that Vince is a great parent, and you trust him. He has been through a custody battle before, and understands the process (the time, money, and energy needed). He supports me because he truly believes Manny is better off under our care.

Any questions or issues that may arise from this email can be directed to my lawyer who is Cc'd. Unless, and I can't emphasize this enough, you have anything to say that is directly related to the day-to-day parenting of Manny do not address it with me or Vince; contact my lawyer.

- Jessica Jacobs

I was at a loss for words. Some of her points *were* valid, sort of. They had a *basis* in truth. My house was torn up. Manny did still have issues with potty training. I did tell Manny his mom needed to learn how to drive, but anyone who looked at her driving record could have told him that. Then there were her claims that I was a pass-out alcoholic. The woman with the DUI was accusing me of being an alcoholic.

Jessica suddenly went from being a drunken cheating whore (Vince's words, not mine) to a standup caring parent. She also said that she was now living in a household without alcohol, and she continued on to say that Manny had nutritious meals every day and went on nature walks all of the time. I didn't know who this person was, but it wasn't Jessica. Jessica wouldn't even know how to spell "adjudicate," let alone put it in a proper sentence.

I went into martial arts that night furious. I needed to break something. My instructor gave me the hardest board possible to break. "Break it, Matt." Veteran members of the class looked on as a white belt was stepping up to break a board that some of them couldn't break. "Matt has something to prove. Break it, with a punch." I didn't break it. I hurt my knuckles instead. I tried again and succeeded. I didn't feel any better though. Now my knuckles just hurt and I was still pissed off.

I would like to call it good timing, but it was really a result of months of work. I found another job. I went in for the interview and aced it. When would I be able to start? Immediately. The job offer came in and I cleaned up my desk, ready to abandon my life as a recruiter. I composed a scathing email to my boss citing the sexual harassment and other blatant violations of basic laws to protect employees. I put my things in my bag. I hit the "send" button and then walked out. I was to start my new job after the weekend.

I collected all of the coins I had in my coin jar and paid for gas so I could drive to work. This new place was six miles away from my house, much further than the two miles I was used to. I couldn't ride my bike any more. Life was changing again, but at least I was making more money again. My new salary was still not as much as I was making when I was married to Jessica, but as least I was moving up in the world.

On Father's Day I checked my mail. I was hoping to find something from Manny. There was nothing from him. There was a card from my mother and a card from Courtney. This was our first contact in months since I had dropped her off at the airport. I first tried calling Manny to talk to him for Father's Day. Jessica had shut her phone off. I tried again later and it was still the same. That bitch.

I hate Father's Day. Since becoming a father, all I had thought about was my own dead father. I thought about how he failed at his job and how much my brother and I would be better off if he would just be alive. I started drinking that night. I was alone, and I had no one to worry about except myself. I called Courtney to thank her for her card. I wasn't in a good place. I was seriously considering Jessica's proposal of Manny living with her. I felt I couldn't go on the way I had been. It wouldn't be fair to Manny and myself. My ability to be a good father for him was directly related to my emotional health. I was reaching the end of my rope. I cried to Courtney on the phone saying that I was considering just letting Jessica keep Manny.

"Okay, are you done now?" Her question was sincere albeit direct.

"Yes."

"Alright, stop it. You are the best thing that has ever happened to that boy. To question your ability to parent him is a disservice to you and to Manny. He is much better off with you than with her."

She believed in me. Even after I screwed things up with her so badly, she believed in me. We continued talking on the phone, glad to reconnect. Our emotions were still there. We discounted the idea of *us* and tried to make it just friends. We started to speak on the phone every night just as before. Courtney believed in me when no one else would. My mother believed in me, but hated seeing me in such pain. She agreed it might be better for Manny to go live with Jessica for a while. Courtney grounded me and gave me motivation.

I was running out of pocket change to pay for gas. I had two dollars left in quarters which would probably last me a few days. I had no idea how I would ever pay for my gasoline, even with the promise of more money from my new job. Most of my paycheck went directly into my mortgage, which was over three months past due. I couldn't lose the house.

A knock came on the door one day after work. It was the middle of July. As I peeked through the peephole I saw a man I had never seen before. I was convinced Jessica had called DCFS again and would want to tour my house. I imagined saying, "Come on in! I know the drill." He didn't want to come in. He was serving me with court papers. Jessica was trying to gain custody of Manny. The complaints in the court document were almost identical to her email.

A court date was set on the paperwork and I needed to do something. I needed to find a way to get a lawyer. I eyed my beat down car in the driveway and figured that selling it might be the only way I could afford to get someone to help, but then how would I get to work? What else could I sell? The only thing worth anything that was still available to sell was my television, and I couldn't fathom Manny being raised without annoying children's shows. Selling my car seemed like the only option at the time, but I would have to register my car in order to sell it, something I had been avoiding for six months because of my inability to afford the sixty dollar registration. It didn't seem like a good idea.

Jessica informed me that she had scrapped her plans to send Manny back to Utah. She suddenly had plans that weekend and called it a "scheduling conflict." I'm certain she was confident the court date would happen before the travel dates and everything would work out in her favor. Unfortunately for her the court date was scheduled after our agreed upon return date. Her refusal to send him back left me with no other option than to go and get my son myself.

Just a few weeks into a new job, with no money to get my son, I started fantasizing about driving my klunker to Alabama to pick up Manny. Perhaps a rental car would work. My mother called me offering her frequent flyer miles. I was saved. My mother believed in me.

Courtney, always a believer in me, sent me the money needed to retain a lawyer. The heavens aligned that week and I was going to be able to do this. I was terrified of Jessica's talk about her "seeing this through to the end no matter the cost." I couldn't afford to do that.

I sent an email off to my new boss telling him that I had to leave unexpectedly to pick up my son. I boarded the plane alone and hoped for the best, knowing that Jessica would not give up Manny without a fight. I started planning ahead just in case.

| FORTY TWO |
Backup Plan
July 2010

I found a reporter at Huntsville Times who mainly reported on the Army base, where Jessica and Vince lived. After calling the police on the Army base and telling them about my situation, I sent an email to the reporter, as advised by my lawyer.

Hi Ken,

I just left you a voicemail and hope that we are able to talk today.

Brief rundown of my situation.

I live in Utah, have physical custody of my son. My ex-wife lives on Redstone Arsenal with her husband (Vince Jacobs, who I understand is the 1st Sgt of the Army base).

I am flying into Huntsville to pick up my son after his parent-time with my ex-wife (6 weeks of summer break).

She is being reluctant about returning my son at the time I have requested, and has been changing the time to within 2 hours of my flight back to Utah.

I have already talked with police on the arsenal, and

they will assist me when I arrive.

The potential story is if the arsenal police are not willing to enforce/uphold an existing court order and allow me the return of my child. Of course if the military are not able to uphold existing court orders, this is an issue.

I am to pick up my son tomorrow (friday) at 11am at the Redstone Arsenal visitors center. This time has been agreed upon previously by my ex-wife. My suspicion is that she will not return him, and I am afraid that the arsenal police would not enforce the existing court order.

Of course your presence would be great, but I know that might be asking too much.

Either way, please call me and we can discuss the situation further. I will be leaving in a little over an hour for the airport so please leave a voicemail if I miss you. I will attempt to get on the Internet tonight from my hotel in Huntsville.

Matthew Timion

I hit the send button. Part of me *wanted* a showdown. I wanted her to refuse to give Manny up and have it turn into some sort of press event where the military police would refuse to uphold a court order. I wanted her to break the law and make it so much easier for her case to die.

Crazy people are unpredictable, however, and unfortunately sometimes even crazy people can act sane. Although I kept checking my phone, I never heard back from the reporter.

I landed at ten o'clock at night. Lynyrd Skynyrd's *Sweet Home Alabama* played on a constant loop in the airport. Mannequins in space suits decorated every part of the building to remind everyone NASA was just a stone's throw away. I acquired my baby blue rental car and went to the hotel. I brought my laptop with me and checked my email. I asked Jessica to have Manny ready at eleven o'clock the next morning. "Absolutely not," she replied. Vince chimed in saying that they had a family lunch planned as some sort of farewell. They were trying as hard as they could to keep Manny as long as humanly possible. I had all of the emails she sent stating that she would have Manny at the base's visitor's center at three thirty the next afternoon, just two hours before our flight. If it came to it I would have to get the police involved.

I drove around Huntsville with nothing to do so to pass time I watched a movie. I would like to say I went sight-seeing, but there wasn't much to see there other than run-down houses and numerous Popeye's Chickens. I just wanted out of that place. I wanted to get my son and leave.

As three thirty came around, I waited at the visitor's center. A red car pulled up with the license plate "JESSICA." It was her. Manny was with her. Vince was nowhere to be seen. She got on her phone and called someone, "Yes, he's here." I told Manny to give his mom a hug. She had gained weight since I saw her last. Her extreme diet of exercise and alcohol appeared to be something of the past. "I will text you when we land," I said. Manny was happy to see me, but he was more entertained by the baby blue car. "Cool car, dad," he said.

He had a suitcase that was mostly empty. He had one pair of clothes and a handful of toys. The majority of the things I had sent with him were not returned. Jessica wasn't planning on Manny staying with me very long. Her light packing was a clear message that she thought Manny returning to Utah with me was just a temporary trip.

"Manny, I'm so glad to see you!" We talked in the car. "How was your farewell lunch with your mom and Vince?"

"Oh, we didn't have a lunch. Vince isn't in town."

"Really? Where is he?"

"Washington D.C."

It figured. Vince had emailed me that very morning about their family farewell lunch. He lied too. I had to stop believing everything those two people said. It was getting ridiculous. Vince had definitely been sucked back into Jessica's crazy web. I wondered if he had decided that fighting her influence was a futile effort. I pictured their house filled with stolen mementoes from restaurants and dive bars, each one with an associated story about some guy they had killed that night.

Manny showed me the picture book his mom made for him. It had pictures from the entire summer. There were pictures of Manny with Vince, Manny with Jessica, and Manny with other kids. It appeared that he had had a great time. I had to battle with the fact that Manny enjoyed himself and was groomed and clean. I was certain Jessica would be able to take care of his physical needs. Knowing she was completely unable to act rationally for the entire time I knew her, I was afraid of her effect on Manny's emotional well-being. I had to stay strong, even if it meant losing my house to pay for the court battle, which was quickly approaching.

We landed in Salt Lake City. I wish I had been happy to be home, but my house represented everything wrong in my life. It was dirty. My dog was a nightmare sometimes. It was the house Jessica and I lived in. It was the house Jessica and Vince had sex in while she was in the basement. It was the house Courtney stayed in when she was in town, and also the house where she had found out about my inability to stay cyber-faithful. I looked at my gnawed-on coffee table and prepared Manny some food. He wouldn't stop hugging me or his dog. He would rotate between the two of us. Happy to be home, he fell asleep on the couch watching television.

It was time to prepare for my court hearing. This turned into another instance of why keeping all of my emails was so great. I responded to every one of her claims. She said that

Manny had not had a haircut since she last saw him. I reminded the court that the last time she saw Manny was a year prior so therefore her claim was ridiculous. This was also a dig at her infrequent visits to see Manny. She claimed I was a pass out drunk alcoholic. I submitted her background check showing her recent DUI and domestic violence dispute with Vince. She claimed I was unable to provide for Manny's basic needs. I included a letter from Manny's vice principal saying that I was one of the most involved parents he had ever seen. I included all of Vince's emails from just four months before where he had called her a sociopath, a liar, a cheater, a drunk, a crazy person, and where he recommended I order supervised visitations. Their being together so soon after his emails only added fuel to the *Jessica is unstable* fire. My lawyer assured me I had nothing to worry about.

I went over the court documents again and again. I wanted to make sure everything was in order. I just wished Jessica would realize how much her instability affected Manny. Regardless of my attempts to shield Manny from the drama, he knew something was going on, and he was confused about it. Before he fell asleep on the couch he told me, "Dad, Mom says I'm only going to stay here for a while and then I'm going back to live with her."

"Honey, I don't know why your mom told you that. This is your home." My disdain for her changed from being the woman who destroyed my illusion of a family to the person who kept disrupting my son and his stability. It turned out that *Protective Daddy Bear* version of myself was a lot more motivated and focused than the *Please Don't Leave Me, Let's Make This Work* version from years before.

| FORTY THREE |
Out of Place
July 2010

There was no way I fit in there. Marble floors and giant columns were everywhere. Ornate wood carvings were on each handrail. Oil paintings of prominent figures from Utah's past were on each wall. I stood there in my grey dress shirt, baggy slacks, and sneakers. I was in the courthouse waiting for my hearing to begin.

My lawyer gave me simple instructions on how to appear. No suit and no white shirt. I still had my suit from my wedding, but there was no way it would still fit. My only dress shoes had been chewed up by my dog months before.

"What about shoes? Can I wear sneakers?"

"If that is what you would normally wear, yes."

My pants were from when I had a thirty eight inch waistline. My tie was one I had acquired while on my Mormon mission from 1998-2000. I was a hodgepodge of dress attire. I sat in the hallway waiting for my lawyer to show up and eyed everyone as they walked down the hallway. I was terrified of seeing Jessica. I knew she would be there. My anxiety was through the roof and just seeing that woman was going to push me over the edge.

"What are you reading?" My lawyer was trying to lighten the mood.

"It's a book about a guy who lives the Bible literally for an entire year." It was a gift Courtney had given me for my previous birthday. It wasn't a religious book, but rather the author's attempt to understand spirituality by taking the teachings of the Bible to a literal extreme. It was my first attempt at reading in years.

"Why would anyone do that? Seems like a waste of time." My lawyer was annoying me. I didn't know why the premise of the book was such a topic worth discussing. I didn't know why his opinion of it was also worth pointing out to me. I put the book down. I couldn't focus on the words I was reading anyway. I wished I had a Xanax.

I was in the courtroom along with twenty other people and their attorneys. We all waited our turn and then got up in front of everyone. Jessica wasn't there, but her attorney was. For something as important as her son's safety I assumed she would have shown up. She was, after all, going to see this through "until the end, no matter the costs."

A woman without a lawyer stood up asking for a time extension on her case. "I'm going into drug rehab tomorrow and won't be able to respond for another 30 days." The commissioner more or less told this woman "tough luck." I didn't know if I should have felt bad for that woman crying in front of the judge, proudly admitting she was going into rehab in order to try to keep her children.

It was our turn. My case number was called.

Jessica's attorney stood up and said something to the effect of, "considering all of the observations my client as reported, we see there is a clear case of neglect and request the court to change custody." His words were so insincere. I don't know if he believed what he was saying, but his lack of emotion told me he didn't believe it. Perhaps he read all of the counterclaims I wrote as well and knew that there was no way Jessica could win. I hoped so.

My attorney stood up and before he could speak the Commissioner injected, "I have read everything, and you have a lot to say." She was looking at me. She was acknowledging that the case I made was a strong one. Jessica had no ground to stand on. Regardless of her lack of proof and unfounded claims (I also submitted the report from the dropped DCFS case), the court had a procedure it had to follow. Whenever there is a report of neglect, abuse, etc., the court needs to appoint a Guardian Ad Litem, which essentially acts as an attorney for a minor child. Now I had a lawyer, Jessica had a lawyer, and Manny had a lawyer. The Guardian Ad Litem's job was to talk on behalf of

Manny and advocate for his best interests.

Jessica's attorney pushed for me to pay for the Guardian Ad Litem. The commissioner said who paid for the Guardian Ad Litem would be determined by how the case unfolded. The commissioner also began the *contempt of court* paperwork for Jessica's failure to pay child support. The state was going to garnish her wages. We submitted a countersuit against Jessica asking to be reimbursed attorney's fees for this entire charade. My counter suit against Jessica was allowed.

I was hoping for some sort of closure that day. I thought everything would be dropped and I would win. I did have a small win that day by keeping Manny and getting child support enforced by the court, but the case was not dropped. The next step was to visit the Guardian Ad Litem and come back to court a month later. I felt like the court battle would never end.

I didn't belong in that building. The last time I had been in that courthouse was when I witnessed the termination of Manny's birth parents' parental rights. Court was for losers and deadbeats like Manny's birth parents. It wasn't for me. Although with my tennis shoes and baggy pants, perhaps I fit in just fine. No, I was better than that. I concluded that Jessica fit in the courthouse very well, but I did not. Why did my life keep getting worse and worse?

I signed a few papers and walked outside. I wished I still smoked. A cigarette would have done me very well at that moment. I noticed a flock of seagulls all fighting over food. There must have been twenty of them going after the one piece of food that someone discarded. That french fry was so lucky. I wanted to feel like that sometimes. I wanted to have twenty beautiful intelligent women fighting over me. A few feet away a single seagull was eating by itself. It had the rest of the package of french fries.

A week later we met with the Guardian Ad Litem. I was terrified. Would he be Mormon and assume that I was unfit because of my tattoos? What if Manny said something and cops showed up? Manny had a tendency to make up stories or exaggerate. This behavior was half due to his background and half due to his extremely creative imagination. To this day Manny is still convinced that Jessica and I once locked him in his room for two days and only allowed bathroom breaks. The truth is he once had a timeout for twenty minutes when he was three years old. To Manny the word "day" meant "a long time" until he was eight years old. He still finds understanding time a difficult concept.

When the Guardian Ad Litem came into the room I stood up and shook his hand. He had one of those limp-wristed handshakes that are not compatible with my family's long line of big hands originally used to plow fields. I felt like I was crushing his bones. This guy must have hated his job. I would hate talking to kids all day knowing that my words and actions could affect them for the rest of their lives.

He took Manny into his office and talked. Thirty minutes later he emerged and wanted to talk to me privately. He asked my opinion of everything and why I am concerned about the welfare of Manny. I explained Jessica, Vince, the domestic violence, the constant moving, and military deployments. I explained the alcohol, the lies, etc. He had already read my file and knew these things. I think he just wanted to hear me say them to figure out if I was lying or not. He told me that he found nothing wrong with Manny staying with me at the moment and would advise the court of his opinion.

Now I had another attorney on my side.

It was approaching the end of August and Courtney was going to fly out to see me. We were going to try "us" again, but it would be different this time. Courtney was not going to move to Salt Lake City. I would have to leave and move to be with her. I was okay with that. Things were going to be better. Even with my mind and body consumed with the details of the court case, always being fearful of Jessica sending DCFS over to my house again, I still had a little energy left to devote to my love life with Courtney. It really wasn't enough energy though.

| FORTY FOUR |
Kate Date
Fall 2010

Manny's teacher wanted to talk to me. I have talked to her a few times before, and I was not too impressed. She appeared to be a veteran teacher with at least thirty years experience. From what I could tell she was younger than she looked. She stood there with her sandy blond hair and a body much too old for her age.

"He has been upset in class. He has been crying because he doesn't know where he is going to live."

"Oh." I knew that this information came from Jessica. It must have been weighing heavily on Manny.

"He said a judge is going to decide where he will live." Manny felt powerless. Even if the choice could be his choice, he wouldn't know what to do. As he saw it his entire future was out of his control. I hated Jessica even more that day.

August 30th, Courtney flew into Salt Lake City to see if we could figure "us" out. We both wanted each other. We had spent months now talking and deciding if it was worth it. It was. I was ready to be the version of myself she deserved. Well, I was ready to try at least. My ability to do anything concerning a relationship was hindered due to the Jessica drama, or rather, my inability to handle the drama properly.

When Courtney arrived again Manny gave her a big hug. He remembered her and wanted to see her.

"Okay," she said, "we have certain rules for this weekend. We do not talk about Jessica and we visit the places my friend Kate says we should."

Her friend Kate was her best friend. Kate helped heal Courtney after our relationship ended. Kate was very wary of me because of the past, and the only reason she would ever approve of me was if we spent the weekend doing the things Kate wanted us to do. So we visited a chocolate shop owned by little people that was also the location of a popular reality show for a while. We also went to a restaurant that was featured on another television show. Just like the Mormons baptize each other in proxy for dead relatives, Kate used us as a way to visit places she wanted to see. Her friend Kate clearly loved reality television.

When Courtney came into my house she said, "Oh, what's that?"

"What?" I thought perhaps someone dropped a one hundred dollar bill on the floor, or maybe she was trying to be cute and use this as a way to compliment me.

"That on the floor." She pointed at a dryer sheet.

"It's a dryer sheet."

"Are you starting a collection?"

"No."

"Then pick it up." This is how she had always been so I wasn't surprised. Courtney loved to point out what I *didn't* do, especially when it came to cleaning. She was the kind of woman that I could spend days cleaning to prepare for only to be passive-aggressively told that I forgot to dust the picture frames. Rarely would there be a compliment on how clean everything else was. Just the picture frames.

This criticism, or as she called it *helping,* extended to my clothes, my hair, my car, my bed, my parenting, my house, my yard, how and when I could touch her, etc. Half of the time I took the "helpful suggestions" in stride and found a way to accommodate her. The rest of the time I took them very personally. She was right though, I did have a dryer sheet on the floor. She was also right that my clothes were old and had holes in them. She was also right that I didn't always behave or react properly. I hated that she was right. It meant I was doing something wrong.

Like I said, I wasn't surprised by her comment. I was used to comments like this from her. That night we laughed and danced in the living room after Manny was asleep. We usually danced to 90's hip hop music that reminded us of high school. We both knew all of the words.

We had our date at Kate's restaurant of choice. We also visited the chocolate shop. Courtney was a little on edge and didn't want their *weird deformed hands* touching her chocolate. I couldn't help but laugh. We bought chocolates for her friend Kate instead.

"I need a drink, let's go back to the house and have a Bloody Mary." It was Sunday, after all. It was the perfect time for brunch.

"Sorry, no vodka."

"Let's go buy some."

"Sorry, it's Sunday. No liquor stores are open." In Utah all alcohol sales are run by the state government, unless you want to overpay for a restaurant or don't mind buying 3.2% beer at the grocery store. Of course these liquor stores are closed on Sunday because Sunday is the Lord's day. Courtney already knew that you couldn't buy alcohol on Sundays. She either forgot or wanted to mention it for dramatic effect.

"Screw it, let's go to Whole Foods."

We took our tomato, basil, and cheese salad to the Great Salt Lake to have lunch. Manny played on the beach and we nibbled on our food. The Great Salt Lake smelled horrible from thousands of years of fish dying in a stagnant pool of water. We walked closer to the lake, avoiding abandoned bonfires from teenagers. Manny took off his shoes and waded. We joined him.

I posed my camera towards us and for the first time took a picture of us together. We had never taken a picture all of those months that we dated before. It was like this could be something real again, assuming I could get over the constant voice in my ear that I didn't dress, groom, clean, and organize correctly.

My mind that weekend was only partially on Courtney. I realized just how much she had helped me. If she had not given me the money to pay for the attorney Manny might not have been with us that day. He would have been in Alabama making racial slurs directed towards crows. The other part of my mind was focused on my uphill legal battle. Why did it take so much money and time to prove I did nothing wrong? Why was a woman with a clear history of mental illness, reckless behavior, and all around craziness allowed to even be granted an audience on this matter? The court case consumed me. I was not okay with the unknown and I was definitely not okay with the thought of Manny being raised by Jessica and her current husband.

Courtney left that weekend on a good note. She told me she finally trusted me again. She believed in me and the past wasn't an issue any more. Like so many times before she boarded her airplane and flew home to Chicago. She landed safely. "Good," I thought, "now I don't have to worry about her dying in a plane crash."

Worrying about people suddenly dying is something I have done as long as I can remember. My grandfather died when I was five years old. While in kindergarten I drew a picture of a skeleton in the ground. Above the skeleton it said, "Ted Huggins is dead." I even remember telling everyone my grandfather was dead for show and tell. Death has been a part of my life for a long time. When my father died with six other people I knew that year it shaped me even more. I could not let someone die. I had to know that he or she was alive and well. It didn't matter that she told me the bottoms of my pants are fringed because I wore pants that were too big.

I went back to work getting ready for my next court hearing. Jessica was requesting a custody evaluator, which would cost us $3,000 plus fees for the evaluator to fly out to Alabama. We were to split the costs down the middle. I started to think that she was trying to bankrupt me out of custody. It was working.

Courtney called the next night. "I am ready Matt. I want a real relationship with you. I want to be your girlfriend. Are you okay with that?"

"I don't know," I said. I had been reflecting on so many things with her. Her "help" was a part of it. It made me feel horrible as if I wasn't good enough. I had never spent as much energy criticizing another person's lifestyle as she had spent doing so to me. I also wanted, deep down, a family. I wanted a woman who had children of her own so they understood what I was going through. She would understand that my picture frames might not be dusted because I didn't have time. She would understand that the dryer sheet on the floor meant that I was doing laundry and folding it, an accomplishment for any man. I wanted to be understood not criticized.

I didn't say that to her though. I told her, "Courtney, I love you and I wished you lived here, but I cannot do this long distance thing. When you are here I am motivated to be a better person, but you're not here. You're far away. I don't know if and when that can change. I cannot leave Salt Lake City any time soon because of the custody case." She was upset. She was furious. She went into a defensive mode; she was angry at herself for allowing this to happen. My answer was exactly what she was afraid of.

"Okay, well then I guess we have nothing more to say to each other."

"I guess not." She hung up. The next day she called back.

"I just feel really sorry for you. Here is someone that

loves you and adores you and your son, and you just throw it all away." I was only listening to her because I cared for her and I wanted to be polite. I had too much else on my mind. "I can never date someone with a kid again, I got too attached. That's making all of this so much more difficult. Matt, you were really good, but what made you great was Manny. Do you understand what I'm saying, Matt?"

"You're saying that the person you really loved was Manny."

"No, I'm saying that the thing I was most attracted to in you was your relationship with your son."

I had turned off the ability to try to have a relationship any more. I wasn't going to give in and say, "Okay! Let's do it!" The conversation ended soon afterwards and I was allowed to get back to obsessing over keeping my son away from his mother who received mysterious black eyes from non-existent CIA operatives.

In a different world, without the court case and a crazy ex-wife, Courtney would have been perfect. I realized that I dated people I wanted to be like.

My first wife came from a Mormon family that were all highly educated. They were strong in their religious beliefs and all ridiculously intelligent.

Jessica was the opposite. She was carefree and fun. She had tattoos and partied. She took risks. She was perfect for the young man I once was, the former version of myself who was trying to find his way out of the Mormon culture that had defined me.

Courtney was smart, beautiful, driven, successful, and confident. I wanted to be driven like she was. I wanted to be successful in my career, not bouncing between jobs in order to get a one dollar per hour raise. I wanted to be like her, but I didn't like the way I felt when she was around me. I had already received so much negative feedback from Jessica about how I lived my life. I looked at myself and only focused on the negative. The last thing I wanted from a partner was someone that joined in the Matt-bashing. I hated being reminded of how much I had let myself go. I hated being told that I wasn't good enough. I wanted to be adored, not fixed. I wanted to be cheered on, not beat down.

I was alone again, but for the second time in my thirty one years on Earth, I made that choice myself. Perhaps Courtney did rub off on me a bit and I took a stand. I decided for myself that she wasn't what I wanted. I set my sights on a family, one that wouldn't look at a piece of clothing on my floor and give me an *are-you-serious* look while mumbling under her breath, "Disgusting."

MATTHEW TIMION

PART 5

| FORTY FIVE |

A Cold Christmas
November 2010

The second court hearing went well. While the commissioner was duty-bound to assign a custody evaluator to our case, she was not duty bound to decide who paid for it. Jessica made no appearance again to court. The commissioner ordered Jessica had to pay the entire amount and was given thirty days to come up with the money. It was a waiting game for Jessica to pay the initial deposit of three thousand dollars. I waited for her to pay the custody evaluator, knowing that I would face talking with a professional trained in recognizing problems with people. The days went on and on. I heard nothing.

Jessica called, drunk. I had no idea what had happened to the sober Jessica from the court documents, but the reappearance of drunk Jessica always eased my looming fears of how the court hearings would proceed. Drunk Jessica was back in control. She talked to Manny for a while. He handed me the phone with a confused look on his face. "She wants to talk to you, dad." I took the phone from Manny's outstretched hands and went into the backyard in order to have some privacy. Jessica and I got into our regular shouting routine right away. She started accusing me of being the villain again. She said I had made all of her friends and family turn against her.

"Does any of this have to do with Manny?" I asked.

241

"No."

I hung up. I followed the letter of the law by letting her talk with Manny. There was no need for her to talk with me.

Jessica repeatedly called back without answer for the next hour. I had to silence my phone. Her drunken voicemails consisted of statements like, "I cannot believe you won't let me talk to my son!" and, "What is wrong with you? I'm going to sue you!" I sent her an email stating that if she tried to call me and not Manny again that I would call the police locally and at the military base where she lived in order to file charges for harassment. She stopped calling, probably partially due to the fact that I had called the police on her military base and made a complaint.

It was October of 2010, and Manny was a demon for Halloween. He loved Halloween. It was easily his favorite Holiday. I wish I had had his enthusiasm for anything, let alone a holiday. I took a picture of Manny's costume\ complete with horns and makeup. I put it on Facebook, and right away Courtney commented on the photo.

Manny looks great...underneath (and on top of) your coffee table needs a little help. Sorry, you know me, and know I would have noticed.

Leave it to Courtney to take a cute picture of my son dressed up for Halloween and turn it into a way to publicly tell me my house was dirty. I would love to say that I had cleaned it up right away due to the embarrassment or that I left it untouched out of protest. I did neither. I cleaned it on its normal schedule. Courtney's comment was exactly just what I needed to remind me of why the two of us would never work out.

In November of 2010 a small local Martial Arts tournament was coming up. I felt confident enough to try. I was still a white belt and wanted to compete. I was throwing everything I had into martial arts. In some ways it was my only outlet for a life filled with dog crap, a troubled son, and crippling debt. It also provided me with some new friends, none of whom were Mormon. All of the people at our martial arts school were either former Mormons or had relocated from the Midwest, never having experienced Mormonism first hand. I wasn't judged for my lack of belief in Jesus' visitation of America after his resurrection. No one there was going to wonder if I secretly wore sacred underwear like the rest of the Mormons. My tattoos were an indicator of my disbelief.

I left work during lunch to register for the tournament. The person running the tournament told me to drop the entry form off at a local community center. I had never been to such a place in America. I must have been the only white person there. The community center was teaching people what they needed to get ahead in America, whether it be English, how to start your own company, or how to file your taxes. It amazed me that such a place existed in Salt Lake City. Compared to the community center, living in a *minority* neighborhood Salt Lake City was a white-bred place.

While driving back to work after dropping off the entry form, my phone rang. I never answered my phone while driving. My fear of other people dying extended to me as well except of course if it was a slow death caused by something like alcohol or fast food. I could handle a slow death. I looked down at my phone while waiting at the stop light and saw Jessica had called. We had not heard from her in well over a month.

"It's Jessica, I just wanted to call and say that I'll be away for a month and I'll be unable to call. Please give Manny a hug for me and tell him that I love him."

I didn't tell Manny about Jessica's sudden disappearance. If I told Manny he would have wanted to call her and he would have been upset when she didn't answer. Where was she going for a month that would prevent her from calling? Did her DUI conviction finally go through? Perhaps she was in rehab. Maybe she was in jail. My mind raced and I searched online for a possible solution using every resource I had. I had no answer. Rehabilitation centers and jails don't normally post lists of their guests.

It was Jessica's year for Thanksgiving and her thirty days without contact prevented her from taking Manny for the holiday. She was required by law to give me thirty days' notice. I didn't like the idea of sending Manny to her, but since we were still in the middle of a custody battle I had to abide by the letter of the law. If she had given thirty days' notice then I had to grant visitation. In some ways her surprise hiatus was a blessing.

The Martial Arts tournament went well. I ranked third and second in two different categories. Manny decided not to participate because he was afraid the tournament would be like one he saw on *The Karate Kid. He* was also embarrassed to be in front of so many people and afraid of getting hit without protective gear.

The season went on. Jessica was still ordered to pay for the custody evaluator, but she never did. My attorney told me to wait it out a bit and see. If she didn't pay for the custody evaluator after sixty days we would make a case to drop everything due to her lack of involvement. I used all of the money in my account to pay my lawyer just to do simple things like emailing me and sending legal documents.

I had become a master of shuffling my bills. I could remain behind on one bill and pay another. I knew I could fall three months behind on my mortgage before the mortgage company got upset and threatened to take my house away. I knew that my phone could go two months without payment before they threatened to disconnect. The thing that wasn't in my budget, however, was the heating bill. My gas bill was around ten dollars per month during the summer. In the winter it would climb to over one hundred and thirty dollars.

I woke up one morning and it was freezing. I looked at the thermostat. It was just above fifty degrees in my house. How did this happen? At first I thought my furnace was broken, but I heard it humming along. I went outside and saw a disconnect notice on my front door. How did I miss the warnings? They're supposed to let you know before they disconnect. I was a pro at disconnections at this point due to my multiple water disconnections. I even had had my power shut off once. I knew the drill.

I checked the water and it was ice cold. No hot water. I called the gas company after taking Manny to school. The air outside made it look like I was a chain smoker. I missed smoking, but there was no way I could afford it. I wasn't going to receive my paycheck for another day. One more day without heat. The timing was horrible. I pleaded with the gas company telling them that I had a minor child in the home and we needed heat.

"We have a number of programs set up for people in need. For example, we cannot shut off the gas if an elderly person is in the house."

"But my son isn't elderly. He's six." Manny was really seven years old at that point, but I wanted some dramatic effect.

"We cannot do anything then. If you pay your bill we can get your gas reconnected within twenty four hours."

We spent the night colder than normal, but I didn't tell Manny the gas was shut off. I inspired him to take a bath instead of a shower. Lucky for me in Utah everyone's stove is electric not gas powered. I boiled a few gallons of water and put them in the cold water already in the bathtub. I put two space heaters in his room so that he wouldn't freeze at night. Luckily we were able to go to martial arts that night to be in a heated place. Perhaps Manny would never notice.

Despite the temptation to just cut the lock they had put

on my gas meter, I paid the bill the next morning. For whatever reason the government frowns highly on that. Cutting the lock could get you jail time even if it were just to provide heat for your family. It was too risky. I had assumed that because I had paid the bill so early in the morning that the gas would be turned on that very day. It wasn't. We went three days without heat. Manny didn't know. He would never have to tell the story about not having heat.

I understand that three days without heat is not the end of the world. I have met many people over the years who have had to burn branches in their fireplace in order to heat their home. They had to do this all winter long. In a weird way I was jealous of them. I wish that I had had a fireplace where I could burn logs to heat my house. The logs in my backyard would have been perfect for that. I could then let the gas bill go unpaid for a while so that I could have afforded to buy Manny Christmas presents. I chose heat over Christmas gifts.

My account balance was always negative. My family had no money either so asking them was out of the question. A man working with an organization called Volunteers of Utah took pity on us. He was Manny's "Life Skills" teacher, which was a group set up for kids identified as *at risk*. We met with him once a week to talk about life lessons and making right choices. In my neighborhood kids that needed that service were a dime a dozen. Somehow Manny fit the mold. This man gave me an address and asked me to come during my lunch break.

I drove up in my beat down car to the address. My car had been without an oil change for over a year and a half. I had just recently renewed my license plates eight months late. I would have to renew them again soon. The volunteer walked me through the makeshift store and told me to pick out clothes, toys, and movies. I was given soap, deodorant, and shampoo. They gave us a winter coat for Manny and a jacket for myself. I received a blanket for Manny that he still has today. All these items were free. I felt so much gratitude. I was beyond the point of not accepting a handout. I needed any help I could get. Thankfully this man saw the need and offered it. It was because of this man that Manny had gifts that year for Christmas. I couldn't afford a thing.

I drove down to Las Vegas for Christmas that year in my car afraid that it would blow up while I drove. Manny slept in the backseat using the only seat belt that still worked. I took my once stolen video camera that had been returned by the police months after the break-in and videotaped Manny opening gifts that year. He thought it was a normal Christmas. He had no idea what we were going through.

On Christmas day, we attempted to call Jessica. Every child should talk to his or her parents on Christmas. Unfortunately she never answered when Manny called. I was hoping she would call back so I spent most of the day waiting for her call. Waiting for her to be a mother. She didn't call. When we called her the phone rang and rang. There was no answer.

We came home and I played a record on my old Victrola record player. It was a hand crank so I didn't have to worry about using electricity. The song *Silver Bells* blared throughout the house, filling us with some semblance of Christmas Spirit.

I loved the sound of records playin, especially if they were old. I would have done so much better in a different century before we had to worry about electrical bills and our gas being shut off. I decided my garden the next year would be even bigger. I wanted to feed us for the entire year. Perhaps it was time for me to seriously try to get a chicken coop. Although we rarely ate eggs, free eggs would be nice.

Jessica called back the day after Christmas. She was hysterical. As Manny sat on the couch talking to her, he looked worried. He looked shocked and horrified.

Jessica was crying and yelling so loudly that I could hear her shrill voice from ten feet away. "Manny, I don't have a job! I don't have any money!" She was sobbing. Why would she tell her son this? I sat at my laptop and wrote an email to Courtney giving her a play by play. Although our friendship was becoming more strained due to the money had given me months prior, Courtney and I were still in contact. She wanted her money back. I was too proud to tell her just how broke I was. Despite the overshadowing debt, she was still concerned about Manny and I.

"Dad, can I send my allowance to Mom? She needs the money." I told him no. Jessica appeared to be unraveling again and she was attempting to bring Manny down with her. I would not let that happen.

The new year was fast approaching and things had to change. I could not have another Christmas like that one. Manny was ignorant of what was going on around us. The effect of being so poor took a serious toll on me. I just wanted that life where there were two parents and we had more money than we could spend. I wanted to be loved again. I wanted to be inspired to be someone better than I was.

My thoughts most nights centered on Courtney, and I wondered if I had made a mistake. I knew I had screwed it up too much to even attempt to try again. I slept on one side of my bed while remembering what it was like when she slept on the other side.

| FORTY SIX |

Just Go Away!
December 2010

Another court hearing. The Guardian Ad Litem was dropped from the case. This happened by the sheer lack of interest by Jessica. She was the one who wanted the involvement with the Guardian Ad Litem. Despite her original intent, her participation in everything she started stopped. Even when it appeared that she was no longer going to pursue the case, I kept paying money for an attorney.

I emailed her receipts for her half of the day care bills. She replied.

Matt, I will be working in January. I should be able to send some money then.

January came.

I haven't been paid yet. What I'm going to do is set things up with ORS to pay you a % of anything I make. Eventually when I have a full time job, I'm will pay you regularly and begin to catch up on what I owe.

Please don't CC [my lawyer] on your emails anymore.

I could only speculate that she could no longer afford her attorney, which in my mind meant Vince had quit paying for her legal fees. A homemaker wouldn't have much of an income.

February came and I was alone still. I have never been a fan of Valentine's Day. I think it's overly commercialized and pointless, but the *idea* of Valentine's Day is wonderful. I would have loved to spend my Valentine's Day with someone. I would have embraced the idea, fully loaded with roses and gifts. Instead I spent it like I had spent my previous Father's Day. Pretending it was a normal day made it much easier to deal with. It was much easier that way.

Work continued on as normal. Poverty continued on as normal. I knew that if I worked hard enough and proved myself to my employer I would eventually make more money. It seemed the salary raise would not happen. I started taking on side jobs to make ends meet. For a while it worked. I would work forty hours a week and then come home and work five hours a night. The money wasn't glamorous, but it started adding up. At one point I actually got caught up on my bills.

Courtney sent me an email letting me know that she was

moving to San Francisco for work. She had been promoted. She had made twice as much as I did. Now she was making more. I was so envious. She still wanted her money back. A few months before she had sent me a text message saying, "Hey, I'm in the Salt Lake City airport. Guess what I would love to get today?" Clearly she thought that obtaining fifteen hundred dollars was going to be an easy task for me. I don't think she fully understood just how poor I was. No, she couldn't have understood. I never really told her.

Although I knew it was probably impossible, I had promised Courtney that I would pay her back. I had daycare, mortgage, and utilities to pay. I could not produce the money she needed. She persisted asking. She would call and send me text messages. Sometimes she would email. I ignored her.

Matt,
It seems that you've fallen back into the cycle of not returning phone calls or text messages, so I'll once again reach out via email.

You had indicated that the money would be paid back to me by the end of January or February at the latest. You stated you had side work monies coming in and with the addition of your tax return you told me that you could pay me back in full.

I have made it very clear that I can be patient and realistic as long as you would maintain open communication with me.

That seems to be something you cannot and are unwilling to do considering this is now the second time you have ignored my attempts to collect money and/or information about the money.

Again, this is your timeline that I'm following for the payment.

I don't think that it's unreasonable for me to expect

you to do one of two things;

1. If your proposed timeline is no longer an option - communicate that with me.
2. Set more realistic timelines for payment as I depend upon that money, and considering the move I just made, i was counting on it at the end of last month.

The way you have been handling (or more to the point, not handling) this money situation is irresponsible at the very least. You're not the only one that needs money, has other financial responsibility, or personal matters that require financial support.

I'm not going to give up my attempt to recover the money owed to me, nor should I be expected to. Please tell me when I can either expect it in full, or what kind of monthly payment plan works for you. thanks,
Courtney

I knew that I had pushed her to this. She was frustrated because I had cut her off and had not communicated with her about my issues. Regardless, I had had enough. Our friendship had turned into nothing more than her trying to collect a debt from me; a debt that was initially a gift. It was a gift for which I was very grateful.

Courtney was the only person who had believed in me enough to help me when I needed it most. Then our relationship went sour because I couldn't do long distance and I was sick of being told constantly what I was doing wrong. I just wanted to be left alone at that point. What was once love had become nothing more than someone I knew constantly asking for money the money I owed her but did not have.

Courtney,
Let me start by stating the obvious: You initially GAVE the money to me. Secondly, you make more than

```
twice (annually) than I do. Third, I am still dealing
with having to pay for a lawyer to fight for my son,
as well as fighting to keep my house.

You only asked for the money back after any form of a
relationship wouldn't work out. I agreed to pay this
money.

It has become extremely clear to me that the extent
of our "friendship" has become nothing more than you
collecting money from me that was originally a gift.

Give me a physical address and I'll send you a check
every month. I'll do this until it's paid off. Other
than that, please stop calling, texting, and emailing
about this. You have made yourself, and your take on
our friendship very clear.
```

I was done with her. I couldn't take it any more. Looking back I know she was being open and trying to communicate with me about the situation. All that I heard, at the time, was someone hounding me for money. This is why people say to never lend money to friends or family. You should only give it as a gift. My pushing her away ruined what could have been a great friendship.

I really don't know if our situation was caused by both of our issues or if the issues were just mine. It didn't matter. I never sent her the money although I had every intention of doing so. I kept falling behind on my bills and daycare again. It seemed like I was in a cycle that would never stop. For those months I felt like I was just falling and out of control. I was the only one who could fix it but I had no idea where to start.

Manny's birthday came and went. He invited some friends over from martial arts, which was turning into our new social outlet. I didn't see my fellow martial arts enthusiasts much outside of class, but at least I saw them three times a week. They were not constantly hounding me for money. They never called me drunk or asked me to have sex with them. I was moving up in the world.

The family who came over from our martial arts class lived in the hills of North Salt Lake City, which I should explain is considered the "rich" area of Salt Lake City. Their house was massive. Their entire house was four thousand square feet. Not including the basement, which Manny and I rarely used, we were living in approximately eight hundred square feet. When they came over one of them said, "Oh, this house is quaint," which is how white Americans say that a house is small.

Our kids were running around and playing. The adults had a beer and were talking. Suddenly all of the kids, running in a pack, went outside and were playing on the sidewalk. The parents from North Salt Lake City stood up in a panic.

"Where did my kids go?" They were stressing out.

"Just outside to play," I said back.

"We don't do that in our neighborhood. No one goes outsides to play." Kids running outside to play was common in my neighborhood. Perhaps that was part of why I liked living in a "bad" neighborhood. My neighborhood was filled with families unable to afford giant televisions and pianos. We could not afford a swimming pool or an exercise room. For fun the kids ran outside and played in the street or played tag. Maybe in 2011 that was how "poor" people lived, but as far as I was concerned it was how I was raised. It wasn't a bad thing at all.

Manny's Spring Break vacation was fast approaching. It was Jessica's turn. With our custody battle still open and still up in the air, I waited for her to give me notice. As much as I hated her at that moment, I knew if she took Manny for the week she wouldn't try to repeat her failed attempt of taking Manny. She wouldn't try to repeat history because it had not worked out for her before. I honestly wanted a vacation from parenting. A vacation from my daily parenting duties would give me a chance to sleep in, maybe go out on a date, or perhaps I could even get the house cleaned while an eight year old tornado wasn't undoing everything I had just done.

From: Jessica Jacobs
To: Matthew Timion
Sent: Wednesday, March 16, 2011 9:03 PM
Subject: Spring Break

Matt,

Vince and I will be visiting Utah in April. Manny's
school break is April 18-22, so I want to coordinate
his pickup and drop off with you. We will be staying
in Kaysville while we are there.

Also, has he had his school pictures taken this year?
If so, I'd like to have a decent size copy (8x10 or
5x7) and two wallet size. Please let me know the cost
of the photos plus shipping, and I'll send that to
you.

Thanks,
Jessica

Jessica seemed to have calmed down a bit. She was
being cordial. Because she gave me proper notice I had had no
choice but to allow Manny's visit with her. Luckily Manny
would stay in town so I wouldn't have to worry about missing a
flight again.

From: Jessica Jacobs
Subject: My Utah Visit
To: Matthew Timion
Date: Tuesday, March 29, 2011, 5:36 AM

I haven't heard back from you. The dates of our visit
will be changing, and we will only be there for a

couple of days. My plan is to pick up Manny when he is out of school and spend an evening or two with him.
Please respond so we can plan this out appropriately.

I could have, at that moment, told her to buzz off. I could have told her *no, you didn't give me thirty days notice, screw you.* Instead I was accommodating. I asked for the dates of her visit. I was told April 4th through April 6th.

Three days before her visit, plans changed again. I had quit telling Manny that his mom was going to visit. I had learned that lesson from Christmas of 2009. Never tell Manny his mom would do anything because there was a good chance she would not follow through.

From: Jessica Jacobs
Subject: RE: My Utah Visit
To: Matthew Timion
Date: Friday, April 1, 2011, 9:40 AM

There's been a change in plans. I won't be able to go to Utah but Vince will. He'd like to stop by and see Manny, drop some things off, and take him to dinner with the girls either tues or wed night. Which is best?

I talked to my lawyer. Vince had no visitation rights. Besides, he had had such a major role in the proceedings over the last year. I didn't trust him alone with my dog, let alone my son. I wrote her back.

Date: Mon, 4 Apr 2011 09:48:30 -0700
From: Matthew Timion
Subject: RE: My Utah Visit
To: Jessica Jacobs

I am sorry, but Vince has no visitation rights. If he has something to deliver, please have him mail it or drop it off during the day.

She replied the next day.

From: Jessica Jacobs
Subject: RE: My Utah Visit
To: Matthew Timion
Date: Tuesday, April 5, 2011, 7:08 AM

Listen, I know you and I want nothing to do with each other. But, the issue at hand is Manny and the Girls. The bottom line is that there are people that love Manny, his step-dad and step- sisters, that want to just see him for ONE evening. Are you really so hateful that you are going to prevent family members from getting together one night because I'm not there? There are two other children (Percy and Sarah) to consider and you're just taking your anger out on me and using the power you have at the moment to be hateful. That is wrong and you know it.

I love it when people tell me what I know. When I was a Mormon, people would routinely come up to me and tell me what I believed and then proceed to tell me why my beliefs were wrong. They never, for a second, asked me if I actually believed what they were saying. They never thought that perhaps my personal beliefs did not always align with the official Mormon doctrine. I hated that.

I refused to trust Jessica and Vince. I would never trust them considering the hell they had put me through over the past year. There was a time when I would have tried to meet in the middle with them for the benefit of Manny, but when I found out about their true characters my job went from peacemaker to protector of my son.

Vince dropped off an Easter basket, rang the doorbell, and left. There was no confrontation. I didn't hear from Jessica for a while after that. Her lack of involvement gave me a sense of peace.

It was late April of 2011 and a number of tornadoes were hitting the Huntsville, Alabama area, where Jessica and Vince lived. I kept refreshing websites hoping to read about casualties. I didn't want Jessica and Vince to die, but sometimes I thought about how her death would solve all of the nonsense I was going through. I just wanted Jessica to go away.

| FORTY SEVEN |

Dorothy?
April 2011

Manny knew the rules. He knew his mom was not allowed to talk to me on the phone. I reminded him of this constantly. "Your mom calls to talk to you, not me." These rules were exactly what made what happened next so difficult.

Manny and I were bored. We didn't have money for a movie or anything else so we decided to go to an event to see dogs ready to be adopted. Manny loved animals. Just being around animals made him happier. While in the car on the way to see the animals, my phone rang. It was Jessica. I gave Manny the phone.

Jessica was hysterical. "A tornado hit us!" She was so loud I could hear her. Manny sat in the seat next to me looking worried. He listened. "Everything is destroyed!" she yelled. "Vince was hurt in the tornado!" Manny's face went from worried to terrified. "Put your dad on the phone!" I told Manny that I couldn't talk because I was driving. What I told Manny was just an excuse. I didn't want to talk to her. I had nothing to say to her that she couldn't say in an email. Manny relayed the message to Jessica. "Tell your dad I'm a tornado survivor!"

"Dad, she said she's a tornado survivor." His voice was shaking. I am certain all he wanted was for me to see his pain and talk to Jessica.

"Manny, I'm driving, keep talking to your mom." By that point her attempt to talk to me had turned into a shell game. I heard her tell Manny to put the phone up against my ear. He tried. I told him to stop. She wailed and cried to Manny about how difficult everything was. A tear formed in Manny's eye. He was upset. She told him to put the phone up to my ear again. I pushed his hand away. In order to avoid talking to Jessica I kept driving for an hour, hoping they would end their call. I should have just picked up the phone and told her to get lost. I couldn't do that in front of Manny though. I was trying to consider his feelings. He didn't need to see me talking like that to his mom.

"My dad says if you want to talk to him you can send an email." Manny was just repeating what I told him.

"But I'm a tornado survivor!" She wore the new status of *tornado survivor* as some sort of badge of honor. Growing up in Illinois, I had lived through tornados myself. When I was in second grade a tornado had knocked down the tree in our backyard and destroyed our jungle gym. It was a sad day for children all over the neighborhood. I had worked at a Boy Scout camp with tornados touching down all around us one summer. We spent the time in our rain gear ready to evacuate campsites into the closest ravine. Despite growing up with weather Jessica had just "survived," I never considered myself a "tornado survivor." I never thought my experiences allowed me any kind of special privilege.

Eventually the phone call ended. Manny and I looked at the dogs and did some grocery shopping. I'm sure we mostly bought canned goods. Canned goods were cheap and easy meals.

"Dad," Manny said. He said my name like he was asking a question. His face looked worried. "I'm worried about Mom and Vince. Mom said he got really hurt. I just keep imagining Dorothy in the Wizard of Oz in the tornado." Manny loved the Wizard of Oz. He would watch it a few times a week. Now one of his favorite movies had become a reminder of how horrible weather can be.

I called Jessica's family to ensure that she was okay. I would have hated for my refusal to talk to her to be unwarranted. I would have hated it if Vince was hurt and in the hospital. Jessica's family told me that Vince and Jessica were fine. Their house wasn't destroyed. The worst that had happened was that their power was out for a few days.

May came and went and there was no word from Jessica. Our lives consisted mostly of school, work, and martial arts. I contacted my lawyer and there was no update on the court case. June came. I still had not heard from Jessica about a summer visit. I sent her an email.

In the first half of the email to Jessica, I put it all out there for her to see - a detailed timeline of her negative interaction (or just plain lack of interaction) with our son. I hoped that seeing it all in one place would give her perspective, but I knew that was unlikely.

Towards the end of the email I wrote the following:

Lately you have been calling again insisting that I talk to you. It upsets Manny, and it especially upsets him when you continue to tell him to do something that I have asked him not to do.

I know that you do not understand most of what I'm going to say, but your words affect Manny. You tell him things that no child should have to worry about. Why did you tell him last summer he wasn't going to live with me? Why do you burden him with your lack of employment, or lie and say that Vince was hurt by a tornado? You repeatedly tell him to give me the phone, and he is extremely confused. You call him and put him between us, making him your errand boy when all you need to do is send me an email.

I am left with the decision that you either do not understand that the majority of what you do affects

Manny, or that you just do not care about his emotional well-being.

And just so you know in advance, if you do decide to take Manny for the summer, he will not go without a return ticket. I will not have a repeat of last year, especially since you are legally obligated to pay for his return trip.

For whatever reason I felt it important to spell out to her all of what she had done. I thought that maybe if she saw the pattern herself, or perhaps acknowledged that yes, she was guilty, that things would change. It never worked. She didn't reply. A week later she sent me a text message saying that there was a change of plans, and she wouldn't be able to afford to bring Manny out for the summer. Her disregard meant Manny would be home all summer, and I would have to pay four hundred and fifty dollars per month to his daycare while I worked. Considering the alternative, the cost was worth it.

| FORTY EIGHT |
Time for a cool change
End of May 2011

At the beginning of 2011 I started looking for another job. I loved where I worked. I loved my co-workers. I did not love, however, that I was being paid twenty to thirty thousand dollars less than the going rate for what I did. Most of my co-workers had been with the company longer than I had been and were able to supplement their income with stock options. I had no stock options. My coworkers had big homes, nicer cars, and disposable income. I had a small run-down house and a car that I had to park on a hill so it would start. The battery barely held a charge, and I had to pop the clutch to get it to go. What was once my dream car because of its amazing fuel economy had turned into a nuisance I could not get rid of.

I received a job offer from a new company located in Sugar House, a small community in Salt Lake City. My new salary would be fifteen thousand dollars more than I was making before, and I would have stock options. I envisioned the company being sold in a few years time and being able to cash out, pay off my house, and perhaps start my own martial arts studio. I loved martial arts. I loved the exercise and the simple nature of it. With my new job offer I talked to my boss.

"I received a new job offer. It's for fifteen *thousand* more."

"Did you consider talking to us about a counter offer first? Have you considered the stock options?" I was in line to receive about fifteen *hundred* worth of stock options if I stuck around for another year.

"The fifteen hundred wouldn't make it worth it. I need to make this change for my family. I cannot afford to live like this any more."

My boss completely understood. Although Utah had horrible salaries, most of the companies were very family oriented. The predominance of Mormons made family-related issues paramount; employers would ask no questions. Family was always first.

I started my new job. I was on the fifth floor of a building overlooking Sugar House Park. This was a stark change from my previous job where I had been in a closet-sized room with two other people. I needed the sunshine. I needed to see something beautiful every day. As the snow melted from the Utah mountains, it filled the lake at Sugar House Park. The lake started to overflow. My new coworkers and I made bets as to when the lake water would run into the street.

We would occasionally eye a cute soccer mom jogging in the park during the middle of the day. I wondered how people were able to afford not working. How could the people jogging in the park have the luxury of such a life? It was like every day was a vacation to them. The last vacation I had had happened years ago. When I had had a vacation from Manny, it was overshadowed with court hearings and custody battles. I envied those people.

In May of that year I decided to try something crazy. While I had been a Mormon missionary, I had lived in the Philippines and I loved the culture. Although I had not been to the Philippines in ten years, I still spoke the language and loved everything about the people, the language, the food, and the country. I thought perhaps my failed love life had more to do with dating the wrong kind of women. Maybe my heart was still back in the Philippines. Maybe what I needed was a Filipina wife. I, like every other desperate man in the world, signed up for a Filipino dating site. These women were in the Philippines. They all wanted American men. I suddenly knew what it was like to be an attractive woman on an American dating site.

When logged in every day to this website I would receive chat request after chat request. I received over one hundred emails a day. Speaking their language made me even more interesting to them. I was a hit. I was popular. Unfortunately, I knew they wanted a green card more than me. I was a means to an end for them. I wasn't the prize.

I sat overlooking Sugar House Park as my phone vibrated with every email I received. The constant attention was too much. I had no idea what I was thinking. There was no way I was going to fly out to the Philippines to meet a woman I only knew online. There was no way I would be able to wait a year for a visa for them to come to America so we could get married without really knowing each other. I wanted someone to see me for who I was and what I had to offer. I didn't need someone thousands of miles away with whom I might not be compatible. I canceled my subscription to the dating website.

Father's Day came up again. I had a card from my

mother that year. Nothing from Courtney. That bridge was burned. Manny's gift to me for Father's Day was a rock. I'm glad I received something from him. I had no money to do anything special for my special day. I had a fifth of cheap vodka, a couch, and a television. I made the best out of my situation. When Manny was in bed I started drinking. For some odd reason I started watching the show *Intervention* all night. *Intervention* is a show where they follow around drug addicts, alcoholics, etc. and film their family staging an intervention so the addicts can get help.

An episode came on featuring a father who was so against receiving help that he did everything he could to avoid receiving help. His children stood in front of him begging him to go into treatment. He left the room. His ex-wife followed him saying that if he did not seek help he would never see his children again. He kept walking. I was reminded of my own father, who was told by my mother to choose between his family and alcohol. "I'm a grown man, and no one can tell me what to do," my father replied. Finally the family on this show wouldn't give up on him. They raced to his house and threatened to get him committed to a mental institution if he did not go into treatment. He reluctantly agreed. He got treatment. A few weeks into living in a treatment facility, states away from his family, he was diagnosed with esophageal cancer. He flew home to receive cancer treatment and be with his kids. He died shortly thereafter.

I was bawling. I didn't want Manny to lose me. I was drinking more than I should have been back then. It was my way to cope. It was my escape. While Jessica's claims of the level of my alcohol intake were not true, I could see that they were not healthy. I didn't want to die. I didn't want Manny to have to experience what I did growing up. I stumbled into the kitchen and emptied out all of the alcohol I had. The kitchen smelled of vodka and wine. I emailed my friend Nadia, who had been sober for a few months. I asked to go to an Alcoholics Anonymous meeting with her. The change and introspection she gained in her life was inspiring. If only I could have some of that.

I needed something to take the edge off though. I bought a pack of cigarettes the next day and smoked a few a day. It was just enough to get my nerves settled. It was enough to get me through the week until the Alcoholics Anonymous meeting. At the very least it would be nice to be around people who were like my father. That was the least I could do.

The next day I sat in my car in traffic. I was agitated by the stresses of life. I lit a cigarette. Little River Band was on the radio.

> *Time for a cool change*
> *I know that it's time for a cool change*
> *And now that my life is so prearranged*
> *I know that it's time for a cool change*

It was time for a change. I had spent years letting life happen to me instead of taking charge. It was amazing how a song about heartbreak inspired me to get healthier. I took inspiration anywhere I could get it though, whether it was in a snowflake, a kitten, or a song by a guy whining about how he was perpetually alone. Come to think of it, I could have just as easily have written that song myself. I too, was perpetually alone.

| FORTY NINE |
And I'm an Alcoholic
June 20, 2011

We were in a basement of a bar in Magna, Utah. The street was run down. The buildings were run down. The entire town was run down. It was my first and only time visiting an Alcoholics Anonymous meeting.

My friend Nadia sat next to me. This was her group. She knew them all by name, and they knew her. There were a number of memorized mantras recited. Everyone else seemed to know them except for me. I sat in silence. It was dark, and there were electric candles on each table. We went around the room, and everyone introduced themselves. An overweight man wearing a shirt that said, "Seven days without a meeting makes one weak" started. "Hi, I'm Dave, and I'm an alcoholic."

"Hi Dave!" Everyone responded.

"Hi, I'm Steve, and I'm an addict." How people described themselves identified their addiction. "Alcoholic" meant they were alcoholics. "Addicts" were drug addicts or perhaps alcoholics too. No one said, "I'm a chain smoker," because they all were chain smokers.

"Hi Steve!" I had heard about these meetings. My father had gone to meetings like these in order to try to maintain his unemployment checks, an unfortunate situation considering his work union required his attendance. After completion of the Alcoholics Anonymous program, my father's union representative mysteriously lost all proof of my father's compliance. My father gave up on life when his work union gave up on him. His work union was against him, just like the rest of the world. He slumbered into a life of two fifths of whiskey a day until he was finally found dead on his leather recliner at home.

At this dark basement meeting I had with me my father's "Big Blue Book," the Alcoholic Anonymous bible. Was I an alcoholic? Was this meant for me? It was my turn to talk.

"Hi, I'm Matt, and I'm an alcoholic." Nadia's friends looked at her with a sense of glee. She had brought someone with her so open to admitting his or her addiction. Admitting you have a problem is the first step of recovery. It is also the hardest one for most people to do. I was just glad to have a friend to be with me while I was there. I doubt I would have ever gone to that meeting without support.

The topic of conversation that evening was "following the steps." The steps are the twelve steps of recovery. People were supposed to talk about how living the principles of Alcoholics Anonymous helped them. They were to talk about how doing so made their lives better. People went around the room, and they talked or passed. Almost everyone talked.

A hardened man across from me told us about how he had done horrible things. Things he couldn't even bring himself to name. One of the tenants of Alcoholics Anonymous is to give yourself up to a higher power. While most of the people around me were not religious they found a way to make the idea of a higher power work for them. A *higher power* didn't need to be a god. The burly man across from me told us, "The judge looked at me and said that I was an animal and wanted to lock me away. He was right. And then the judge dismissed the charges. Whatever saved me that day is my higher power. I will never go back to jail again."

The man next to me talked about making amends for your prior mistakes. This man, who you would assume the worst of if you had ever met him in real life, was a leader in the community. "I have been making my list for years. I have forgotten so many things that I did while using. Some people remind me of stuff I did and I add it to the list. I will be able to reach out to those people eventually." I looked at him and knew that he was being honest.

It was my turn. I talked about what brought me there. I talked about my father. I had no lesson to share about how living the steps of the group had helped me. I was just happy to be there, in the dank basement with a bathroom that I was afraid to step into. I was happy to be around people who didn't need drugs or alcohol to be happy. Those people were my heroes.

The violent ex-con had a moment where he changed his life. The man next to me also had a moment where he wanted to change. They had all hit rock bottom. My life felt like it was close to joining them at the edge of despair. If anything, I enjoyed being there with those people because I wished my father were in the room with us. I wished he had had the strength to stop. I realized my father had never had the personal conviction required. My father never stood a chance against life. He wasn't meant for this century either. My father would have been happiest living in a cabin in the woods and fishing every day.

The meeting ended and everyone said the serenity prayer.

God grant us the serenity to accept the things we cannot change, courage to change the things we can, and wisdom to know the difference.

We walked outside and smoked. Everyone was smoking. "One vice for another," I thought. Smoking only hurt the individual. At least no one was driving drunk or having sex with strangers because of his or her pack-a-day habit.

Nadia came back to my place and we talked a bit. My house was in disarray mostly because I was about to refinish my hardwood floors. Not drinking made me awake more than I was used to. Not drinking kept my brain running at three in the morning. I had to find things to stay occupied.

When I stopped drinking I noticed a difference in myself. I had more energy. I lost nearly 20 pounds in two months. My martial arts skills were increasing. I was no longer sluggish.

In July I received a text message from Courtney.

`I understand the no contact thing, but what medication were you on to help with your stress? I am having a very difficult time here.`

I told her that Prozac worked wonders for me after my divorce. I told her to stay away from Paxil as it only made my anxiety worse. "By the way, I have not had a drink in over a month and have lost over 10 pounds." She used to comment on my drinking and my belly. I wanted her to know I was making my best effort to become a better person. She replied with, "great!" And that was it.

That summer was a sober and productive one. I concluded that while my drinking had become more of a crutch that I was comfortable with, I was not a hard core alcoholic like my father or Jessica. My father used to bring a six pack of beer with him to work so that he could have a beer, or six, during the day. My drinking was mostly tied to my stress level. Since I was in my new job I finally had enough money to survive. I was almost caught up on my bills.

My new boss pulled each of his new employees into a private meeting one at a time. "We don't have the funds to pay for this pay cycle," he said. "We're working on acquiring new funds, but it might take a while. We're offering to pay you with stock this time around." Everyone said yes except for myself and one other person. There was a company meeting a few days later explaining the situation. "We had an investor willing to pay ten million dollars to us, but he wanted too much ownership of the company. We're looking for other investors." We were not going to be paid. I went home that night upset, but optimistic. I reverted back to the similar routine of applying for another job. It was late August of 2011. My gamble to make my life better was a losing bet. I was happy though that I had it in me to try.

I called my previous job begging to come back. At first when I showed up to meet with my former boss, he didn't recognize me. I was thirty pounds lighter than when he had last seen me three months before. They understandably hesitated about my return. They were afraid I would leave again if another higher paying job came up. I vowed my dedication to them. I pointed out that my friends had put themselves on the line to get me the opportunity. I couldn't let them down. Low pay was better than no pay. Working for no pay was exactly the situation I was leaving. I couldn't work for free. I had to support my Manny.

September of 2011. I called my mother for our regular check in.

"Yes Matt?" She sounded upset.

"I was just calling to see how you were." I am the first to admit that I, a grown man, talk to my mother at least three times a week. We often call to talk about our days and nothing more.

"Well.... shit... I wasn't going to tell you this yet, but your grandma died."

My grandmother died. She had, by the force of sheer stubbornness, stayed alive longer than she should have. She was the woman who had had a quintuple bypass surgery and kept eating fast food. This was the woman whose idea of a home-cooked meal was cold beans and a tuna sandwich. She often called me "Little Miss Susie Homemaker" when I told her about the quilts I was making out of old t-shirts. I usually called her once a week just to touch base.

I got in my car and drove towards the liquor store. I bought some tequila. My grandmother's death was too much for me to handle. After Manny went to bed, I had two drinks and fell asleep. Maybe I didn't need the crutch of alcohol, but sometimes it was helpful. I was back to making less money again, but this time I would try my hardest to keep stay on top of my finances. I would try my hardest to stay ahead. I would live a life that would make my grandmother proud.

The school year had just begun. Manny was in third grade. He was happy and didn't talk about his mom any more. There were no more outbursts. It had been a year since he had last seen her and the longer he went without her, the better his behavior became. Jessica's lawyer had contacted my lawyer and had agreed to drop the case against me if I agreed to drop my counter motion for legal fees, which totaled to more than three thousand dollars. I declined the offer. Jessica went silent once again.

| FIFTY |
Perspective
Fall 2011

"I've been doing this for 25 years. I cannot give you a diagnosis because I'm not a doctor. What I can tell you is that I have seen kids *like Manny* over the years, and if they do not receive some sort of medication they will turn to drugs and alcohol."

Manny's third grade teacher was a godsend. She had noticed Manny's inability to focus and gave a recommendation. She spoke from decades of experience.

We saw a doctor and Manny was prescribed with medication to help with his attention issues. Normally I thought medicines like Adderall and the like were overly prescribed. I thought symptoms like lack of focus were just kids being kids. If Manny shared my genetic makeup I would have easily said his issues were due to stubbornness and laziness, not biological in nature. Since the only thing I knew about Manny's genetics was my short interaction with Ariel and Peter, I called Ariel's new family. Ariel was on Adderall, and the new medication had caused a huge improvement in Ariel. The possibility of a biological cause for Manny's behavior wasn't a big surprise since Manny's biological mother had tested positive for methamphetamines shortly after giving birth to him.

The new medication started and his behavior and attention issues at school started to get better. Manny was no longer running around the house screaming. He didn't sit on the floor during class and pick at the carpet. He was no longer obsessively picking his fingernails. He was focusing. Our routine was the same. I worked, he went to school, and I picked him up. We both continued martial arts and progressed towards getting our black belts. I loved attending having a regular activity with him, a real father and son activity.

When I was six or seven years old there was a father and son picnic in our town. Actually, the place I grew up in was so small it was considered a "village." Everyone had a parent to go with, except for me. My mother and other mothers in the area knew I needed someone to fill the void. My father was passed out drunk or just had no real desire to be a part of the father and son activity. An old man came by our house and took me to the church where the picnic was to be held. I was thrilled that I had a father figure although it was only for one night. As a father myself, I refused to be an absentee father like my own father. As much as Manny hated martial arts at the moment, he would always be able to say his dad and he did something together.

As a Mormon missionary I spent two years always with someone else by my side. The only "alone time" we had was in the bathroom, and that wasn't always true. In the Missionary Training Center in Provo, Utah, we all showered in a common room. We all stood around looking at the ceiling so we could not accidentally glance at another naked person's body. After two years of constant interaction, coming home from my missionary experience was horrible. There was nothing but silence. There was no one else around. I was too acclimated to always having someone else by my side.

I had always wondered if Mormons married so young because of the silence after mission. Perhaps they were feeling lost and afraid after coming back from their missions. Perhaps they didn't want to adjust to being alone. Maybe this is why I jumped into a marriage so quickly with my Mormon wife and then so hastily with Jessica. It would explain why I needed female attention so much all of the time. Those two years helped shape me into the lonely person I had become.

I was coming to peace with being alone though. I wasn't really alone. I had my son with me, after all, and Jessica was not much of a factor in our lives any more. The string of female groupies I had years before, thanks to my job in radio, were all non-existent in my life. Besides, I didn't have time for dating. Considering how long I had been out of the "dating" game I doubt I would have been very successful at dating anyway. The solitary life was growing on me. I was still broke, but I had learned how to adapt to my financial situation. I didn't have a girlfriend or a wife, but I had my son. At least I had him.

Being the lone single father had its advantages. Long gone were the days when young single women were attracted to me. The younger girls liked that I owned a house or a motorcycle. They liked that I worked in radio or that I had tattoos. Introduce the kid, however, and they were usually gone. The good ones stayed, but I wasn't in the right frame of mind to really be with them. Since my projected persona had changed due to my insistence of keeping Manny with me, the only women who ever showed any interest in me were married women.

"You're like chocolate to me," a mother said to me at martial arts one day. Her two daughters were in our class. The mother watched her daughters, and me, kick, punch, jump, and sweat. "You're like chocolate to me," she said again.

"What do you mean?" I was trying to understand her metaphor. After all, English was her second language and as far as I knew chocolate was something bad where she came from.

"I know I shouldn't, but I just want to sometimes." Since Manny and I had gone to a birthday party with her daughters a few months back, this woman had had a fixation on me. She was very bold and upfront. As enticing as her offer was, I couldn't be *that* person. As attractive as she was I knew what it felt like to have your wife sleep with another guy. Nope. Couldn't happen. She kept flirting with me for a while before changing her daughters to a different class schedule. "It's just hard for me to see you sometimes." Her changing schedules was a relief.

She wasn't the only one. A number of married women propositioned me. I started to wonder if they felt there was something safe about me that said, "I sleep with married women." What was I projecting? Why did women from high school find me on Facebook and start talking dirty? Their husbands were in the next room. Why was this somehow *okay* for them?

It all became clear. They were dissatisfied with their husbands. They wanted their husbands to be a father to their children not the guy who helped pay the bills. They saw me and somehow put me on a pedestal. I was a father, and a damn good one at that according to them anyway. I was not bad on the eyes. I followed my heart and these women loved that. I was new and exciting.

And they were all married women.

It started becoming rather annoying to have to tell married women over and over again that we would never work out. Where were the single women? I guess it didn't matter though. Not really anyway. I had learned to accept I would be alone for the rest of my life, and I was okay with the idea.

Of all the women in my life the only person who I could have ever seen myself with, Courtney, was long gone. I had not heard from her in months. I had not been romantic with her in over a year. I knew that my actions had made any chances of a relationship with her again impossible. I had earned my solitude. I deserved it. I opened myself up and let the cool nothingness sweep over me. "Being alone is okay," I told myself. And it was.

| FIFTY ONE |
Assimilation

Autumn 2011

I looked into the mirror on my wall. The mirror was surrounded by pictures from my life, my grandparents' lives, and my parents' lives. There was a photograph of my family when I was in third grade next to a photograph of my father's Vietnam era basketball team from the Navy. My father was the only white player on the team. To the left I saw a photograph of my grandparents from the late 1940s, and next to it was a picture of Courtney and Manny from the Oktoberfest in 2009.

The mirror revealed something amazing. I was now covered in tattoos. I had seven of them. I had two on my upper right arm of the Philippines and the Aztec sun on my left wrist. I had a car and microphone on my right forearm. On my back was a giant scene from Don Quixote, which I had always loved because it symbolized a man living his life they way it should be not the way it was. On my left ribcage was Da Vinci's Vitruvian Man. My latest tattoo was Korean words spelling out the version of martial arts that Manny and I had come to love.

I had assimilated. I had become exactly what I had first criticized when I came to Utah. I was covered in tattoos. I had joined the hippy liberals, and I had a giant garden with thirty tomato plants that year. Like all of the other adult teenagers in Utah, I had had multiple sexual partners, both consecutively and simultaneously. I had experimented with over consumption of alcohol. It was official. I was no longer an outsider. Utah had become my home. My formerly emotionally shattered self had become open to the influences of the world around me. I had assimilated into this weird culture that I used to observe and mock. I had become the epitome of an ex-Mormon minus the need to talk about Mormonism all of the time.

When I had lived in the Philippines during my two year stint as a Mormon missionary I did my best to assimilate into their culture. My appearance was a giveaway that I didn't belong, but that didn't stop me. I wanted to learn the language, the culture, and the food. I wanted to understand the rituals, the clothing, and the customs. In some way I did this because I knew it would make me a more effective teacher. I wanted to belong. When I came home from the Philippines my mother had introduced me to the woman who managed my new apartment building. My mother had acquired the apartment for me when my step-father proclaimed he would in no way ever want to see me or "my kind" again. Living apart was better for all of us.

"Nice to meet you!" The manager said to me.

"Nice to meet you din!" I replied back. "Din" is a *Tagalog* (Filipino) word for "as well," or "also." I had spent so much time speaking the language and living in the Filipino culture that assimilating back to American life was difficult. Because my experience coming back to America was difficult, I started to wonder if I ever *could* leave Salt Lake City. I had become a full fledged member of the tribe. Everything about me screamed "Former Mormon," from the tattoos to the cigarette hanging out of my mouth.

Everything I knew, from the culture to the customs of the area had become second nature to me. They were second nature to my son as well. I knew liquor stores were closed on Sundays and it no longer bothered me. I knew the best time to shop at a big box store was also on Sunday because half of the population was at church and not allowed to shop on Sundays. I knew twice a year you never go to downtown Salt Lake City because the Mormon Church was putting on their semi-annual General Conference and the traffic was horrible. I knew on Saturdays that the Farmer's Market at Pioneer Park was the best place to get fresh produce and see yuppies selling beaded jewelry. Could I survive somewhere else? Would it be just as difficult as leaving a country and a culture that I had grown to love? Would I have to learn how to speak American again as I had to learn how to properly speak English again when I came back from the Philippines?

I didn't know, and I didn't care. I was staying. The thought of leaving, the overwhelming process required to sell a house worth less than I owed, or paying off credit cards I had neglected to pay for over a year was too much to handle. I would rather just sit there and let the status quo happen to me. I would rather just *be*. It was exactly what I had done for so long.

It was Thanksgiving of 2011 and the only place I could go was to a friend's house. Nadia had invited us to spend Thanksgiving with her family first, but I declined. It would have been weird to be the third wheel anyway. My own mother had just moved from Las Vegas back to our home state of Illinois so going to Las Vegas was out of the question. A family from martial arts invited us over. The people in our small martial arts community were becoming my family. They took us in and helped us when we had nowhere else to go. I loved it. I loved that they had it in their hearts to reach out to us and take us in. If we had nowhere else to go I would have simply made a chicken while Manny and I watched one of his favorite movies for the 50th time.

Manny called Jessica that night and she didn't answer. As long as the effort was made, I was okay with it. She called back later than evening and they spoke for a few minutes. Manny was having too much fun playing with other kids and their conversation was short. She called back a few days later and wanted to talk to me after she talked with Manny. She wanted to know what Manny wanted for Christmas, she and couldn't understand him when he told her. I was feeling very forgiving that day. After all, her court case had gone nowhere. I won although the cases were still technically open. I had nothing to fight with her about. Her behavior was so clearly wrong in so many ways that I did not see how talking about it even mattered. I got on the phone with her.

"Maaatt." She had been drinking, but she wasn't drunk.

Well, she wasn't as drunk as I was used to her being, so in my mind she was just buzzed not drunk. We talked about gifts for Manny, and just as I thought the conversation was over she continued. "Listen," she said, "I pulled some shit with you, and you pulled a lot of shit with me. But I'm willing to let it go for Manny's sake." Arguing about the specifics was irrelevant. I could let it go too. "Matt, I dropped the case against you months ago!"

I don't know why she thought the case was dropped, but she was wrong. "If you think the case is still open you have a horrible lawyer. I dropped it." I asked her why her family doesn't contact Manny. "Maaaatt. My dad wants to talk to Manny but doesn't because you have an open court case against me." She was referencing my counter-suit for legal fees. Somehow her father not wanting to talk to his grandson was all my fault. Suddenly the conversation changed directions again. "Things are great with us here. I'm an AA now. Both me and Vince are both AAs."

"AAs?" I had to ask.

"Yeah, Alcoholics Anonymous." I knew what *AA* meant, but never once had I heard someone refer to themselves as *an AA*. I had even read the entire *Alcoholics Anonymous* handbook and had never once seen that. "Yeah, I just got my silver chip, and Vince is getting his soon too." I didn't ask what a silver chip was. Members of *Alcoholics Anonymous* received chips for milestones of sobriety. The colors of the chips, however, are irrelevant. Every local meeting can have whatever colors they want. I had only spent one meeting in AA and I had only read the book one time, but I could tell that her terminology was off. Alcoholics talk about their chips in number of days not colors. Something didn't bode well with what she was saying and how she was saying it. Her lingo was all wrong.

"That's good Jessica." I found that playing along with her instead of confronting her usually made her say more ridiculous things.

"Yeah, I know how much that means to you because of your dad." I couldn't believe she was bringing that up, but I had learned to let what she said roll off of me. I could pick it up later, dissect our conversations, and figure out the truth behind her words. "I'm there so often and am so good they want to hire me to be a full time counselor." I knew that what she said was a lie. One of the best things about Alcoholics Anonymous is they have no paid members. The entire program is volunteer-based. I put one more thing on the list to look into the next day, if it even really mattered, which it didn't.

I didn't know what her agenda was with everything she was saying. I'm guessing she wanted me to know she was doing better and was sober. She wanted me to know that her issues with alcohol were gone as she attempted to convince me of this through slurred speech.

I said to her, "Let me update you on all of our friends." I was grateful we were communicating again. We both agreed communication between us was long overdue. I told her about Nadia divorcing her husband and about Alan's mom dying. I told her that Tyson, who lived with us for those two months, had become a professor at Princeton. I told her that my brother had divorced his wife and was living alone with my niece. We discussed people who were at one point her best friends, her closest confidants.

"I think that's really sweet and all, but I don't know why you're telling me this." I just listened. Interrupting Jessica only led to fights. "These people all abandoned me. They all threw me away and chose you over me. The memory of that hurts me. I don't want to hear about it." So I stopped.

"I'm proud of you Jessica for stepping up and facing your addiction. We need to talk like this more often."

"Yes, we do."

We didn't talk like that again. Our talk was a one time

deal. A few days later she wrote me an email.

Hey, Vince and I will be in Utah over Christmas, so I'd like to figure out a time to pick up Manny. We will arrive on the 22nd and stay through the new year. Please let me know what works out best. Thanks.

It was her year to take Manny for Christmas. I couldn't do anything about it, but I really wanted to.

I tried not to focus on her weird story about a silver chip and becoming a paid counselor for Alcoholics Anonymous. Focusing on her so much is part of what led to the demise of Matt and Courtney. Her behavior affected my life too much already. I needed to let it go.

Jessica showed up on Christmas Eve to pick up Manny. She was staying with Vince at Vince's ex-wife's house for the holiday. Vince brought me a package of fireworks that he picked up in Alabama. "This is the good stuff. You can't get it here." A giant box filled with explosives would usually make any man happy. I had to wonder if they were going to call the police and tell them that I had illegal fireworks. Just in case I left the fireworks untouched. At least his fingerprints would be on them, which would prove they were driven across state lines. That's a federal offense.

I hated that my mind worked that way. I hated that I had to always think of a backup plan just in case a nice gesture was ever secretly a ploy to take Manny away. My anxiety, although warranted, was unnecessary.

Christmas day came in 2011. Jojo caused the only noise in the house. I had no one to talk to so I sat in silence. Manny's childish voice was nowhere to be found. The one person I wanted to see the most that holiday was off with his mother for five days. I didn't know the address where he was staying. I refused to impose myself on friends during this family holiday. If I had done that I would be the equivalent of the drunk uncle sitting in the corner drinking his fifth egg nog before 10 in the morning. I would be the guy invited over out of obligation. Spending the holiday by myself was better. Besides, being alone was something I had mastered. I was good at it.

I sat at my dining room table and browsed the Internet on my laptop. A few weeks prior my friend asked me if I thought his sister-in-law was cute. I did. He said we would hit it off and had a lot in common like being divorced, having tattoos, being a single parent, etc.. Anything was worth a shot, but she lived in Southern California. Maybe she was the kindred spirit I was looking for. I saw that she logged into Facebook.

"Hi Michelle," I wrote.

"Oh, hi!" She wrote back.

| FIFTY TWO |

Michelle
Shortly after Christmas 2011

For the first time in five years, I felt ready to be in a relationship. A real relationship. I was okay being alone. I had worked on myself during those years. I felt that I could offer someone a person worth loving. I was ready for a real deep connection. When Michelle and I started talking, I put myself out there no longer afraid of being hurt and no longer always thinking about protecting myself like Jessica had taught me to. I felt healed.

Michelle seemed to be the answer. She was smart, which I find attractive. She was tattooed, which made me feel normal being around her. She was a single mother of a hyper kid much like Manny so she understood the unique challenges of my life. She was recently divorced from a controlling guy who she should never have married. Actually, she was recently separated, not divorced. She had just moved back into her mother's house. Her son's father wasn't a part of the picture much so she understood this part of my situation too. We seemed to have a lot in common from the initial conversation.

Our relationship evolved fast, too fast. I did my best not to control the evolution of the relationship so that it happened organically. We talked every night and sent each other text messages every day. We video chatted often and she let me talk to her son Charlie. Charlie and Manny also video chatted.

I think we were both trying to fill a missing piece in our lives. While I had long embraced being a single parent, romantic solitude wasn't what I wanted. I don't know what she wanted, but she did not want to be a thirty-three year old single mother living her in mother's house. She did not want to have to share a blow up mattress with her seven year old son. She was seeking that other person, the one that would solve her problems. I was seeking the other person who could accept me and would be okay with my ADHD child, my dog, my cats, and would be able to understand just exactly how difficult it is to do it all alone.

The pieces seemed to fit. We got along. We planned for a meeting in February of 2012. Meeting up in Las Vegas made the most sense since it was between the two of us. Our children would meet each other in person and play.

Our initial meeting went great. Spending our time going to various places around Las Vegas, mostly for the kids' sake, was a blast. Having room service and watching movies in the hotel room made us both feel like we already had this little family. Everything seemed so right. It was as though it was meant to be. We were officially a couple.

On this trip both Manny and Charlie put on their hoodies, and they were identical. While Charlie was a year younger than Manny, they were the same size. From behind they appeared to be twins. We walked the casinos and the Las Vegas strip with two children dressed identically alike. We were "those parents" who dressed their children the same.

Friends of mine began asking who Michelle was. They

wanted to know all about her, knowing the trouble I had dealt with when I was married to Jessica. Every single friend of mine was elated for me. Every single one of them cheered me on. "It's about time," they said. Their feeling was exactly how I felt too. It was about time.

We had a plan. Michelle was going to move to Utah to be closer to her sister and brother-in-law. She was going to move to Utah in order to be closer to me too. She started talking about her plan to move in March of 2012. Her goal was to move in June when Charlie was done with school for the year. She talked freely about her plans to relocate with her son and with my son. "There is no way," I thought, "that she should be lying about this. There is no way she would say this and possibly hurt these kids with a lie."

I envisioned a life where she would live nearby. She would enroll Charlie in the same school as Manny. "Charlie is my best friend," Manny told me. "I cannot wait for him to move to Utah." Charlie and Manny began video chatting more and more frequently. They were developing a real friendship together.

Charlie asked Michelle, "Mom, can you marry Matt?"

"Why?" It seemed to be so out of the blue and unexpected.

"Because when people talk in class about having a brother or sister, I want to tell them I have one." He, of course, was referencing Manny. He wanted Manny to be his brother. I started to think that all of the years of pain and parenting all by myself were paying off. This woman wanted all of the same things I did. She wanted her son to be with my son. She wanted this fantasy life that I wanted too.

I was so wrapped up in the emotion and the romance that I didn't see the red flags.

"I don't know why you want me Matt. I'm just so ordinary." I didn't think she was ordinary. I thought she was great. "You could easily find someone better." I didn't think so. After she started talking like this it persisted for weeks.

I began wondering if something was going on that I didn't know about. She seemed to be spending a lot of time with her tattoo artist getting tattooed. Was she cheating? She couldn't be. I realized that my default reaction was that people were cheating on me. Jessica's behavior years back still stuck with me and somehow tainted my view of relationships. Michelle insulting herself and telling me that I could do better than her should have tipped me off. I just assumed, that my gut reaction was influenced by how Jessica had treated me years before. Instead of acting on my suspicions I had opened myself up for the first time in years and I was letting life happen. I was a willing, open, happy participant in this long distance relationship that would be a close distance relationship when she moved to Salt Lake City in June.

In April of 2012 Michelle came to Utah with her mother and son for Easter.

Easter came. I asked Michelle's brother-in-law when I should show up at his house for dinner. "I don't know, ask Michelle," he said. Michelle didn't give me an answer either. She just told me that she arrived. I packed Manny and a few bottles of wine into the car. We drove up to Cottonwood Heights and parked the car. Over a year before I had been at that house during our first and only "poker night." I had fully planned on holding the next poker night, but after seeing how my friend lived with his big house and family, I rescinded my invitation. I had always assumed that all of us were broke. I was the only one.

I saw Michelle. I gave her a big hug. Something was different. It felt more like a *friend* hug than a *boyfriend* hug. I shrugged it off. The kids played while the adults drank wine. It was ridiculously boring and wonderful. I longed for boring and normal. I had arrived. The night ended and Michelle was supposed to spend the night with me. She and Charlie were supposed to spend the entire week at my house. It was her idea.

We drove back to my house and went to sleep. Manny's new best friend Charlie slept in the top bunk in Manny's room. My dog Jojo slept in my bed between Michelle and myself.

The next morning we all woke up and dressed for church. I put on my wedding suit and Manny put on the only dress clothes he had, which wasn't much. Being properly dressed wasn't too important though. I saw many people at the Catholic Mass hadn't dressed up for the occasion. Some did, but it was not abnormal to see people in jeans and polo shirts.

Michelle seemed to reluctantly hold my hand. She whispered in my ear, "I'm afraid I'll burst into flames here."

We left the mass and went to a park to have lunch.

"Hey," Michelle said, seemingly uncomfortable with what she was going to say next, "I cannot stay over tonight. My sister is upset that I'm not spending time with her and wants me and Charlie to sleep over at their house." I had no issue with those sleeping arrangements. After all, she would be in town all week and she would only be away for *one night*.

The kids had an Easter egg hunt and Michelle's sister kept introducing me as "Michelle's boyfriend" to everyone. Could this be my new family? I was oddly okay with the idea. I was okay with the boring regular exchanges. I was alright with the occasional Catholic church attendances. I welcomed it.

The next day Michelle sent me a text message. I had not heard from her all day, which was abnormal for her. Her lack of communication was especially weird as she was in town. I expected for us to make plans to see each other every night. The text exchange went as follows.

Michelle: *Hi.. so I'm feeling overwhelmed by all this. I think i need to take things way back.. things are going too fast 1:44 PM*
Me: *I had a feeling you were reluctant recently. 2:02*

PM
Me: *what does "take things way back" mean to you? I'd like to know what you are thinking. 3:58 PM*
Michelle: *I just want to be alone right now 6:43 PM*

Just like that, it was over. Michelle had driven ten hours to break up with me over text message. I can say I saw it coming. I knew something was wrong. I knew she was hesitant. Why didn't I talk to her about it and try to prevent it? Why didn't I try to communicate what I was observing? I had become too confident in the idea of she and I, and it was nothing more than fantasy.

I was heartbroken. For the first time in years I had finally been able to open my heart to someone. I had finally been able to be in a healthy place and look towards a future.

All I wanted to know was why. *Why?* Why had she done this. What was wrong with me? What did I do wrong?

After a week of seeing new pictures of Michelle on her sister's Facebook page, I sent Michelle a text message asking her those very questions. Why did this happen? By that time she had removed me from Facebook and blocked me. I had no idea what I did wrong. I had no idea why I deserved any of what I was receiving. Looking at her pictures at the Tracy Aviary all I could think was that I was supposed to be there. Manny was supposed to be there. When I sent the text message to her I assumed she was back in California. I was wrong. I didn't get a reply for another day.

Sorry I was driving yesterday. I'm sorry for the way things happened.. I just realized that the reality was not what I want. I'm sorry for hurting you

I didn't hear from her again. It felt like my entire world was crushed. Manny's world was crushed too. Manny loved Charlie. Manny loved Michelle. Manny had bought into the idea of Michelle and I as much as I had. I should have been a better father and protected him from the potential let down, but it all seemed so real. It all seemed like it was going to happen. Over the course of a week the future we had planned was gone as though it never existed.

I should have known better than to throw everything into one person. I should have known that her "I love yous" were too early. I should have known that she had just left a marriage, and as a result was emotionally incapable of what she was offering me. She wasn't ready for anything. She wasn't ready for me.

I was oblivious to something that should have been obvious to me. All I knew was that I could throw my entire self, my entire being, into another person, and that they could accept it or not. She chose not to. This "all or nothing" approach might have scared her off, but I really doubt it. Her own issues scared her off. My friend, her brother-in-law, told me, "I quit trying to make sense of Michelle's actions a long time ago."

She was different from Jessica, but honestly not by much. I started to ask myself why I could fall for someone so similar to Jessica. Looking back, she only told me what I wanted to hear and left out what she really felt. I was duped again. What was wrong with me that I could not see it for what it was?

My heart hurt. I sat at my dining room table aching because the person I had trusted and wanted to be with had rejected me. Looking back though I didn't put up much of a fight. I really wonder how much I truly wanted her. Perhaps I just wanted the *idea* of her.

PART 6

| FIFTY THREE |
Late Apology
April 2012

The breakup affected me more than I thought it would, and I felt like I was spinning out of control. Michelle and I had had a future planned. I was going to have a family and I would be able to be the resident expert on Salt Lake City. My fantasy future was all gone in the blink of an eye.

I should have realized that Michelle was right and our relationship was moving too fast. I also should have recognized that anyone who would break up with me in a text message was not the kind of person I wanted to spend my life with. Instead of holding my head high knowing I was the better person, I cried. I wallowed. I was angry and confused. I listened to love songs and I lamented about how much I hurt. What I really wanted were answers. I wanted to know what I did wrong so that I could fix it. Truthfully, I was also upset because my ability to find anyone to date was nonexistent. Michelle had shown up like a miracle and I was relieved. I had put all of my eggs in one basket with her and when the bottom of the basket fell out, I was left with a mess, one I hated to clean up.

Suddenly nothing made much sense any more. Why was I still in Utah? What was keeping me there? For the few months before the breakup, the idea of Michelle and Charlie made living in Salt Lake City seem like such a good idea. With Michelle gone the only thing that kept me there was my house, which I was so upside down in that walking away seemed like a better option than staying behind on payments. We also had martial arts, but we would be able to find another martial arts class elsewhere if we left.

Manny and I walked into martial arts one night and participated in the family class like normal. When the adult class came up I just looked at the instructor and told him, "I don't have it in me to do this class tonight. I have too much on my mind." That is how it continued for a while. This image I had built for myself, of what my life would be, was suddenly shattered. Honestly the image I had built for myself had been a facade for a long time. All that was required to shatter it was heartbreak. Everything I had built up over the years finally showed itself to me for what it always was: just a dream I would never be able to realize at least not in Salt Lake City.

How could this happen? How could someone do this to me? I kept reminding myself that I was a real catch, I was the prize and Michelle was losing out. Suddenly, like a wave of revelation, I realized I, too, had done this same thing to other people. I had led Courtney on and had inexplicably vanished from her life. I had strung Krystal along for almost a year and was indifferent when she left. I was emotionally incapable of having a relationship with many women since Jessica but I went through the motions anyway. It felt like Karma. Perhaps I had earned the heartbreak. Maybe life teaches you lessons iso you to learn how much you have hurt other people. Hopefully when that happens we learn and never repeat the same mistakes again.

I started seeing Michelle in a different light. Nothing was wrong with me. It was all wrong with her. She wasn't emotionally ready, and really what did I expect? She was still technically married to her ex-husband. She had just ended a relationship, and it was stupid of me to think she had the emotional capacity to be in another relationship so soon.

It had been almost a year since I experienced my first and only meeting at Alcoholics Anonymous. The twelve steps to recovery included one I loved. It was step number nine.

Made direct amends to such people wherever possible, possible except when to do so would injure them or others.

For once I knew the pain I had caused other people. Finally I felt the same pain myself. I had to reach out to these women I hurt and apologize. I had to start with the most obvious one: Courtney. I had had time to think about my relationship with her over the two years since I had last seen her. Now that my head was clearer and I had some perspective, I knew that she was the one that "got away." Her criticisms of me were not criticisms of my character. She was the only one who had seen me for me and accepted me. She loved Manny. I loved her. She had at one point discussed moving to Salt Lake City and starting a family with me. I messed our relationship up badly by shutting her out. It was April 21 and I sent her a text message. I saw a picture of her on Facebook and was reminded of how beautiful she still was.

Me: for what it's worth, and I know it isn't much, but I'm sorry for how things ended with us. You were right, I was wrong. I totally get what I must have put you through back then, and I'm sorry. Cute pic with your sister btw. 9:27 PM
Courtney: No biggie 12:35 AM
Me: it is. Just wanted to say it. You at least deserve an apology albeit overdue. 12:36 AM

And that was it. She didn't reply again. At least I apologized and let her know that I knew how she felt. I had acknowledged the pain I caused her. I didn't blame her for not responding to me any further.

I did this same thing for a number of other people I had dated over the years. They all responded kindly. One said the gesture was sweet but she had been happily in a relationship for the last three years. Another told me that she waited for me for a long time, knowing my potential. She was about to be engaged to her boyfriend. At last I wanted to reach out to Krystal. I wanted to apologize. I finally understood. I understood how much I hurt her by being unable to commit to her. She never replied.

I wanted to live my life as authentically as possible. I wanted to acknowledge the pain I caused other people. I wanted never to repeat my mistakes again.

When Manny found out that he would never see his best friend Charlie again he began crying. "I know honey, it hurts, but you didn't do anything wrong. We'll find a way for you to contact Charlie again." I knew the words I spoke were not true. The chances of us talking to Charlie again were small. I wanted Manny to have hope though. I wanted him to stop hurting too.

I started living my life differently at that moment. I started seeing my life for what it had become. I was perpetually broke. I couldn't keep my house clean. I had a job that I loved but would never pay the bills. I would never be able to save money. I wanted a woman in my life who wasn't emotionally crippled by Mormonism. The only good things in my life were Manny and martial arts. I was starting to only have enough energy for Manny. My life plan shattering helped me realize I had overextended myself with martial arts, gardening, pets, work, side work, and Manny so much that I could really only pick one or two of them.

My initial apology to Courtney opened the door for us to begin communicating again. I called her on the phone one night to share with her a ridiculous story I heard. I knew she would be the only person in the world who would find the story as hilarious as I did. Courtney and I had always had the same sense of humor. After laughing with her for a bit, I decided to go for broke. I had to tell her more about my feelings. She had to know how I felt about her. She had to know I never stopped loving her.

"Courtney, you were the one that got away. You told me that you felt sorry for me because you loved me and Manny and I just threw it all away. You were right. I wish there were a way for us to try again."

"Matt," she replied. I had a feeling she was expecting this from me. "You made me feel like the only woman in the world when I was with you. *Us* won't work though. We've both tried that too many times and it cannot happen again. Honestly, I wanted the family and everything with you, but if I were honest with myself I didn't want to move to Salt Lake City. I wasn't ready to be a stepmom. I don't know if it would have happened anyway."

"You've always been so important to me and I never stopped caring about you."

"We can meet up for lunch sometime and laugh about old times, but you and I will not happen again."

I was okay with "us" never happening again. I felt it important to express my feelings and see what would happen. I had earned her rejection. I had behaved so poorly with her that I knew the odds of her saying yes to me were a long shot.

Courtney's new job was as a director of her company. Part of her responsibilities included her traveling to retail stores on the west coast. Her company had just opened a store in Salt Lake City and she was scheduled to come out in June. We were going to have lunch and catch up. I would have taken any version of her in my life again. If I couldn't have her as my girlfriend, I would be happy with her just being my friend. I felt great knowing I could start down the path of patching things up with her.

Jessica had little to do with all of the revelations I was experiencing. She had little contact with Manny during that time period. She was back to her once a month phone call and promises of sending gifts to Manny which would never arrive.

I kept talking to Courtney on the phone, glad to hear her voice. I was so happy I could talk to her again, even if she was in San Francisco and I was in Salt Lake City. She still was my dream girl. I hated that it had taken so much for me to see her for who she was, and I hated that I was way too late to do anything about it.

| FIFTY FOUR |
Karma
May 2012

It was May 20th and an eclipse was going to be visible in Utah. The sun was supposed to be 90% covered. I prepared for Manny and I to see this once in a lifetime event together.

The eclipse began. Slowly. It was only 10% covered but it began.

Manny and I went outside with our viewfinders from the planetarium. The entire neighborhood was outside waiting to see.

We went down the street to a friend's house to watch the eclipse with all of our children together. A man across the street was looking at the sky wearing a welding mask. I kept holding the viewfinder up to my eyes to take a look.

I had missed Halley's Comet when I was in grade school. It came and went while I slept. I did not want Manny to miss an almost total eclipse.

And then the sun began to be almost entirely covered by the moon. Manny and his friends all took turns looking into the viewfinder. Some of them had homemade contraptions made from shoeboxes and tinfoil to view the eclipse.

It was breathtaking.

As I watched two giant celestial bodies cross paths, my mind was heavy with Courtney and our past relationship. The relationship we had years before never really had a chance.

Things were moving along with us, and although our phone conversations were only a new addition to our friendship, I was optimistic. I never stopped loving her after all of these years. I had recently told her that she was the one that got away. I knew it was true. If any woman in this world was "the one," it was her. I had messed it up years ago. Just like the sliver of the sun poking through from behind the moon, I felt fortunate that I had a sliver of a shot with her. It was an opportunity I was not treating lightly, and one that I would not give up on.

Viewing the eclipse, my world shifted into focus.

We were all so small compared to the sun and the moon. If we were so small and insignificant, what did life matter? What was the point? I had been trying and trying and trying to make something work since Jessica had left. Anything. All that life handed me was more despair. Nothing was working.

And then it all snapped into place. As I was looking at the eclipse through the viewfinder, I couldn't help but think of the only person I wish I had been with to share it. It was Courtney.

What mattered to me was the life I wanted to live and the person I wanted to share it with. What mattered to me was the pain I had caused her, and how something like that could never happen again. What mattered to me was how much I missed her in my life and how I could never let her go again.

That day a celestial event happened, and the truth is that it wasn't unique. Eclipses happen all of the time. But for one moment, for one singular second of heavenly bodies intersecting and making me realize how small we all were, I had no choice but to learn life can be meaningless, unless you give it meaning. Courtney was it. She had always been it. It was as clear to me as the crisp shadows on the ground. It was as bright to me as the sun in it's full glory.

The eclipse passed and the novelty wore off, but I

remained affected. The perspective I had gained made me want to see the world, my world, through those lenses for the rest of my life.

I threw away the viewfinder because I have little reason to stare at the sun again. What I gained that day, a little perspective about the important things in my life, was something I've thought about every day since.

"I love you," Courtney told me. We had been talking on the phone every night for weeks. It was late May of 2012. I was visiting my family in Las Vegas due to some unforeseen family issues. The entire situation was horrible and stressful to all of us. "I love you, Matt," she said again. She already knew how I felt about her. She knew that I never stopped loving her. Her feelings were coming around too. We both loved each other.

I spent my days elated. Happiness was something that was easily accessible now. The rejection by Michelle was no longer on my mind. Why would it be? I had someone better. I had someone that I had wanted for so long. I had a second chance. Well, it was a third chance, and it was a chance I was not going to mess up. Had I never reached out to her and apologized my third shot with her would not have been possible. The fruits of my actions were starting to become abundant. Good things really *do* happen to people who try to do the right thing.

My normally plush garden was filled with weeds. My backyard was full of sticks and wood, and I didn't care. Courtney was coming soon to see me for our lunch date. She was falling for me again, and I wouldn't let anything get in the way. She was all that I wanted, and if it meant me and Manny moving to San Francisco to be near her I was going to do it. Salt Lake City was had worn out its welcome with me.

Courtney visited in June, and then she visited again that month for my coworker's wedding.

"What I really want," she told me one night on the phone, "is to end up in Chicago again. By this time next year I want to be in Chicago."

"I would like that too," I replied. Suddenly my life had direction again. I needed to get out of Salt Lake City and get back to my roots. I needed to be closer to my family and the friends I had had since I was ten years old. It was time for a real change, and knowing that Courtney was going to be a part of it made my potential future that much better.

At first I started thinking that I would wait until April of 2013 to move to Chicago, which was when my company offered it's annual bonus. After a week or so of contemplating my options, however, I decided I needed to start looking for a way out right away. I figured I could start applying for jobs in Chicago and if I couldn't find anything I would be in the same situation I was in at the moment, I had nothing to lose.

After applying for just a few jobs in Chicago I was surprised by the response I received. I started receiving calls from giant companies all over the country. I received calls from Home Depot, Walgreens, Sears, Adobe, and Apple. I started to feel pretty important again. I felt desired.

Courtney and I both went back to Illinois for the fourth of July where we introduced each other to our respective families. Things between us were difficult, especially considering the distance and our history. We were both determined to make it work. It was during this trip that I drove up to Chicago and had a number of job interviews. I walked into one interview thinking it was not going to be a good match for me. And then I walked in the door. It was perfect. The people were perfect. The environment was perfect. They thought I was perfect too. They gave me a job offer on the spot.

I had two weeks to get my affairs in order. My new job wanted me to spend a week in Chicago for on-the-job training. They were going to fly me to Chicago and pay for my hotel. I felt like a rock star.

I had had no idea that my skillset and experience would

elicit so much praise and attention. I still had to deal with selling the house and paying off my delinquent debts. Somehow though, it all made sense. Somehow I was going to do it. I had just enough money to retain a lawyer to file for bankruptcy. That was my plan. Wipe the slate clean and start over.

But I had to do it just right. I couldn't just leave. I had to tell Jessica. I had to give her proper notice. Jessica had just moved to Arizona because Vince had changed military bases. This meant Jessica was closer to me and Manny. Her being closer was something I wasn't okay with.

Luckily though we were moving far away.

Jessica was talking about taking Manny for a month during the summer. The visit was supposed to happen every year. This time Manny's visit would be to Arizona, and when Manny went to see Jessica and Vince, he would fly out with his step-sister who also lived in Utah.

I would have loved to have protested the visit but I could not. It was her legal right to take Manny. I needed the break. I needed alone time to just be an individual. I needed to get ready for my move - our move - away from Salt Lake City and all that had caused me pain over the years.

We went to the airport. My plans for the summer included my first week at my new job in Chicago and a trip out to San Francisco to see Courtney. Without Manny's trip to Arizona, I would not have been able to do any of those things. I put Manny on the plane and met Vince's ex-wife for the first time. I saw Manny's step-sister, who I had not seen since she had come over to my house with Vince for Easter years before.

The plane took off and I went home sad. I hated it when Manny was away, even if it meant I could get so much accomplished. Courtney called me. I cried to her about my son being gone. She wanted to see me. She had booked a flight to come out to Utah so she and I could just have some time to ourselves without Manny. She was doing everything she could to make "us" work.

Jessica had called me to tell me that the flight was diverted due to weather conditions. I wouldn't know when Manny landed in Phoenix for a few hours more. Courtney and I planned our childless weekend together. The phone rang again. It was Vince's ex-wife. I had to get off of the phone with Courtney and answer the call.

"This is Alison. Did you get a call?" She sounded upset.

"Oh, the flight was diverted." I assumed she was calling about the flight being diverted because of weather. There was no other reason for her to be calling me.

"No, Matt, from the police." I went into panic mode. Why would the police be calling me? What happened? Alison quickly gave me the phone number of the police officer who had called her. I called right away.

"My name is Matt Timion. I am told I needed to call you."

"Yes, My name is Officer Smith. Do you know a Jessica Jacobs?"

"That is my ex-wife."

"She came to pick up your son at the airport completely intoxicated. We would like your permission to send your son back on the next flight."

It looked like Karma was affecting more than me.

| FIFTY FIVE |
Download Spiral
July 2012

"I'm calling just to apologize to you. Matt. I'm sorry for what is happening." It was Vince on the phone. "I just want to call to apologize for Jessica's actions. I am sorry." At least he was man enough to take some responsibility for his crazy wife, Manny's mother.

Just thirty minutes before Vince had called I was on the phone with Officer Smith. He was explaining the situation to me.

"This is just nuts," Officer Smith said, "I've never had to deal with anything like this before." In the background I heard Jessica alternating between yelling and sobbing. "My husband is in the parking garage!"

"Do you understand what is happening here?" The officer in the background asked her.

"Wait, what? Can we leave now?" It sounded like Jessica didn't even know where she was.

"We're sending the kids back home to Utah." The officer's voice was stern and unwavering as if he were telling a three-year-old that eating toothpaste was not a good idea.

"I'm not drunk!" She started sobbing again. "What's going on? My husband is in the parking garage waiting for us."

Officer Smith told me they had sent a patrol car to the parking garage in search of Vince. He was nowhere to be found. His absence surprised me since Jessica had told me just weeks before that Vince was going to take the entire summer off to spend with Manny and his daughters.

From: Jessica Jacobs
To: Matthew Timion
Sent: Wednesday, July 11, 2012 12:27 PM

Hi Matt,

Here are the details for Manny's flight. He'll be flying unaccompanied this Saturday. We have him sitting next to Sarah on the way down and I'll pick them up in Phoenix. Percy will be down a few days later because of her band activities. We have a BBQ set for Sunday with my Dad & Beth, my uncle Dan and family, and some neighbors that Manny might remember from Alabama (John-John and Lauren) as well as some new neighbors. We had a delay with housing on post, they just got us in and delivered the household goods as of yesterday. We have a playground directly behind

our house and all the neighbors seem to congregate there in the evenings. There are TONS of kids and the adults are very nice and social. Manny is going to have a great time :) And, Vince will be on leave for the entire time Manny is here, so we have a lot of stuff planned... observatory, wildlife, hiking, biking, pool, etc...
Hope your Illinois trip was fun, call/email if you have any questions or concerns.

Jessica

"Sir," I interrupted the police officer while he was talking with Jessica. "I have primary custody of my son. I want him back now."

"Wait, you have primary custody? Why?" This was a common question I received. Why would a *man* have primary custody of a child? In hindsight I should have responded with, "Well, look at her," but instead I told him our entire history. I'm sure he really didn't want to hear it. "You have primary custody, are you certain?"

"I can email you the divorce decree right now."

"Okay, I'm going on record right now acknowledging that you're telling me you have primary custody of your son." He turned the phone away and spoke to Jessica, "I'm talking to your ex-husband, and he says he has custody of your son. We're sending him back to Utah."

"Noooo!" She screamed. "I have custody. My son was only visiting his dad for a little while."

"Are you certain you have custody?" He was asking me again. Understandably he had to do this to be thorough. I told him again that I would email the divorce decree at a moment's notice if he needed it. "We're sending them back," he told the other officer.

I hung up the phone. Everything I had planned for the summer was looking like it wouldn't happen. It was all going to be ruined because Jessica couldn't stay sober long enough to drive the children back from an airport. I just couldn't shake that woman. She was going to keep ruining my plans and Manny's life as long as she continued breathing.

Officer Smith called me back later that evening to tell me that Jessica had been charged with Child Neglect. They then put her in a cab to go to a hotel. I wished they had arrested her. This was going to be the proof I needed if the charges stuck.

***

Months later I was able to procure the police report. Jessica apparently was escorted down to the lobby to get a cab. The police officer noticed that she had urinated herself during all of the commotion. She was put in a cab to go sleep off the alcohol in a hotel. While the police were writing their report, they received a call about a drunk woman walking around the parking garage trying to get into her red Dodge Durango. The police sent out a patrol car and found Jessica sitting in her car. Since she had no keys in her hand they could not charge her with DUI. The police did, however, send her to a drunk tank for the night.

***

I spoke with Vince's ex-wife Allison and we both knew where we would be that evening. We went to the airport to pick up our kids. We sat next to each other in the terminal and compared war stories. "Vince knows she's crazy Matt. He sat me and my husband down one day and told us about everything she's done. We told him to run and that she was nuts. He told us, 'What you're telling me is exactly what people with three letters after their name have told me, but I love her.'"

Vince knew she was crazy. He knew knew about her mental imbalance going into the marriage. He knew she was unfaithful, a pathological liar, and a severe alcoholic. He knew she was capable of everything she had just done to both our children. He still let Jessica drive four hours to pick up my son and his daughter knowing what could happen. Vince knew that Jessica would be attracted to alcohol like a moth to a flame and could never be left alone.

Alison told me that she didn't really know Jessica too well though. "What about Christmas when they stayed at your house?" I remembered Manny, Vince, and Jessica stayed with her just six months before.

"They didn't stay with us. Vince wanted to but Jessica didn't. They stayed in a hotel." Over the years I had wondered *why* someone would lie about having stillborn babies, working for the CIA, or being a professional mixed martial arts fighter. The kind of person who lies about those things is the same kind of person who lies about having custody or where she was sleeping for a few days. Deception was as much a part of her daily life as drinking four cups of coffee a day was to mine.

Earlier that evening I had tried to call Jessica's father when I initially heard what was happening at the airport. My call went straight to voicemail. I found out later that Jessica had called her dad completely drunk while at the airport bar. Instead of protecting his grandchild from being driven home by a drunk woman, he turned off his phone. Jessica's family had always viewed her bout with motherhood as nothing more than a phase or a show she was putting on. Manny was merely a prop to show off to other people. She wasn't a real mother, and as a result Manny wasn't really part of her family. Her father's indifference was proof of how little Manny meant to him.

The plane landed and except for a few janitors Alison and I were the only people in the terminal. Our kids were the first off of the plane. Manny's step-sister was crying. Her eyes were swollen, and she was still sobbing. She had witnessed the entire altercation between crazy-drunk Jessica and the police.

She was terrified. Manny looked at me confused. He thought I had called the police and asked for him to be sent back as if I suddenly changed my mind about his summer trip. "Why am I back, Dad? I want to see my mom." Manny had sat in the police station at the airport while his mother yelled and slurred her speech, but he had no idea what had happened. He had witnessed her stumbling all over herself and being confused about what was happening. Manny had zero comprehension of what it all meant. If you think telling your child Santa Claus isn't real is difficult, try explaining to your nine year old that his mother got drunk and messed up their summer.

Manny came home still confused. I fed him dinner and put him to bed. Jojo was next to him having sensed that Manny needed the extra attention. The next morning Manny woke up and said, "Dad, is my mom still drunk?"

"I don't know Manny." I had not heard from Jessica or Vince since the night before.

"If she isn't drunk, can I go back and visit her?"

"I'm sorry honey, but your mom messed up her chance to see you this summer." A tear formed in his eye, and he ran off to bury his head in his pillow. Manny did not want to talk about what happened at the airport for months afterwards. He did not want to talk to Jessica on the phone for weeks. He pretended the whole event never happened.

At the last minute, I had to purchase Manny a ticket to go to Chicago with me. This erased any chance I had of filing for bankruptcy. I had no idea how I would entertain a child while I was working full time. My time in Chicago was to be my first week at my new job. I was supposed to be showing them all just how amazing I was. Luckily for me my mother stepped in and told me she would take Manny for a few weeks so I could have my week in Chicago and I could visit Courtney in San Francisco.

I eyed my house, which was half empty, and was excited that I would only be in Utah for another month. Not only did I need to escape that place, but I needed to get as far away as possible from Jessica. I needed to do it for my sake and most importantly for Manny's sake.

For a few weeks before Jessica's drunken airport showdown, Courtney was afraid of how I would tell Jessica that Manny and I were going to move. Jessica could have reacted poorly and taken me to court over the sudden life change. This could have been a way for her to try to continue her court case against me for custody. The court case was still open.

On the phone that night Courtney said to me, "At least you don't have to worry about telling Jessica you're going to move. Really Matt, what can she say now?" She was right. Jessica's opinion and role as Manny's mother were non-existent as far as I was concerned. Manny and I were on to bigger and better things.

| FIFTY SIX |
Taste of a New Life
Late July 2012

Touchdown. Our plane landed in Chicago's Midway airport and my mother was there waiting for us. Although I had grown up just hours away from Chicago, I had only been there a few times. My mother was equally ignorant of how to get around the city.

Under the cover of darkness, we drove to the hotel where I was to stay. My new company got me a room for the entire week. After driving around Chicago's Loop for what seemed like an hour we finally found the hotel.

"Manny, we can stay for the night or we can go back to my house," my mother told Manny.

"Let's go to your house!" He was excited. A three-hour drive was ahead of them and they would not get to my mother's house until around midnight. I grabbed my bag and checked into the hotel. The hotel was in an old building, built when people took real pride in the buildings they made. It had marble floors and ornate decorations. I felt like I had stepped into a time machine and was whisked back into the 1920s. The only place I had experienced that in Utah was at the courthouse.

I stepped outside at nine o'clock in the evening. I was hungry and on the hunt for food. Having lived in suburbs for most of my life I was completely unprepared for what I was experiencing. There was traffic. There were trains overhead. There were people everywhere. Lights filled my view, and I knew Chicago was in my future. There was a certain *energy* about that place. It was like listening to a jazz album and just feeling the groove of a certain song. Standing on Wabash and Adams filled me with something I had never experienced before. I loved it.

Even though I was working I viewed that week as my first real vacation in years. The last vacation I had was also to the Midwest, years before, with Jessica and Manny. I remembered walking downtown Chicago with them thinking how overwhelming the city was. I was overcome with fright that I would never find my way and wanted nothing more than to retreat back to our simple Utah life. On this trip though, it was different. I was different. I was no longer afraid of the people, the buildings, or the enormous size of everything around me.

The next morning I walked into my new job, ready to learn. I was ready for a new beginning. The exposed brick walls and old hardwood floors made feeling creative so much easier. I sat at my new desk and literally rolled up my sleeves to work. With my tattoos on full display I realized that no one had commented on the permanent pieces of art on my arm. No one even looked twice. I was so used to being the outsider. Not in the big city though. Tattoos were as common in Chicago as hot dog vendors, and having them said nothing about the person wearing them. I blended in.

Instead of taking the train back to the hotel, I walked. I wanted to see the city. I wanted to see the people all around. I was not alone in my desire to walk. It seemed like everyone was walking. People in business suits and sneakers were on every side of me. I walked past the Sears Tower and recognized a small convenience store I had gone to years back with Jessica during our visit. Back then the place scared me, but this time it seemed quaint.

Memories of the life I had lived with Jessica no longer haunted me. I would have looked at that same store years before and felt the sadness of a lost love, a lost life. Memories of the person I loved were gone because I had realized that person never existed. The Jessica I knew wasn't a real person. She was an invention, made up to win me over. The newest version of her sat somewhere in Arizona, probably trying to protect herself from the consequences of her actions. If she was the same as she was when I was with her, she would find a way to dodge punishment for showing up drunk at the airport. Someone would always rescue her.

Jessica called while I was away, but I didn't answer. If Manny had been by my side, he would have certainly not wanted to talk to her. I had nothing to say to Jessica anyway. My time in Chicago was *my* time not hers.

Before my trip Courtney gave me a list of places to visit while in Chicago. I visited every single one of them. I was experiencing the sights and sounds of a city she wished she still lived in. Our plan to move forward together was still going to happen.

I visited Oak Park, just outside of Chicago, and put down a deposit for an apartment. It took almost every cent I had, but my future was cemented. I was officially relocating.

In a blur, the sights and sounds of Chicago came and went. My week by myself was relaxing and eye opening. I arrived back in Utah and instantly began throwing more useless things away. How had I accumulated so much *stuff* over the years? I only had a month to get ready to move, and I had to empty my house in a short amount of time. I found a new home for Jojo, and then I arranged for my cats to be taken as well. I was saying goodbye to everything that used to matter to me, and I was okay with it.

Manny was still in Illinois with my mother and he loved everything he did that summer. "Dad, I want to move here!" he told me.

I boarded another plane to visit Courtney in San Francisco. Walking into her apartment I noticed a stark difference between how she lived and how I lived. Her apartment was clean like she had a team of professional cleaners come through every day. No wonder she was so disgusted with how I lived. By comparison I was living in a trash heap.

We spent four days acting like tourists and soaked in the city. While I enjoyed walking the Golden Gate Bridge with her and I had loved every restaurant we went to, I was happiest spending time with her. I didn't need the sights and sounds of a grand city. I just needed her. She was who I wanted to visit. We walked down a hill, and she grabbed onto my arm at the bottom. I looked into her eyes.

Could I spend the rest of my life with this woman? Could she really be the one? Absolutely. I cannot imagine two people who were not meant to be together willing to go through the back and forth that Courtney and I had endured over the years. She was worth waiting for. For her, I was worth the heartache I had caused her and the months apart until we could be closer together.

"I just realized something," she told me. "I'm never going to see your house in Utah again. I'm never going to see your dog or cats again."

"I know," I said, realizing the gravity of what she was saying. She was going to miss those things. I was going to miss them too.

"This is really happening, isn't it?"

"Yes," I replied. Life was moving forward and after years of living in survival mode I was finally coming up for air. Courtney was there holding my hand and proud of me for the changes I made.

| FIFTY SEVEN |

A Life Uncommon
Late August 2012

"Do you need this?" My friend Diane yelled from my kitchen. I had no idea how long she had been there or how she got into my house. I had just come back from the airport to drop off Manny. He was flying all by himself again, but this time he was going to be picked up by my mom in Chicago. Suddenly my house was filled with people.

"Matt, do you need this?" Diane persisted.

"Nah, throw that away."

"Do you need any of these dishes you left?"

"Nope." I had already packed everything I needed to bring with me from the kitchen. I heard a loud crash and glass breaking.

"I love throwing away other people's stuff," Diane said, "I cannot do it for my own stuff, but when I get the chance I love throwing stuff away." The sound of more glass breaking filled the house as Diane threw cups and mason jars onto the trash bag on the floor. "Okay," she said, "where to next?"

My house was being emptied by Diane, Nadia, Mary Ann, and Nadia's kids. My former roommate Alan was there too to help with the heavy lifting.

As weird as it sounds, the best place for me during the makeover of my house was receiving was out of everyone's way. They were on a junking rampage and throwing as much away as possible. All of the items they had tossed had sentimental value to me so I could not bring myself to throw things away. They had no problem smashing glass and filling garbage bag after garbage bag with relics I had once held so dearly.

I stepped outside of my house to smoke. I knew I was not going to be there much longer. In my driveway was a moving truck almost filled with furniture, clothes, and everything else I had decided to keep. I could not have loaded that truck myself. Friends of mine who I had not seen in years dropped everything they were doing, came over one day, and helped load the truck. These friends were not part of the ex-Mormon group, but rather friends I had made along the way. Some of them were Mormon and some were not. It didn't matter what they believed. They were helping me. They were my friends.

I had spent so much time in Salt Lake City searching for a community, wanting to *belong.* My experience in Mormonism led me to the ex-Mormons, who were my community for so long. That community faded and I spend years just surviving while I parented Manny. My dreams of family and belonging somewhere all faded.

Sitting on my front porch Mary Ann came outside in tears. "Matt, you have no idea how hard it is going to be for you to leave. You're such a great friend." Her sobbing made it difficult to talk. "I am so happy for you, but you're such a big part of our lives." I wanted to feel emotion for what she was saying. I wanted to want to miss her and her daughter. I wanted to be sad about moving, but I couldn't. I was thrilled, and I knew that one day I would look back at Utah and miss all of the people and places, but it wasn't that day. That day I was focusing on getting out. That day was a day of work and moving forward.

I realized then that I had had a community all along. People traveled from almost an hour away to help me load a moving truck. Other people left work early to help destroy mason jars while throwing them into garbage bags. Old high school friends who happened to be in town came over and helped load the truck. Nadia and her kids picked up everything they could and threw it away while Alan was there to help take my cats to the Humane Society. The community I envisioned, and so long sought for, had been in front of me the entire time. The only missing component was me. I had never reached out to those people and asked for help. I had never seen what was right there.

After realizing that the friends I had were in fact my long lost community, I had to come to grips with the fact that I was moving the next day. I would most likely never see some of them again. The life I had lived in Utah had been an interesting one, but it was certainly an uncommon one.

It was time though. It was time to move on.

I sat in an empty house that night with my television on the floor. I checked my laptop for any new messages. There was one, and it was from Jessica. A week before I had sent her the following email:

Date: Tue, 14 Aug 2012 15:41:18 -0700
From: Matthew Timion
Subject: Manny
To: Jessica Jacobs

Jessica,

In a text recently you admitted to having had made a "huge mistake." Of course you were referencing your child neglect charge. To put it bluntly, a "huge mistake" is an understatement. Just so you know, I am in contact with the detective on the case and continue to get updates as it progresses.

I am Manny's custodial parent, and as such, I need to look out for his emotional and physical well-being. Your behavior could have easily hurt or killed yourself, Manny, and his step-sister. It is entirely *unacceptable. This is also not the first time you have endangered yourself (and others) due to alcohol. It is the first [time] that you put minor children at risk (that I know of).*

Just so you know, I asked Manny if he wanted to talk to you a number of times after he came home. He said no. I have quit asking him if he wanted to call you and am waiting for him to want to call you himself.

Simply put, your behavior over the years has done more damage than good to Manny. He regularly sees the school counselor over abandonment issues. Every time he talks to you, or sees you, it gets worse for a while. He gets confused, angry, and will usually have a total meltdown because your side of the family wants nothing to do with him.

I am not writing this as some form of debate. It's fact. Any attempt you make to argue with me over his reactions and feelings will not be reciprocated.

Due to your inability to control your drinking even for a few hours and put innocent children at risk, I do not feel safe leaving Manny alone with you. Vince was right to recommend supervised visitation years ago. Also considering that you told the police at the Phoenix airport that YOU in fact have physical custody of Manny, I cannot trust you to not lie again to anyone in authority.

Because of your "huge mistake" I had to spend $800 of my own money on a last minute plane ticket for Manny to accompany me on a business trip. Add this to the thousands of dollars you have cost me over the years in legal fees, plane tickets, and unpaid day care (which you refused to pay). Your behavior HURTS Manny by depriving him of money/resources. Your actions cause him pain. As I mentioned, he has such a difficult time processing it that he cannot even talk about it most of the time.

I started looking at jobs months ago out of state.

One of the benefits (at the time) was that we were going to be moving closer to you and the flights would be direct. I started this process long before you told me you were moving to Arizona.

I was offered a job in Chicago, and I accepted it. We will be moving by the end of this month.

The environment is great there, the schools are stellar, and we will be close to extended family that Manny knows.

I would encourage you to recognize what effect your behavior has on Manny. If you cannot be the kind of mother he needs, then please stop trying. Manny will be a better man in the long run if you did. What you are doing now is hurting his chances of ever being a well adjusted adult. I cannot sit by and let that happen.

I do not expect a reply from you, nor do I really want one. There is nothing to debate or discuss concerning Manny's reactions to years of your behavior, the seriousness of your actions, or our move.

If you really love Manny, do the best thing for him and stop hurting him. That either means you need to get REAL treatment for your serious substance abuse problem (as well as behavioral disorders) or just stop contact all together.

All future communication between us will occur over email or through our attorneys.

Regards,

Matt

It took her a week to reply, but she finally found it in herself to write me back.

Matt, the way that you communicate with me is aggressive, I'm not sure what you're trying to accomplish, because I do not present any threat to you and the aggression doesn't hurt me, it ultimately hurts Manny. I made some poor decisions that day at the airport, but it doesn't mean that I'm a bad person or that I don't love Manny. I wasn't charged at all, and you're not in communication with any detective- you just made that up. And, I don't believe at all that Manny doesn't want to talk to me. Also, when you've contacted my Dad and siblings, it hasn't been well-received. You're not part of our family, Manny is, but not you. In the end they're on my side. That sentiment is clear.

I wish that you would get over your grudge against me and we could just teamwork Manny. I'm upset with you right now, but I'll let the negativity drop for Manny's good, whether or not you're willing to do the same.

I somehow doubt she will ever understand her actions. I was certain that no matter how many times I spelled out her hurtful behavior, she would never change.

The doorbell rang and my long time friend from Southern California was there to buy my car. We sat drinking beer, discussing Mormonism, and smoking cigarettes before parting ways. He was another friend who was always so close geographically that I never took advantage of. I had had friends all along willing to help.

I made a few more runs to the dumpster with filled trash bags before calling it quits that night. The next day was a day to remember. Talking with Courtney that night on the phone I could think of nothing but the future I had planned with her, and the unknown of the adventure I had just begun.

| FIFTY EIGHT |
Leaving Salt Lake City

August 26, 2012

Why was my phone ringing? Why was it still dark? Why was I asleep on the floor? It was late August of 2012 and my few days following up to that moment had been a whirlwind of garbage. Literally. After throwing away half of my possessions I still had more *stuff* than I knew what to do with. I had worked late into the night filling up garbage bags, big black ones, with random garbage throughout the house. Old clothes, books, and VHS tapes all went into these bags. Random photo albums Jessica left behind, sketches from my stint as an art major, and useless picture frames went into those bags. I drove throughout the neighborhood and found a place to throw them away. A house was being remodeled, and there was a giant dumpster in front of the house.

The phone rang again. Who was it? Why was my head pounding? It was six in the morning, and my friend and former roommate, Alan, was calling me. An empty liquor bottle sat on the floor next to me. I couldn't waste the liquor. This explained why my head hurt. It also explained why it was six in the morning. Alan was going to drive out to Chicago with me in the moving truck. It was six in the morning because he was there for the move. I was sleeping on the floor because my bed was packed. My living room was littered with electronics that I didn't want along with cleaning supplies, blankets, and a vacuum cleaner.

I didn't have time to finish throwing things away. Even if I had the time, my garbage cans were overflowing and had no room. I was going to leave my house just like it was with a truckload of cleaning supplies and miscellaneous items throughout the house.

That was it. I was leaving Salt Lake City. I closed the back of the moving truck and we drove.

I didn't say goodbye to my neighbors. I didn't even tell

them I was moving. They started to figure it out themselves though when I had parked the moving truck in my driveway. As soon as I had pulled out of the driveway, a swarm of people from the neighborhood descended on my house to grab anything I had left behind. My gas grill, which wouldn't fit in the moving truck, was taken away. My electric lawn mower, useless for Chicago apartment dwelling, was wheeled down the sidewalk. All of those *things* that were such a part of me at one time were left behind. The *stuff* I had acquired over the years was no longer a part of me. They were ready to be a part of someone else's life, someone else's story.

At a stoplight I called Courtney. "I'm on the road," I said.

"Baby! I'm so excited for you!" She loved that I was making such a positive change for our lives. She always saw the best in me. She always knew my potential. In the years since she and I had first started dating the first and second time, I had changed from someone who *talked* about making life better into the person who actually followed through and made my life better.

I drove past the liquor store for the last time, and I knew I might never see it again. That place would become part of someone else's story when they learned that it is closed on Sunday and the only parking you can find is a block away. I was okay letting it go. The streets that had become so familiar to me would be missed, but they would be replaced by new streets in a new city. Hopefully the new streets wouldn't be subjected to the annual "undie run," where people run a 5k wearing nothing but their underwear. This annual display of flesh was just a way to show how *free* the runners were from the "oppressive" dominant religion. I wasn't going to miss that. I wasn't going to miss both the overt and silent signs of rebellion over something that no longer mattered to me.

We passed the Gothic bar where Jessica and I used to dance.

Someone else could dance with their friends there and drink way too much. I no longer needed it. We passed the park where the Farmer's Market was normally held. Another single father could carry his four year old while just trying to fit in with the local liberals. I no longer needed that place. The early morning air was still a little cold, and my head still hurt from saying goodnight to the liquor the night before. It was time to just relax and be done with it all.

Alan took his turn driving. We listened to Johnny Cash on the radio. We were mostly silent. *Highwayman* was playing and as we drove past the mountains we began approaching Wyoming. Utah was now literally and figuratively in my rearview mirror. It was a part of my past. So many people and places I would never see again were behind me.

In front of me were great wide open plains of nothing. It was an empty landscape waiting for buildings to be built, for lives to be lived. I sat in the cab of that moving truck driving at sixty-five miles per hour, wondering if I should have any regrets about leaving a city that was supposed to be my home for the rest of my life. I had no regrets. Despite moving away from friends and the house that I had once loved, not a single ounce of me wondered if I made a mistake. Nothing was holding me back.

With the road in front of me, I thought about the great wide open plains of my own life that were waiting ahead of me. There were stories to be told and memories to be made. I thought of the life I could have with Courtney. I thought of the opportunities Manny would have in a city with a good educational system. I thought of how my journey in Salt Lake City had prepared me for a life where I no longer needed it. I was finally ready.

For the first time in years a genuine smile came across my face. I was happy.

THE END

PROLOGUE

Manny: Manny is adjusting well to life outside of Utah. It has not been an easy transition for him, but he has amazing strength and unprecedented resiliency. He still has issues with his mother, but has not seen her since the incident at the airport.

Ariel: Manny's brother Ariel is doing well with his family in Utah. His life is infinitely better where he is now. I am grateful such an amazing family was able to take him in.

Peter: I know Peter kept running away from his foster homes to his grandmother's house – to the point where the Utah Foster Agency stopped trying to stop him. He was aging out of the "system." He has a lot of anger towards Jessica and I for promising him a home all of those years back. I hope one day he reads this and finds me. I also hope he is able to find peace with his mother and family. He never asked for the life he was given, and he did not deserve it.

Jessica: Jessica still lives in Arizona with Vince. She still calls once a month and child support is unreliable at best. Jessica was never prosecuted for child neglect since the children were never technically in her care unattended. Once again she got away with it. The system can only do so much, and she has beaten it repeatedly.

Vince: Vince received a promotion at work when they moved to Arizona. While he does not have physical custody of his children he appears to be doing a great job with what he has. He once told me that "living with Jessica is enough work as it is."

Courtney: Courtney and I are still together. We have been navigating through a long distance relationship for almost a year now, and it appears the end is in sight. She plans on moving to the Midwest shortly. Our story has been long, difficult, and often times heart-wrenching. I am horribly lucky to have her in my life again.

AUTHOR'S NOTE

Writing this book was no easy task. It involved pouring over old court documents, reading years worth of emails, and interviewing so many people who witnessed all of the events described. There were a number of events that I had totally blocked out of my memory until I began the research process. Remembering them all has been difficult but I am ultimately grateful for putting the pieces together again.

A number of people have asked if I fear legal repercussions from Jessica over the book. The answer is no. I went above and beyond to ensure nothing about Jessica can easily be attributed to her. All of her identifying features (as well as Vince's) have been changed.

Every event in this book took place just as I described it. While I am positive Jessica could say that my version of events were not accurate I am aware that no two people remember the same thing in the same way. During the writing process I took painstaking measures to ensure all of the emails and text messages were accurate. They can be subpoenaed in court if need be. I also have multiple people willing to testify concerning the majority of Jessica's outlandish claims and actions. Luckily for me I was not the only one she told about being a CIA agent, murdering another person for her *other job*, and her stillborn babies from her first marriage.

Ultimately this book was a burden to write. It was a wonderfully healing burden. I carried around these stories and experiences for years. Now that they are on paper I do not feel the need to keep them in my heart and head.

As a result, Manny and I are better for it.

I thank you, the reader, for letting me tell my story as it happened to me.

THANKS

While I was writing this story I reached out to a number of people asking for feedback. The result was that on any given day over a dozen people were commenting on parts of this story; offering suggestions and clarifications.

I would like to thank, in no particular order:

- Archie Egbert – for helping me relive some of the early days
- Katie Sheen – for ensuring my facts were straight and for being one of the best friends I have ever had.
- Iris Jean James – for believing in this story and encouraging me – your words had more effect than you know,
- Rory McDaniel – for keeping me entertained while I wrote and pushing me forward
- Peter Huggins – when I was afraid the story was too much about Jessica you said, "it's sort of like saying that movie about the giant nuclear grown lizard should have more information about the City of Tokyo." You were spot on.
- Cat Palmer – We have been friends for so long, and talking to you about this process has inspired me greatly.
- Kathryn Duncan – for "getting" what this story was all about and giving me big, general feedback – it was much appreciated.

There were dozens that read the book and gave great feedback. I do not have room to name them all, so if I missed you I apologize profusely.

I would also like to thank Benji Smith, a friend I have had for a decade, who helped motivate me during the process of writing this. Benji was busy writing his own story while I was writing mine. He kept me going when some days the task of writing and reliving everything seemed too much to handle.

To Nicole Yabut for editing the book. You took the 10th revision and turned it into something I am happy to share.

To my mother for being there on the phone the night I

called when Jessica dropped the bomb on me. You listened to me day in and day out for a year as I tried to process it all. Needless to say you raised two extraordinary men who want to do what is right regardless of the consequences. While the consequences are often times difficult to handle please be proud of the moral character you instilled in your children.

Lastly I want to thank Courtney for her role in all of this. She listened to me as I talked about the writing process night after night for months at a time. Courtney's love and encouragement not only help make this book possible, but her love for me gave me the fortitude required to uproot my life for the better. It is a debt I will never be able to repay.

LEAVING SALT LAKE CITY

18594889R00174

Made in the USA
Charleston, SC
11 April 2013